# FAIRNESS,
## COLLECTIVE BARGAINING,
## AND INCOMES POLICY

# Fairness, Collective Bargaining, and Incomes Policy

BY
PAUL WILLMAN

CLARENDON PRESS · OXFORD
1982

*Oxford University Press, Walton Street, Oxford OX2 6DP*
*London Glasgow New York Toronto*
*Delhi Bombay Calcutta Madras Karachi*
*Kuala Lumpur Singapore Hong Kong Tokyo*
*Nairobi Dar es Salaam Cape Town*
*Melbourne Auckland*
*and associate companies in*
*Beirut Berlin Ibadan Mexico City*

*Published in the United States by*
*Oxford University Press, New York*

*British Library Cataloguing in Publication Data*
*Willman, Paul*
  *Fairness, collective bargaining, and incomes*
  *policy.*
  *1. Wages 2. Collective bargaining*
  *I. Title*
  *331.2'1    HD4932.B/*
  *ISBN 0-19-827252-9*

*Library of Congress Cataloging in Publication Data*
*Willman, Paul.*
  *Fairness, collective bargaining, add incomes*
  *policy.*
  *Bibliography: p.*
  *Includes index.*
  *1. Wages—Great Britain. 2. Collective bargaining—*
  *Great Britain. 3. Wage-price policy—Great Britain.*
  *I. Title.*
  *HD5015.W53    331.89    81-22429*
  *ISBN 0-19-827252-9 (U.S.) AACR2*

*Set by Richard Clay (S.E. Asia) PTE, Ltd.*
*Printed in Great Britain*
*at the University Press, Oxford*
*by Eric Buckley*
*Printer to the University*

# PREFACE

The purpose of this book is to give a very partial account of the factors underpinning the use of arguments about fairness in the collective bargaining context. A number of readers may suspect that such arguments are merely the façade for a deep-seated cynicism on the part of negotiators about the equity of negotiated solutions. I hope to show that there is more to it than this, but I ought to stress at the outset what this book is not. It is not a philosophical text, and will not therefore seek to pronounce on what is fair or unfair. It is not an economics book, and will not attempt to assess the relative importance of economic and extra-economic forces in wage determination. Finally, it is not a psychological study: the reader will not find that fairness is analysed in terms of the operation of individual cognitive or perceptual frameworks.

At the outset, I decided that the idea of fairness was of such conceptual complexity and that instances of its impact on social behaviour were empirically so elusive that a restrictive theoretical approach and empirical base were essential if anything were to come out of the research. I was interested primarily in the policy issues raised by the problem of fair pay, and so chose to focus on social actors' definitions of fairness in a collective bargaining context. This is primarily a study in industrial sociology and industrial relations.

An earlier version of this work was submitted as a D. Phil. thesis, and my greatest thanks go to my supervisor, Rod Martin, who provided valuable advice and constant encouragement. I am grateful to John Corina and Alan Fox for supervision at various stages of the research; to Willy Brown and Paul Edwards who read and commented on earlier drafts; and to Pat Bissette without whom the empirical work would not have been possible. None of these are responsible for the flaws which remain in the study; they are of my own design.

PAUL WILLMAN

*London*
*July 1980*

# CONTENTS

# ABBREVIATIONS

*Trade Unions*

ACTS     Association of Clerical, Technical and Supervisory Staffs (the white-collar section of the TGWU)

ASTMS     Association of Scientific, Technical and Managerial Staffs

ATAES     Art, Technical, Administrative, Executive, Sales and Clerical Section (white-collar section of SOGAT)

AUEW     Amalgamated Union of Engineering Workers

EETPU     Electrical, Electronic, Telecommunications and Plumbing Union

GMWU     National Union of General and Municipal Workers

NGA     National Graphical Association

SLADE     Society of Lithographic Artists, Designers, Engravers and Process Workers

SOGAT     Society of Graphical and Allied Trades

TASS     Technical and Supervisory Section (AUEW)

TGWU     Transport and General Workers' Union

TUC     Trades Union Congress

UCATT     Union of Construction, Allied Trades and Technicians

*Other*

ADO     Assistant Divisional Organizer (AUEW)

BPIF     British Printing Industries Federation

DE     Department of Employment

EEF     Engineering Employers' Federation

FOC     Father of the Chapel (NGA and SOGAT)

FTO     Full-time Official

JIC     Joint Industrial Council

JSSC     Joint Shop Stewards' Committee

MOC     Mother of the Chapel (SOGAT)

# INTRODUCTION

During the economic debate at the 1974 TUC conference—the last under free collective bargaining for some time—Lawrence Daly asserted that 'Congress believes in a free collective bargaining system that will give to all workers a fair living wage and a decent standard of life.' In arguing for the compatability between free collective bargaining and fair wages, Daly was reaffirming the conventional wisdom of the British trade-union movement. His statement also echoed a belief which has informed one strand of public policy at least since 1891. From the first Fair Wages Resolution adopted by the House of Commons to Schedule II of the Employment Protection Act (1975), fair pay has been legislatively defined as the rates established through the institutions of collective bargaining.

However, this view of collective bargaining as the means for achieving a 'fair' wage has been by no means universal in the post-war period. For many, collective bargaining involved 'smash and grab' techniques by the powerful, creating a wages 'jungle' wherein those without bargaining power were severely disadvantaged. Far from setting 'fair standards', wage bargaining was seen to be a self-interested, unprincipled activity, generating unjustifiable inequities based only on differences in bargaining leverage. From this viewpoint, equity in pay could not be guaranteed by collective bargaining: in fact, it could only be ensured by setting restraints on the exercise of bargaining power. The usual means of achieving this has been through incomes policies. Although income policies may be seen as purely economic devices, devised to restrain cost-push pressures towards inflation, they are usually presented as having an ethical content. This view of incomes policy has been influential at least since the publication of Allan Flanders's *A Policy for Wages* in 1950, and governments presenting incomes policies subsequently have invariably had recourse to notions of justice and equity in encouraging acceptance.

During the same 1974 debate in which Daly emphasized his commitment to free collective bargaining, the TUC General Secretary espoused a different view, which was to be more influential over the following three years. He saw a vote for the Social Contract, ultimately for restraint on the operation of free collective bargaining, as 'an assertion of our demand for a social system in which need, not power and not privilege, determine how the fruits of our economic advance are to be shared out'. And, for the years 1975–8, the trade-union movement by and large agreed. However, at the end of 1978, during what has been termed the 'winter of discontent', the final phase of the Social Contract was dismantled by workers in the public sector and the road transport industry who, under the pressure of rising living costs, were clearly unconvinced of the ethical content of incomes policies.

This raises several questions. For the majority of workers in this country, is fairness to be achieved through collective bargaining, or through the regulation of such activity through incomes policies? How do arguments about fairness come to have a place in collective bargaining, and why is their moral content so difficult to enshrine in an incomes policy? Finally, given recent sociological argument about the relationship between rising expectations and inflation, how do workers' views about fairness in bargaining influence those who actually do bargain? In view of the way in which the Social Contract ended, such questions about rank-and-file conceptions of fair pay are particularly important.

This monograph provides some empirical evidence in these areas. It attempts a study of fair pay conceptions, of attitudes to collective bargaining, and of collective bargaining arrangements at plant level during a period of incomes policy. It examines events at the place where the impact of rank-and-file pay expectations on bargainers is likely to be most keenly felt, namely at the plant level, and where the success of incomes policy is determined in practice by its degree of acceptance by bargainers. The plan of the book is as follows. Chapter 1 outlines the problem to be tackled in detail, and the deficiencies of previous work in the area. Chapter 2 details the analytical approach which will be adopted here: Chapter 3 then describes the background to the case-study analysis and the important features of the sample, indicating the techniques used in research. Chapters 4 and 5 present the bulk of the data on fair-pay conceptions, and Chapter 6 reintroduces the analytical model to help summarize the findings. Chapter 7 presents data dealing directly with fairness and incomes policy; Chapter 8 assesses their sociological relevance, and seeks to make some recommendations about future incomes policies.

## CHAPTER 1

# THE PROBLEM OF FAIR PAY

## INTRODUCTION

Arguments used by different parties in industrial relations are frequently affective or moral. Particular practices and procedures, substantive claims and settlements may be referred to as 'fair' or 'unfair' by management, by trade unions, or by government. Legislation prompted by government involvement in the industrial relations sphere has enshrined concepts such as 'unfair dismissal' or 'fair wages'. Yet appeals to standards of fairness or equity do not always appear to yield solutions to industrial relations problems or disputes: conflicts of interest can rarely be reconciled by appeal to such independent standards. This is especially so where the conflict at issue concerns pay.

There are at least two schools of thought why this should be so. The 'hardheaded' approach suggests that the use of moral arguments in industrial relations is mere expedience because such arguments are used only to conceal naked self-interest. This view is echoed by Wooton, who refers to 'smash and grab' techniques of wage-fixing, and by Lockwood.[1] It is an argument which discounts rather than explains the use of notions of fairness.

There are several objections to be made to such a simple diagnosis. Firstly, as Hyman and Brough note in the introduction to their own work, 'appeals to the principle of fairness often display all the indications of sincerity: and the commitment of one side or the other to a particular notion of fairness often appears to exert a significant influence on the actual course of industrial relations.'[2] Secondly, it is difficult to explain the continued use of moral arguments if it is assumed that they are merely a façade. Presumably, continued cynical use of such arguments in an unjustifiable fashion would so devalue the 'moral currency' of industrial relations that sympathy and support would cease to be encouraged by their use. Successive attempts to discover bargaining resources in moral arguments would meet with diminishing returns, and their popularity would decline. This does not appear to be the case. Thirdly, Daniel's empirical evidence shows that negotiations may involve a relatively complex mixture of moral argument and pragmatism;

moral 'reference points' are crucial to subsequent bargaining over exact amounts.[3] Influential conceptions of fairness do appear to persist, and the 'hardheaded' approach appears overly simple.

The second school of thought acknowledges this influence, but argues that the standards of fairness need not be unifying. Clegg, for example, observes:

In the absence of dependable evidence, I would suggest that it would be commonly thought to be fair in the modern U.K. for the Steel Company of Wales or Fords to pay more to the driver of a 5-ton truck than does Westmoreland County Council. I do not see how this is reconciled with the proposition that it is fair to pay the rate for the job to postmen in Dagenham, Swansea or Keswick. So long as the general public holds contradictory notions of fairness, it is impossible to erect a consistent system of remuneration on the basis of fair comparisons which would prove generally acceptable.[4]

These 'contradictory notions' may generate a number of problems. The idea of an absence of consensus over the basis of income inequality—that 'any occupational group seeking a pay increase is likely to be able to find some kind of legitimation for pressing its case'[5]—is central to Goldthorpe's writings on the sociological basis of inflation.[6] Phelps-Brown's explanation for the 1968 pay explosion relies heavily on ideas of rising rank-and-file expectations of fair pay rises, while Hyman and Brough conclude that, while some general consensus exists on the nature of income inequality, 'the structure of incomes is not necessarily stabilized: a process of leap-frogging claims and settlements may occur'[7]. These 'parochial' problems are seen as capable of escalating into severely destabilizing tendencies within the established economic order. Similarly, these 'contradictory notions' prevent some measure of stabilization being introduced. Goldthorpe clearly feels that incomes policies—and indeed several types of 'normative regulation' of economic life—are jeopardized by the absence of coherent principles of income distribution.[8] Moreover, John Corina suggests that the decay of incomes policies is assured, since they must fail to create consent 'where social valuations of incomes, within a given income distribution, are confused and often obscure'.[9]

Inconsistent, contradictory or obscure views on the fairness of incomes differences are clearly seen by several observers to create problems for the social and economic order, and to prejudice attempts at stabilization, such as incomes policies. However, when one seeks to go beyond such generalizations about inconsistency or obscurity to specify the substantive content of these influential notions of fairness, and to ask why they should be problematic, one is hampered by the absence of any detailed empirical analysis of their use in collective bargaining.

This monograph will be concerned to look at this area: to analyse the use of arguments about fair pay in collective bargaining and their relationship to incomes policy. The latter part of this chapter will look at the existing evidence with a view to developing an analytical approach which can provide the basis for an empirical analysis. However, it is necessary at the outset to be clear about the meaning of terms such as "fairness" and 'fair pay' and to establish whether this clarification can shed any light on their use in collective bargaining.

## THE IDEA OF FAIRNESS

The idea of fairness requires some reference to the idea of equality of treatment, or justification for inequality of treatment. Fairness may occur in exchange—in this case in the effort bargain—or in distribution, in the treatment of groups in apparently similar situations according to the same criteria. In exchange, the 'fair' situation is one where there is an approximate perceived balance of advantage between the two or more parties concerned, in terms of the relevant contributions they make to the exchange and the advantages they glean from it. For Runciman, who follows Rawls in regarding justice and fairness as coterminous; 'We may say that injustice is held to arise when either two men with unequal investments receive equal profits, or two men with equal investments but unequal costs receive the same reward and therefore a different profit'.[10] Fairness in exchange thus has to do with the equity of bargains.

In distribution, fairness entails that equals should benefit equally, and that any inequalities of benefit should be justifiable in terms of relevant and socially operative criteria.[11] Fairness in distribution thus has to do with the justification of inequality: inequalities will be seen as unfair where no basis for them is seen to exist, and fair where such a basis *is* identified. Similarly, equality will be seen as fair where no discriminating criteria are identified but as unfair where such valid criteria are ignored.

The principal exchange with which I am concerned here is the effort bargain; the exchange of a certain level of effort for a specified reward. The distributional aspect is a concern with differentials of income which follow from the striking of innumerable effort bargains. And the concern here is with what types of effort bargain and what patterns of differentials will be considered fair or unfair by any or all participants. Posed in this way, it is apparent that these formal definitions of fairness are of little assistance, since the principal omissions are precisely the conditions of both sociological and policy-making interest: namely, the problems of what basis of identity for equal or unequal treatment is operative, what is defined as 'equality of treatment' or 'equality of investment', how much inequality is justified by a particular difference, and whether one view of all of these matters prevails universally.

A more sociological approach is required to deal with these issues on an empirical level, and in this connection, the work of Runciman is of considerable interest, since he employs perhaps the most comprehensive philosophical model of fairness—that of Rawls—in an evaluation of various forms of inequality in modern British society,[12] and he makes use of the concept of relative deprivation which is similar to the idea of fairness in distribution with which I am concerned here.[13]

Central to the contractual theory which Runciman adopts is the idea of a situation, *logically* prior to the formation of vested interests, from which actors may evaluate principles of, for example, income distribution, without prior knowledge of their own location in a social structure to be based upon them. In this situation, 'To make a claim on the basis of justice . . . is not merely to claim what is seen as a right, but to claim what is a right only if it derives from a principle to which the claimant would have subscribed before knowing whether he might not be the loser, rather than the gainer, by the acceptance of it.'[14] After applying this principle to modern British society, Runciman concludes that certain inequalities are unfair, and derives several principles—and a rank ordering of them—with radical implications for the social order.[15]

Rawls's model implies that inequality of rewards can only be 'fair' to the extent that it improves the absolute welfare of the least advantaged.[16] It is possible to object to this formulation on several grounds. Chapman, for example, argues that justice cannot be considered as coterminous with fairness,[17] while Runciman himself cannot resolve several difficulties inherent in Rawls's ideas.[18] Nevertheless, Runciman's own adaptation of some long-standing ideas about fairness is of the greatest relevance here since it relates the philosophical problem of fairness to the sociological one of the selection of reference groups. Runciman's argument implies that one can analyse, and perhaps evaluate, the empirical standards of fairness held by social actors in terms of reference group selection. The sources of feelings of inequity are in principle specifiable.

Valuable though Runciman's approach is, it cannot be adopted wholesale here, for three reasons. The first two concern his use of the contractual model itself. He notes; 'Since the agreement envisaged by the contractual model is to be supposed to be on principles, not on practices, it cannot be used to yield any specific formula by which the inequalities in a society should be fixed.'[19] Yet the focus I wish to adopt here—on the 'parochial' issues of collective bargaining—involves looking in detail at the possibilities for success of particular collective agreements and incomes policies that are essentially formulaic. Secondly, the Rawlsian agreement on principles occurs prior to the formation of vested interests: actors agree to the application of principles with no knowledge of their effects. Such candour does not enlighten the bargaining process, where information is unevenly available, and may be conceded or distorted during negotiations. Thirdly, his research design is not adapted to generating results relevent to collective bargaining. His subject matter—the spontaneous feelings of relative deprivation revealed by a variety of social actors—differs from my own, which is concerned to analyse the use of arguments apparently based on relative deprivation within the institutional context of collective bargaining as organizational phenomena. I shall elaborate on this distinction in chapter 2.

Philosophical approaches to fairness are thus not useful in dealing with the problem as I have outlined it. However, a considerable amount of sociological data and industrial relations analysis of direct relevance is available, and it is to this that I now turn.

## EMPIRICAL WORK ON FAIR PAY

Two types of sociological data are relevant here. The first indicates the existence of a broad consensus on relative occupational worth, the second that manual workers tend to select as comparative reference groups other groups of workers in substantially the same position as themselves. Both types assisted Hyman and Brough in their definition of the problem of fairness as 'parochial'. I shall deal with each in turn.

On relative occupational worth, Hilde Behrend asked her respondents what were the appropriate amounts of pay for different occupations, then compared these amounts to produce a rank ordering (rather than by asking respondents to produce a rank-ordering themselves). Her results show that in broad terms there appeared to be a high level of consensus across the whole sample over the rank ordering of occupations. There were tendencies for lower placed respondents to wish to 'collapse' the income distribution by bringing the lower-paid up and, conversely, for higher placed ones to give higher amounts as fair pay for the top occupations.

Moreover, there appeared to be specific instances of lack of consensus about the ranking of individual occupations in the manual stratum within the context of an over-all agreement as to the location of this stratum itself.[20]

North *et al.* asked respondents to produce rankings of manual occupations and generated complementary results.[21] Asked to rank twelve manual occupations in order of estimated worth, respondents gave answers which contrasted markedly with the actual hourly and weekly earnings of these occupations.[22] There was apparently some consensual pattern to responses, but the report does not indicate its extent. The findings may be regarded as a more extreme example of one aspect of Behrend's findings; there is far less consensus on rankings among manual occupations than there is in ranking manual workers as a whole at the base of the occupational hierarchy.

Setting these results against the findings of reference group analysis demonstrates the sociological basis for 'parochial' disorder. Runciman found that manual workers tended to compare their pay principally with that of other groups of manual workers, rather than with those outside of the manual stratum. He notes that 'less than a quarter of manual respondents at most could be described as choosing a specifically non-manual reference group' and that 'the disapproving references by manual workers to non-manual are the smallest single category of all.'[23] His conclusions are substantially replicated in a survey carried out thirteen years later by Daniel, who found no evidence of any growing sense of relative deprivation or widening of comparative reference groups over the period, and concluded that 'the differences in pay that exist between the broad social groups in our society are irrelevant to the acceptability of an incomes policy to wage and salary earners . . . it is peoples' position relative to others in the same class that influences their evaluation of their own circumstances rather than their position compared to that of people in other classes.'[24]

Valuable though this data is, it is of limited relevance to the problem at hand. It provides a context within which questions about fair pay under collective bargaining may be asked, rather than providing any of the answers. The finding that manual workers have consensual views of relative occupational worth and choose comparisons over a restricted range cannot explain the problem I have outlined; more detailed and specific data is required on such areas as the perception of and attitudes to differentials between jobs 'adjacent' in the accepted hierarchy of worth, the precise basis of comparison selection within the manual stratum, the acceptability of specific incomes policy measures and the relationship of all such attitudes to collective bargaining behaviour. Although data exist in all of these areas, they do not amount to an adequate approach to the problem.

For example, Behrend's work on pay and price perceptions reports the findings of a number of sample surveys conducted in the United Kingdom and Eire between 1966 and 1971.[25] The findings of these surveys about the absolute *amounts* of fair pay, fair differentials and fair pay rises are hardly relevant now, but the findings about the *form* of perceptions certainly are. Her general findings are that underlying the consensus on occupational rank orderings is a concern to 'collapse' the range of income differences, and that definite absolute amounts constituting 'low pay' at the base of the income structure could be quoted. Most respondents saw fair pay differentials and fair pay rises in terms of absolute amounts rather than percentages, and these absolute amounts were slow to adjust to inflation. The rate of increase of prices appeared to be the basic framework for the assessment of pay rises, respondents having an expectation of pay increases without any change of contribution. Finally, her respondents appeared less concerned to compare levels of earnings than to focus on the size of pay increases: they were consequently concerned with 'pay increase differentials'.

These findings have obvious implications for policy. Writing in the early 1970s, Behrend found a 'communications gap' between policy makers and the general public, the latter being unfamiliar with terms like 'inflation' and making no connection between wage and price increases. This has probably become less of a problem, but the form of perceptions of differentials and policy measures remains important.[26] Her findings indicate in particular that policy designers must concern themselves with low pay and with incorporating cost-of-living compensation into incomes policies.

I have noted that the problems of the more general data arise from a failure to consider the specifics of comparison selection and the details of fair pay. But both general data and more specific analysis share the fault that they take insufficient account of the organizational processes which influence the conduct of collective bargaining, and thereby the way in which such views of fairness might influence the use of moral arguments. Reliance on social survey techniques cannot assist a fruitful understanding of the process of wage determination: bargaining behaviour must be studied in a more direct fashion. The use of moral arguments in collective bargaining is influenced less by the attitudes and behaviour of individuals randomly distributed throughout the social hierarchy than by the attitudes and behaviour of occupationally-similar individuals acting as members of specific bargaining units subject to specific sets of social pressures.

A reliance on 'opinion-poll' type samples tends to encourage single-factor explanations of the success or failure of policy measures. Behrend relies on a 'communications-gap' explanation for the failure of incomes policies; others, such as Fosh and Jackson, on the relationship between the policy-forming government and the social location of its electorate.[27] But what one needs to know is why particular groups of workers within the broad mass of the ignorant or politically opposed reject specific measures, while others might acquiesce.

Part of the problem is, as Daniel notes, that respondents' 'frames of reference' in answering social survey questions might differ from those employed on a day-to-day basis.[28] But, equally, one cannot fully understand the success or failure of incomes policy measures without looking at the response of trade-union organizations to them. As Clegg notes, 'the desire to win trade union support generally has played a considerable part in most policies', and indeed the most recent incomes policy was designed by Congress.[29] Similarly, the breakdown of incomes policy has been directly related to the relationship between the TUC and member unions.[30] Again, the important issues concern the behaviour of specific groups and organizations in collective bargaining.

The need to consider collective bargaining institutions also emerges clearly from a consideration of the use of wage comparisons as moral arguments in bargaining. Industrial relations analysts do not see wage comparisons simply as indications of feelings of relative deprivation. According to Lipset and Trow, union leaders select references to other groups so that the ensuing comparisons will engender sentiments strengthening and supporting the position of the spokesman.[31] Brown and Sisson contend that there are substantial organizational advantages for both management and trade-union negotiators in the use of stable comparisons.[32] In this, they clearly follow Ross: 'The ready made settlement supplies an answer, a solution, a formula. It is mutually face-saving. It is the one settlement which permits both parties to believe that they have done a proper job, the one settlement that has the best chance of being "sold" to the company's board of directors and the union's rank and file'.[33]

But this type of analysis does not directly analyse this process of 'selling' since it does not include any reference to the substantive conceptions of equity held by the 'rank and file'. Lipset and Trow seldom mention 'membership sentiments', but Brown and Sisson make a number of assertions about reference group selection and change and about bargaining awareness which are incapable of substantiation by the data presented. As a consequence, there is again no analysis of the social processes internal to bargaining units which mediate between members' conceptions of fairness and trade-union bargaining policy. The weaknesses of this analysis are just the opposite of those of the attitudinal analysis discussed above: if the former is exclusively concerned with the 'normative input' to collective bargaining, the latter is too concerned with the 'output' in terms of a set of bargaining practices and income differentials. Neither analyses the operation of conceptions of fairness *within* the group and indeed no such analysis exists. Consequently, an exploration of *variable* conceptions of fairness is incomplete. So, for example, Brown matches up wage movements in forty engineering firms for the period 1972–7 to general ideas about equity derived from Behrend,[34] without analysing shopfloor bargaining behaviour itself. But given the generality of the social-psychological assumptions an explanation of the differential propensity of any two bargaining units to experience problems of fairness is elusive. As Corina's analysis of the 1948–51 incomes policy—and indeed popular accounts of the demise of the Social Contract—have shown, the relationship between rank-and-file aspirations and union policy is crucial to the success of incomes policy. Yet no comprehensive analysis of this relationship exists.

I am arguing the case for a detailed empirical analysis of fairness in specific collective bargaining situations, in such a way as to:

(i)   take account of rank-and-file conceptions of fair pay;
(ii)  relate these to bargaining activity by detailing intra-group processes in bargaining;
(iii) indicate the contingencies which may account for variance in the use of moral arguments in bargaining; and
(iv)  relate these findings to the design and administration of incomes policy.

I will seek to outline an analytical approach fulfilling these conditions in the next chapter. Before doing this, however, I want to make some points about the over-all theme of this study.

First, the approach offered here is sociological rather than economic. It might be argued by certain economists that a concern with the sociological basis of fair pay is mistaken, since the forces of supply and demand are always and everywhere the most important determinant of wage levels. However, there is by now a good deal of literature emphasizing that economic forces leave a range of indeterminacy within which industrial and political forces influence the process of wage settlement,[35] and several economists, notably Brown, are concerned with the nature of these 'extra-economic' forces. In any event, the concern here is less directly with the impact of conceptions of fairness on particular wage levels or structures than with their impact on the generation of bargaining arguments.

One may further distinguish between, on the one hand, the policy-oriented approach with treats the problem of fair pay as an industrial relations issue in the narrowest sense and, on the other, the sociological approach which sees the problem of fair pay as one aspect of the over-all problem of the legitimation of income inequality. The former approach seeks *solutions* to the problem in the reform of bargaining arrangements or the application of specifiable principles, such as those enshrined in job evaluation schemes, to differences in income and to wage bargaining. From the latter perspective, apparently 'parochial' conflicts have their origins in important features of social structure, and what becomes remarkable is not that certain pay problems within establishments or industries are so intractable, but that feelings of inequity are so localized. Given that differences in income in modern British society are so large, and that many appear to be unjustifiable in any language of expediency or ethics, what is surprising, given the disruptive potential of certain well organized groups, is that the redistributive implications of so many articulated feelings of fairness are so limited. There tend to be few points of contact between the two: the former approach appears superficial to some sociologists, while the latter appears almost as an admission of defeat to those with practical concerns. It is my ambition in this monograph to establish at least some modest basis for dialogue by using sociological techniques to establish the basis for policy measures; consequently, the next chapter opens with a brief statement of the underlying theory.

## CONCLUSION

In summary, the problem is as follows. Arguments about the fairness or unfairness of particular pay levels or differentials are frequently used in collective bargaining, and are apparently influential. But they do not necessarily provide solutions in pay bargaining: in fact their influence is extremely problematic. No adequate empirical analysis of fairness, collective bargaining and incomes policy exists, and this monograph will seek to provide some data in this area by looking closely at the ideas about fair pay held by different groups of workers and the impact that these have on collective bargaining over pay. It will try to draw conclusions which have direct implications for the acceptability of incomes policies.

The basis for the study is an analytical approach to the operation of pay bargaining. It seeks to substantiate some of the claims made in this chapter about the peculiarity of moral arguments in collective bargaining by indicating why one might expect variable usage of moral arguments, and then spells out the major contingencies which will help to explain such usage.

## CHAPTER 2

# SHOPFLOOR PAY BARGAINING

## INTRODUCTION

In their discussion of fairness, Hyman and Brough came to rely on the idea of ideological hegemony as an explanation for the 'parochial' nature of discontent over inequities. Workers are seen as socialized into acceptance of work obligations and limited pay horizons so that 'just as "the employer or manager receives an employee who is already socialized and trained in obedience", so he receives an employee whose normal pay horizons do not extend far beyond those in kindred occupations.'[1] But the use of moral arguments in collective bargaining is characterized not only by its lack of ambition but also by its inconsistent, variable, and *ad hoc* nature, and explanations of the latter cannot be produced by such a generalizing framework.

This incompability and variability of arguments is obvious when one looks at the justifications used in pay negotiations. Bernstein's study of pay increase justifications in arbitration decisions in the United States unearthed 'differential features of work', 'productivity', 'comparisons', 'financial position of the employer', 'cost of living' and 'substandards of living'; Ross's earlier study revealed a similar pattern.[2] In the United Kingdom, Wooton has noted the availability of conflicting criteria for pay claims,[3] while Daniel found that the major arguments used by trade unionists were 'ability to pay', 'productivity', 'cost of living' and 'comparibility'. While there is some over-all consistency in the set of arguments unearthed, in particular circumstances different elements of this set may be used. Some of them may be mutually exclusive, and it is important to understand the basis of selection. Different forms of argument may imply different forms of substantive settlement, while disagreement over the 'correct' argument may generate conflict.

This chapter will seek to explain the basis of selection of moral arguments. The next section will seek to explain why one might expect such variance to occur in collective bargaining. Subsequently, a model of shop-steward activity will be presented which seeks to outline the influences on union representatives' choice of arguments in negotiation, and the principal contingencies which might affect the operation of the model will be discussed.

## FAIR PAY AND COLLECTIVE BARGAINING

Any conceptualization of this variable practice must deal with the peculiar relationship between the ethical basis of many bargaining arguments and their instrumental, opportunistic use. One gains little by saying simply that this ethical basis is inconsistent: one must go further to explain how this inconsistency affects bargaining practice. Obviously, straightforward ideas about value consensus are of little use here, be that consensus 'spontaneous' or 'manipulated'. It is more profitable to see the set of commonly used arguments in bargaining as a vocabulary of motives, in Mills sense of the term.

For Mills, motives are primarily social, being directly related to situated action. His argument is worth quoting at some length.

As over against the inferential conception of motives as subjective springs of action, motives may be considered as typical vocabularies having ascertainable functions in delimited social situations.[5]

we might assume that conduct is motivated by the *expectations* of others which are internalised from the roles which persons enact, and that important aspects of such motivation are the vocabularies of motive which are learned and used by persons in various roles. Motivation thus has to do with the balance of self image with the appraisals of others.[6]

In this particular context, the observation that motivational vocabularies have institutional anchors is particularly important.

The choice of a motive which is ascribed to some conduct pattern reflects the institutional position of the actor and of those who ascribe motives to him.[7]

From this perspective, variable and divergent use of moral arguments is to be expected, even where one can point to substantial areas of general agreement about the *sorts* of argument to be used. The vocabulary may be used for different purposes in different situations, and access to it may be unevenly distributed; it may be accepted in broad terms by different parties, but the uses to which it is put may reflect both the differing types of acceptance and shades of meaning which specific elements of it may possess.

The advantages of this perspective on fair pay are, first, that it sheds light on the nature of 'parochial disputes' within a broad overarching consensus; one need not posit implausibly divergent value systems to explain conflict, since motive avowal and imputation may cause conflict even 'within' one set of justifications. Secondly, one is encouraged to move away from general motivational theories, and from discussion of general perceptual 'frames of reference' in explaining the use of moral arguments: if the avowal of motives is situationally determined, the contingencies outlined below take on a particular importance. Thirdly, the idea that motives may have institutional anchors focuses attention directly on the nature of institutions within which moral arguments are used: in the context of fair pay, these are predominantly the institutions of collective bargaining.

In his classic analysis, Allan Flanders noted that collective bargaining is concerned both with economic and managerial relations: that is, both with setting the terms for the sale of labour, and with regulating the exercise of managerial authority in deploying, organizing and disciplining the labour force after it has been hired.[8] The problem of fair pay as I have defined it thus arises in an institutional context where issues of power as well as issues of payment equity are bargained and where questions of control over jobs and the value of jobs are not easily separated. The striking of an 'effort bargain'—relating a 'fair day's work' to a 'fair day's pay'—may involve conflict both over the nature of effort and the amount of reward. Although the data below focuses largely on comparisons, effort-bargain issues cannot be ignored.

These issues have been considered in detail by Baldamus, who makes a distinction between permanent pyramidal structures of inequality and more variable, flexible bargaining over effort which is consistent with the discussion of the previous chapter. He argues that, given the indeterminacy of measures of effort, distributional questions to do with appropriate differentials are necessarily made on a normative basis, and that questions of the value of effort are dependent upon questions of the 'control over the means of industrial administration'.[9] In considering the effort bargain he notes the close link between effort expenditure and wage expectations and the extent to which neither side of the effort-reward bargain can be considered in isolation: 'all judgements on effort values are a combination of effort and wage expectations: the evaluation of the right effort is inseparably fused with judgements on appropriate earnings.'[10] Moreover, the question of fair pay is premised upon collective organization: 'Nobody could argue about fair or unfair distributions unless a structure of groups whose members have similar interests within the group, but where the groups as such have conflicting interests, already exists'.[11]

If bargaining over effort and over reward are so closely related, and if both types of bargain are heavily influenced by questions about control within industrial organizations, particularly questions of trade-union control over work, then this obviously has implications for discussions about fair pay. 'Fair' pay settlements will have to do with a range of collective bargaining issues such as how the settlements influence collective organization, how intra-group and inter-group relations are affected and whether control over work is enhanced or damaged. The 'equitable' bargain, like Ross's 'responsible' pay bargain, is to be defined in terms of its effect on collective bargaining arrangements rather than any broader criteria.[12]

It is now possible to draw certain parallels between the way shop stewards bargain over pay and over effort; in particular, between the development of rules of job regulation and the use of moral arguments in pay bargaining. Though substantially different in a number of respects, both are accommodative responses regulated by workers' representatives in line with identifiable principles: that is, the use of moral arguments, like the development of rules of job regulation, must be acceptable both to management and to the steward's constituents. In what follows I shall rely heavily on Brown's analysis of 'custom and practice' rules.

Both Brown and Rimmer have looked in detail at the development of 'custom and practice' rules of job regulation.[13] I am concerned here only with the three main areas where useful parallels with the use of moral arguments can be drawn.

First, custom and practice rules have a basis in managerial prerogative. Although particular custom and practice rules may be opposed by managers, more generally their development is premised on the assumption that management has the right to give orders. Hence Rimmer:

> In internal job regulation, management does not have to appeal to custom and practice to establish a rule since its commands are legitimated under the general heading of managerial prerogative. But workers generally possess no recognised right to make rules governing their conditions of work. They must either engage in collective bargaining to establish joint rules, or find indirect methods of elaborating rules. One such method is to describe practices which develop through exploitation of management weakness and aberrations as customary rules or 'C & P'. Particular concessions are sometimes applied out of context and individual precedents are interpreted as demonstrating the existence of a rule. Thus work groups will use the term 'C & P' to establish the legitimacy of a rule which benefits them.[14]

Managerial acceptance of particular practices—or their failure to reject them—is crucial in establishing the legitimacy of a rule. The parallel I wish to offer here is that similarly the use of moral arguments by stewards is heavily influenced by their acceptability to management, but, conversely, once managers have accepted the validity of an argument, they cannot easily refuse to endorse it in future.

Secondly, custom and practice rules may develop 'as a flexible social institution over long periods of time'.[15] They are not ephemeral, but define the employment-transactional relationship in a fundamental way: their survival and development is independent of institutional reform in rule-making.[16] Custom and practice rules may develop over time in one location, and may vary between locations at the same point in time: the nature of development depends on the industrial context. Similarly, ideas about fair pay may vary in detail between locations and over time; they set the ethical context within which transactions occur and are equally fundamental to the employment relationship.

Finally, the four principles of shop steward activity identified by Brown as the organizational constraints on the development of custom and practice rules can also be seen as constraints on pay bargaining. These four principles are:

(*a*) the search for unity among members of the bargaining unit;
(*b*) the search for equity among members of the bargaining unit;
(*c*) the maintenance of good bargaining relationships with management;
(*d*) the reduction of uncertainty in relationships with management.[17]

Stewards seek to control custom and practice drift in line with these principles. Given the relationship between 'C & P' drift and wage drift, it is a plausible suggestion that these principles are applicable to both sides of the effort bargain, and that stewards' success in exerting control over one side can be related to success on the other. But the pressure on stewards to make advances in pay bargaining is likely to be greater than that to make advances in job regulation, and the attempt to increase earnings is always potentially at odds with those principles. Members' ideas about 'equity' in pay increases may be incompatible with other steward goals. In considering fairness in collective bargaining, members' views are only one influence.

I want to suggest that the use of moral arguments can be seen as a form of accommodative reaction by trade unions which seek to develop bargaining resources out of managerial prerogatives, that such arguments are both used manipulatively as a 'vocabulary' and that they are subject to certain principles, and that, being based on the resources for collective organization to hand, they are extremely variable. Just as custom and practice rules indicate workers conceptions of equity in effort expenditure, so moral arguments about pay indicate feelings about equitable rewards, and one can use knowledge of the former to help study the latter.

The conceptualization of moral arguments in collective bargaining as elements of a vocabulary for negotiators within a specific authority framework and co-ordinated by identifiable rules indicates how tangential to the problem is the evidence presented above. To understand fairness in collective bargaining, one needs a model outlining the relationship between 'spontaneous' feelings about fairness and the bargaining context, and an idea of some of the contingencies which influence the way this relationship changes. In the remainder of the chapter, I shall try to provide both.

### THE BARGAINING MODEL

The starting point here is the observation made by Pedler and subsequently analysed in far greater detail by Batstone *et al.* that leadership behaviour is a feature of shop-steward activity. Pedler notes that stewards perform notable 'informal leadership' functions such as the initiation of action and the 'filtering' of members' grievances.[18] Batstone *et al.* suggest that many features of the day-to-day leadership behaviour of shop stewards both embody and are in pursuit of the basic principles of trade-unionism. They derive a four-way categorization of shop stewards[19] on the basis firstly of the degree to which the steward plays a representative or a delegate role and, secondly, the degree to which trade-union principles are pursued. Fig. 2.1 is reproduced from their book.

FIG. 2.1. *Pursuit of union principles*

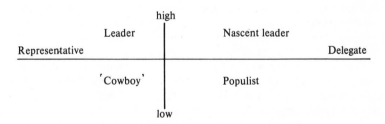

In practice, Batstone *et al.* concentrate on leaders and populists, since the two axes in Fig. 2.1 are related. The leader plays a representative role *and* pursues trade-union principles successfully. The populist lacks both the commitment to trade-union principles and the ability and desire to be a representative. Populists, empirically the most common type in the cases studied, tend to act as delegates.[20] The leader acts in pursuit of trade-union principles—independently, to some extent, of the immediately-held views of his constituents: the populist, by contrast, tends simply to reflect such views—and their ambivalence.

Leadership—seen as representative behaviour in pursuit of a specific set of goals—is not presented as a personality matter: it is a sociological rather than psychological conception. The ability to be a leader is seen to be dependent upon certain 'resources' which are present to varying degrees in the work situation. The most important of these 'resources' are:

(i) A payment system which assists the continuous involvement of stewards in the determination of members' life-chances;
(ii) A high level of peer as opposed to supervisor—subordinate contact in the work situation;
(iii) The availability of information and 'expertise' through the network of shop stewards and the link, via this, to a larger body of legitimatory trade-union ideology;
(iv) The existence of mutually profitable rule-breaking relationships with management in bargaining;
(v) The degree to which the technical system of production generates crises which require the involvement of a steward for their solution.

These are the features of work which allow the union to achieve 'institutional centrality' in work and which, by extension, assist the pursuit of 'trade-union principles'.

As I have noted elsewhere, some of the difficulties with Batstone *et al.*'s classification stem from their inability to define 'trade-union principles' in any precise way.[21] Because I want to use their framework here in order to discuss the relationship between stewards' bargaining tactics and the more 'spontaneous' feelings of equity held by their members on particular issues, a more precise idea of the principles stewards pursue is needed. Similarly, I wish to differentiate between the issues on which stewards will be representatives and those on which they will merely be delegates: a concern with representative *behaviour* rather than *orientations* is thus appropriate. These requirements entail some changes to Batstone *et al.*'s approach.

The first change is simply to define 'trade-union principles' operationally in terms of Brown's four principles of shop-steward activity discussed above. These principles are somewhat indeterminate and organizational: indeterminate in that it is not clear what they imply in particular circumstances for wage differentials without a great deal of ancillary data, and organizational in that they imply some purpose 'beyond' achievements such as unity and profitable bargaining relations. However, both the collective bargaining correlates of these principles and the wider goals they serve are empirical questions which I shall deal with in Chapters 4 to 7.

The second change is to treat representative behaviour as issue specific. One might expect a representative role to be adopted where a steward has access to the necessary information, but on other issues, where the matter is 'central to the norms of the group', the steward may simply be a 'mouthpiece'.[22] Whatever the differences between domestic organizations, it may be the case that, *within* an organization, stewards are more likely to lead on some issues than on others.[23] Leadership may thus be seen as a feature of shop-steward behaviour in particular situations, rather than as a general role-orientation of particular stewards, and the ability to adopt a representative role may be to some extent a function of the sort of issue involved.

An alternative definition of leadership can thus be offered, stressing these changes. Leadership may be defined as initiatory action on an issue on the part of the steward, the characteristics of which are defined by allegiance to shop-steward principles rather than to the immediately-expressed wishes of the membership. The steward's ability to lead may depend on his allegiance to trade-union principles, which thus act as constraint and resource, and on practical success. Allegiance to trade-union principles legitimates steward leadership, but this allegiance must be combined with some practical success if steward power is to continue. And stewards will need to justify their independent action in terms of wider principles if it is to be sustained over time.[24] The ability to lead will also depend on members' conceptions of equity and their relation to the principles stewards pursue. For example, if a group have individualistic conceptions of payment equity, the stewards' job will be more difficult: I shall deal with this in more detail later in this chapter.

Consequently, one may distinguish within any group 'leadership' and 'normatively central' issues: the former are ones on which the steward exercises freedom of action, the latter are those where he is merely group spokesman. The stewards' role thus combines representative and delegate behaviour, and his issue-specific leadership behaviour will be directly defined by his adherence to trade-union principles, his substantive bargaining success, and the relationship between shop-steward principles and members' equity conceptions.

In this connection, Ross notes that wage bargaining is poorly adapted to rank-and-file control.[25] In pay bargaining, Ross alleges, the rank and file are extremely dependent on leadership guidance in pay matters as to what is possible, equitable or acceptable: there are two facets of this. On the one hand, the rank and file rely heavily on leadership expertise; 'The reason is not that the leadership has wrested dictatorial power from the rank and file, but that it alone is in possession of the necessary knowledge, expertise and skill to perform the function adequately.'[26] On the other hand, 'there are no administrative devices which will entirely eliminate the need for careful management of the wage bargain so as to hold the organization together.'[27] Not only are unity and equity dependent upon the elimination of sectional claims within the bargaining unit, but the maintenance of a good bargaining relationship with management depends on the ability of the steward to plan his policy in a predictable manner.[28] The pursuit of trade-union principles depends upon the ability of the steward to manage and manipulate systems of argument over pay independently of the immediately expressed interests of his members: if he cannot, then sectional claims or individual earnings movements may destroy equity and unity.

Pay issues are thus among those on which stewards are likely to lead. However, since the basis of this leadership is the possession of greater information and expertise than the membership, one can make a further sub-division. Where the situation requires negotiating skill, bargaining awareness, good contacts with representatives elsewhere and a sound knowledge of pay rises elsewhere, the members are likely to cede responsibility to the steward: the typical situation in this respect might be the negotiation of a pay increase. On the other hand, there may be pay issues which are 'central to the norms of the group' and in which the steward's freedom of action is greatly curtailed by the existence of definite preferences within the membership. The structure and size of differentials may be one such issue. On a day to day basis, however, stewards seek rises on the basis of existing structures of differentials rather than seeking to alter that structure itself.

Whether the issue is concerned with affairs internal to the bargaining unit or external to it, in the selection of wage comparisons, steward leadership is always open to challenge by the membership. Ross identifies the situations where stewards' leadership on pay issues is likely to be challenged, namely

(i) where there exists 'a strain upon established standards of living brought about by an inflation in the price level or by a reduction in take-home pay', and

(ii) where members make 'an invidious comparison with the wages, or wage-increases of other groups of workers'.[29]

These are both situations where the leader cannot legitimate his pursuit of shop-steward principles by pointing out to his members the substantive wage successes following from such a course of action.[30] The pursuit of the principles in specific situations is dependent on success, which may be gauged in terms of outside occurrences, such as the level of wage increases elsewhere. The leader steward will attempt to manage the impact of such events on his bargaining unit and on his members' attitudes, in his role as 'link with the outside world'.[31]

This management function is identified in observable patterns of shop-steward behaviour. Partridge identifies an evolution of functions, as shop stewards manage this 'gateway' function with increasing success. Initially, the steward is simply a spokesman for the group, but subsequently 'disseminating', 'monitoring' and 'liaison' functions are adopted so that ultimately the steward develops a fuller leadership role in motivating the workgroup and influencing its values.[32]

The role of wage-comparison choice is particularly important in this respect. The types of comparison made by stewards in their bargaining role may be selected with specific organizational goals in mind, and contrasted with the more 'informal' feelings of discontent which members typically experience in selecting reference groups. The steward, in his attempt to define the group's links with the outside world and manage the systems of argument relevant to negotiations, may seek to control or even to discount members' grievances so derived.

With this process in mind, the following distinction may be proposed, between

(i) 'bargaining comparisons': those quoted by officials/representatives in negotiations, or in dealings with members, for collective bargaining purposes and the furtherance of equity principles; and

(ii) 'informal comparisons': those quoted by members (or stewards) as instances of discontent/satisfaction with relative wages, but having no formal role in collective bargaining.

This distinction has obvious parallels with that between 'leadership' and 'normatively central' issues made above: it seeks to distinguish membership feelings from bargaining arguments. It is substantially the same as that made by Hyman and Brough, between 'primary' and 'secondary' comparisons.[33]

These types are more usefully distinguished in terms of their functions than in terms of the formal features of the situations in which they are used. The central characteristic of the former type is that their *tactical* element is pronounced: they are seldom ostensibly advantageous to the groups quoting them—in fact their use normally serves to highlight relative disadvantage. Yet, because they are typically for use in a bargaining context, their success, in assisting in securing a particular wage deal, depends upon the degree to which they limit the scope of the inequality highlighted.[34] In contrast, the typical absence of a formal role for members' comparisons means that they may be the basis of more 'spontaneous' feelings of relative deprivation. In particular,

(1) they need not be designed to elicit a positive response in a bargaining situation;
(2) they need not always elicit feelings of discontent: informal comparisons may be 'favourable' where bargaining comparisons are unlikely to be so.

They may, 'horizontally' at least, be more flexible and less consistent over time than bargaining comparisons since their justificatory role may be less exacting: industrial boundaries and occupational distinctions within the manual stratum may be less significant. Nevertheless, they may be an important influence on bargaining behaviour to the extent that they generate discontent which the steward must deal with, either by exerting his informal authority or by providing substantive solutions by translating such discontent into the appropriate 'systems of argument'.

The degree to which this analytical distinction is evident in practice is an empirical question which may be related directly to the leadership problem outlined above. Stewards in pursuit of trade-union principles are likely to select disadvantageous comparisons on the basis of information available to them about groups in broadly similar industrial relations situations. The availability of information in this respect, and the necessary supporting expertise to follow up such a claim rely heavily on the contours of union organization—both formal and informal—which will tend to reflect those of the company or industry. One would expect leader stewards—having better network contacts—to have more information about comparative rates of pay than populists, since such information is a resource which may be withheld. In accordance with this leadership role, the leader steward will attempt to be the main channel of communication with other groups. Informal comparisons need not be so limited and may, from the point of view of a predictable bargaining relationship with management, be diffuse and random.[35]

Ross feels that informal comparisons originate out of work— 'over the clothesline'—and are consequently extremely damaging to the worker's self-respect. In comparison, considerations such as employer's profits and worker productivity are far more remote, but are seized as supporting arguments once the original feeling of injustice is created.[36] This process may, of course, act in reverse if 'clothesline comparisons' are generally favourable; for example, if the worker is employed in a high-paying plant in a generally low-wage area, or if the worker's wages are high in comparison to those of his family network.

The central point is that, for stewards, comparisons which are based on other identifiable work units and the weighing of elements of one wage bargain against those of another group are potentially unifying and subject to control by their knowledge and expertise. Feelings of discontent which are, for example, based on comparisons with neighbours or invidious comparisons of after-tax earnings or with prospective unemployment benefits, all of which may vary between individuals according to social networks and family situations, are not potentially unifying, nor are they systematic enough to be conducive to good bargaining relationships with management.

In the first place, they may be very unpredictable.[37] Moreover, the quality of information available to members and upon which 'informal' comparison is based may be far less systematic than that required in bargaining: it may not, for example, be clear which measure of earnings is being quoted, particularly if the information is acquired in casual conversation. Gross and net earnings, earnings before and after addition of shift and overtime premia, and the consistency of comparative earnings over time are all variables which influence the bargaining validity of the comparison made. In addition, the steward will wish to know some details of the work and working practices of ostensibly similar groups, so that the entire effort bargain can be evaluated, in case the comparison has unwelcome bargaining implications. Similarly, impressions of pay settlements culled from the press and impressions of the sorts of rises needed to compensate for price rises may be imprecise.[38] Where stewards must argue with managers on a relatively systematic basis, imprecision or inaccuracy in reporting information which is the basis of argument can lead to unacceptable loss of bargaining advantage.

Stewards typically attempt, by contrast, to manage the use of comparisons in pursuit of trade-union principles: they want the wage comparisons they quote to be disadvantageous, unifying and plausible. However, in many cases they also want them to be manipulable within the constraints of the bargaining relationship.[39] There may be, as Brown and Sisson and Ross note, organizational advantages in the use of comparisons, but stewards concerned to stress their substantive successes in bargaining will find unwelcome the 'follower' conception which consistent use of the same comparison might imply.[40] The extent to which stewards can manage the use of comparisons depends very much on the extent to which they establish the independence of steward action within the bargaining unit: this is the paradoxical, and difficult, aspect of the use of bargaining comparisons. Stewards will wish to use disadvantageous comparisons as a bargaining 'lever' in certain instances, and will seek membership support for the bargaining initiative. However, they will not wish for this use of comparisons to reflect on their bargaining success, since this is to some extent the basis of their leadership: members must accept wage comparisons, but not assume that they are always chasing better-paid groups. A steward using a particular bargaining comparison may thus characterize it one way in discussion with management, and quite another when talking to members.

One can look at the difference between bargaining and informal comparisons in Runciman's reference group terminology. Runciman notes, on the one hand, that any individual may be a member of several different membership reference groups simultaneously; these may, in turn, be the basis for a number of different comparisons with other groups. On the other hand, he notes that an individual may seek an 'egoistic' (individualist) or 'fraternalist' (collective) solution to relative deprivation. According to my distinction, stewards will wish to ensure that,

(a) the membership reference group which is of greatest salience for the individual on pay matters is coterminous with, or at least not inconsistent with, the boundaries of the bargaining group of which he is a member, and

(b) that the fraternalistic solution, based on the entire membership reference group within the bargaining unit or, better still, on the bargaining unit itself, will be adopted in preference to the egoistic one.

FIG. 2.2. *Reference group selection and bargaining attitudes*

|  | Relatively deprived because of own position as member of group | |
|---|---|---|
|  | satisfied | dissatisfied |
| **Relatively deprived because of group's position in society** — satisfied | *A*<br>apathetic | *B*<br>egoist |
| **Relatively deprived because of group's position in society** — dissatisfied | *C*<br>fraternalist | *D*<br>griever |

The situation may be further clarified by reference to Fig. 2.2, which is largely a reproduction of Runciman's Fig. 2. The four categories may be labelled as illustrated; of the two categories I have labelled myself, the 'apathetic' is one whose satisfaction with all relationships may not be supportive of the representative's ambitions in bargaining, while the 'griever' may be a threat to the unity of the group. The representative will seek to encourage all his members to make comparisons of type $C$, and his selection of bargaining comparisons will reflect this; they will tend to be fraternalistic and to encourage fraternalism. Members, by contrast, may be satisfied with wages so that they will not support a bargaining initiative (type $A$), wish, for example, to work a great deal of overtime, or at a 'rate-busting' pace without worrying about the collective repercussions of this (type $B$), or display an unmanageable militancy fuelled only by purely personal grievances (type $D$). The bargaining comparison will tend to be in support of collective advancement, whereas informal comparisons may have vastly different implications.

I have presented these two distinctions—between leadership and normatively central issues and between bargaining and informal comparisons—as clear cut. But the precise relationship in each case is an empirical question. If stewards and members think alike, members preferences may closely correspond with steward principles, and the distinctions may have little force. Where they do not think alike, and the distinctions are easily made, stewards may experience problems in reconciling their principles with members' wishes. Stewards will seek to rectify this by encouraging the 'bargaining awareness' of their members; that is, an awareness that conflicts of interest can arise over aspects of work, and that negotiations can take place. A growth of this awareness is likely to be associated with a developing knowledge of the earnings of other groups, and a questioning of differentials between them. As the shop-steward system develops, and the workforce becomes integrated as a political unit, informal comparisons may become uniform.[41]

The usefulness of the two distinctions is thus inversely related to the bargaining awareness of the membership. This broad 'leadership' model of steward activity on pay will be used where appropriate in the empirical analysis in subsequent chapters. The model, however, points only to general trends and says little about the determinants of the substantive pattern of fair pay conceptions within a bargaining unit, and of attitudes of fair pay between bargaining units. It must be supplemented by a consideration of particular features of the industrial relations situation which may affect the bargaining unit. Broadly speaking, the important issues concern the coverage of the bargaining unit and the collective bargaining context in which it operates.

## THE BARGAINING UNIT: INTERNAL INFLUENCES

I have stressed that shop-steward activity on pay can be characterized broadly in terms of the pursuit of unity and equity between constituents and the maintenance of a good bargaining relationship with management involving a minimum of uncertainty. The internal structure of the unit will define the extent to which and the manner in which shop stewards achieve this principally because, in any situation, the steward will attempt to achieve a working consensus on issues rather than one which is based on a reference to any 'wider' theory of fairness. Fairness is operationally defined in terms of equity within specifiable organizational limits.

One of the crucial determinants of the steward's ability to realize trade-union aims is the occupational composition of the bargaining unit. Different occupational groups may have very specific ideas about definitions of 'skill' and occupational relativities. Certain of these definitions may be mutually exclusive, and the difference may not be resolvable by reference to technical criteria, since the definition of skill may be 'social'. As Clegg notes

In the past, skill generally meant the practised ability to perform a difficult task or group of tasks. More recently, technical knowledge has come to constitute a greater part of many skills. For the purposes of industrial relations, on the other hand, a craft is a social institution based upon a set period and form of training and the reservation of certain jobs for those who are undergoing and have completed that training.[42]

The problems of unity and equity may be greater where a bargaining unit contains workers of different skill levels: it is not merely that problems may arise over the existence of differentials, they may also arise over their size and definition. The classic case in this area depicts a convergence of skilled and semi-skilled earnings as a consequence of payment by results. However the problem is not peculiar to this situation: semi-skilled earnings are extremely variable in relation to skilled, even where external influences such as national agreements seek to impart uniformity.

Problems may also arise since bargaining units normally contain several distinct work groups.[43] What is at issue, then, is the steward's ability to establish the bargaining unit as the primary

membership reference group on pay matters, where other potentially divisive bases might suggest themselves to members. The
contours of union organization must accommodate to the basic
structure of industry, defined by managerial interpretations of
technological requirements, in order to establish the basic identity
of interest for collective action. This is a complex area, but essentially what is at issue is the steward's management of wage relationships between what Dunlop has identified as job clusters; 'defined
as a stable group of job classifications or work assignments within a
firm (wage-determining unit) which are so linked by (1) technology,
(2) the administrative organization of the production process,
including policies of lay-off, transfer and promotion or (3) social
custom, in that they have common wage-making characteristics.'[44]
In the short term—and as far as shop stewards are concerned—job
clusters can be regarded as given by technology and managerial
control systems. Stewards must co-ordinate the activities of workers
in different 'job clusters' in bargaining in order to avoid divisive
sectionalism.

The size of a bargaining unit is thus critical, in that the likelihood
of a diversity of interests on any particular problem increases as
more distinct groups are embraced by the same bargaining unit. It is
critical to wage-bargaining activity in a number of other respects
also. Beynon notes that the influence a domestic organization may
have on the larger union depends on its membership.[45] In the same
vein, Batstone *et al.* have traced a positive relationship between
steward leadership and constituency size,[46] and Boraston *et al.* note
a relationship between the size of an organization and its achievement of independence from the larger union.[47] It is clear from
Batstone *et al.*'s analysis that the development of a sophisticated
shop steward organization integrating and co-ordinating action on
pay would only be possible on the basis of a large bargaining unit.

I have argued the importance of the idea of leadership on pay in
the model above, and it is important to note that leadership is based,
not merely on the resources of the work situation, but also on the
institutional definition of the shop-steward's role in union rule
books. Hence, in the AUEW, a steward can raise any question of
concern to his members, provided that it cannot be settled in discussion between the foreman and the man or men concerned. This
leaves the limits of steward authority open.[48] In SOGAT, also, the
rule book contains a clause to the effect that the F.O.C.'s word on
certain matters is 'final': thus establishing *by rule* a certain amount
of independence of action.

In practice, the application and observance of such rules is an empirical question: they are resources on the basis of which stewards may establish independence from the membership. Different officers may be constrained by the membership to different degrees: this is clear from Batstone *et al.*'s discussion of the 'tiering' of shop-steward organization, and some tendency towards 'hierarchy' in steward organizations appears widespread.[49] The rules of election, tenure and function are none the less important.

A further feature of particular importance is the representation ratio or pattern of representation. If there is a high steward–member ratio, it is likely that members' grievances will be less likely to be 'sifted'—at least at this first level of representation. Moreover, if grievances may be settled at this level, without recourse to the steward committee, members may receive a better service (defined in terms of the proportion of personal grievances to which they receive a satisfactory solution). More significantly, if there is a substantial rate of turnover of stewards combined with a high representation ratio, the number of members with steward experience may be high.[50] If a number of members are *au fait* with the problems of shop stewardship, this may serve to increase the number of opinion leaders on whom the steward can rely and to emphasize to the remainder of the membership the problems faced by the steward, and so ensure him a sympathetic hearing at mass meetings and other occasions where he is answerable to members. There may be size effects here too. Smaller bargaining units with a reasonably high turnover of stewards may be advantaged in the achievement of bargaining awareness. There appears to be a positive relationship between steward continuity and size of bargaining unit.[51] These contingencies of size and structure are important influences on the achievement of equity and unity. The obvious hypothesis is that larger bargaining units appear to have greater equity problems to the extent that they embrace a wider variety of interests—but this must be qualified by acknowledging that their resources and bargaining power may also be considerable.

The pursuit of shop-steward principles is likely to be influenced considerably by the policies of management and the control systems in operation. The relationship between management policy and collective bargaining has been analysed in detail and in different ways by both Brown and Batstone *et al.* Brown has traced a relationship between systems of managerial control and the development of 'distortions' in the payment system: the different concerns of different management departments—with 'getting the job out' or with close cost control—may conflict.[52] Batstone *et al.* have shown how, in the context of different management–steward relations, management may provide information to stewards in bargaining. This is particularly the case where leader stewards engage in strong bargaining relationships with management. In such cases confidential information is exchanged and each is concerned to protect the relationship with the other party.[53]

On the most general level, Terry has shown how management may 'sponsor' the formation of shop-steward organizations in order to overcome problems posed by rationalization and change, and elsewhere I have traced a relationship between sponsorship and the policies of shop-steward organizations.[54]

More specifically, management practice may structure bargaining expectations through the payment system, the choice of which may affect the pattern of internal differentials and reflect over-all managerial 'style'.[55] There is a close relationship between managerial policies and the steward's achievement of equity and unity. Defective managerial control systems may increase the difficulties of co-ordination faced by shop stewards by setting discordant precedents or generating uncertainty.[56]

It should not be assumed, however, that the role of management is always facilitating; managers co-operate with leader stewards in pursuit of their own divergent goals. The other side of the coin, so to speak, is the withholding of information, the undermining of equitable pay structures where they contradict some definition of efficiency and the imposition of restrictions on steward activity. The extent to which shop stewards can arrive at the pay structure which they most favour may depend on the degree to which management are concerned to limit the total cost of the wage bill rather than define relations between its elements.

## THE BARGAINING CONTEXT

The individual bargaining unit operates within constraints set by the structure of collective bargaining within the plant, company, industry, and area. The bargaining power possessed by the unit itself may be defined by 'external' contingencies such as the rate of unemployment[57] or a strategic location in the production process.[58] In particular, the bargaining behaviour of groups will be at least in part determined by the autonomy of action permitted by trade-union structure.

Within the workplace, the bargaining unit may embrace all manual workers in the plant, or it may be one among several. The former situation has been analysed by Batstone *et al.*, and it is with the latter that I am primarily concerned here. In this instance, the bargaining unit will have a set of 'horizontal' relationships with other domestic organizations of manual workers in the same plant or company. Certain features of these bargaining units are important for patterns of wage comparison and influence on the larger trade-union structure—for example, their bargaining strength, occupational composition, payment systems, size and bargaining dates. Relative bargaining strength will influence the problem of wage leadership, as will the timing of bargaining.[59] Occupational composition will influence the availability of comparisons, given the tendency of workers to delimit reference groups narrowly. The opacity of payment systems will also influence the tendency to compare earnings.[60] The availability of information is extremely important. It is generally assumed that earnings information is more readily available within rather than between plants. Where bargaining is fragmented, this need not be the case, as competitive bargaining may generate pressures to conceal rates of pay. In any case, 'casual' information flows may be very inefficient in communicating rates and workers may find factory wage structures opaque.[61]

More systematic information may be available where bargaining units within a plant are covered by a Joint Shop Stewards Committee. The importance of a steward network such as this is clear from Batstone *et al.*'s analysis and Goodman and Whittingham also emphasize the information-pooling aspect of JSSC activity.[62] However, while such developments may be common in the motor industry,[63] multi-unionism in other industries may generate different patterns of unofficial organization. For example, where two craft groups are employed at different locales within a company or industry, the contours of organization may follow occupational or craft lines rather than geographical ones, and Combined Committees may develop, particularly where bargaining units are small.[64]

Since communications improvements may spread information about bargaining strategies as well as about earnings,[65] such developments are important. In their absence, contact between stewards may be rare and information exchange infrequent: Boraston *et al.* note that AUEW stewards employed in different plants of the same company were not in frequent contact, even within one geographical area, and that the quarterly shop-stewards' meetings were not used for information exchange.[66] Given the stringency of information requirements for bargaining purposes, the development of unofficial organization is crucial.

The information available to the stewards from the formal union may be minimal. Within the AUEW, for example, the full-time officer may be a source of earnings information, as may convenor or steward membership of the District Committee,[67] but involvement with both is a contingent rather than essential feature of shop-steward activity. Boraston *et al.* discuss in detail the patterns of contact between local or unofficial organizations and the 'formal' union, particularly the full-time officers. They distinguish between the independence of the workplace organization from the formal union and the scope for workplace bargaining permitted by national or company agreements: high independence and a wide scope for workplace bargaining do not necessarily go together—the relationship may be more complex.[68] Batstone *el al.* make a slightly different distinction: they note that strong domestic organizations may be both independent of and isolated from the formal union, and that contact may be limited to branch attendance by individual members. Their classification is as follows:

(*a*) integration/isolation 'refers to the extent to which the domestic organization accepts the larger union's role in determining their own actions'. This distinction classifies organizations in terms of the degree of consensus they have with the larger union on goals and rights.

(*b*) Dependence/Independence classifies organizations in terms of dependence upon the formal organization to achieve goals: 'A domestic organization is classified as dependent upon the larger union when it has to have frequent resort to the latter in order to achieve its goals.'[69]

These distinctions define the autonomy of the domestic organization: in both formulations, independent organizations—often powerful—will have no reliance upon the full-time officer. Isolated organizations will have little contact with the officer, branch or district committee. And organizations where the scope for workplace bargaining is considerable may develop policies on a wide range of issues which differ from those promoted by the formal union. The position of an organization on these continua will define not only the amount of contact it has with the full-time officer, but also the quality of contact in terms of the influence the full-time officer is able to exert: his role may differ in different situations. More autonomous organizations will have correspondingly greater freedom to arrive at a rate structure which stewards feel best suits the particular equity requirements of the bargaining unit. Within the AUEW, even where the full-time official is involved, there may be little District Committee control. As Boraston *et al.* found in their study: 'The test of any settlement which he (i.e. the District Secretary) negotiated with management of a local firm was its acceptability to workers in the plant, rather than the approval of the

Committee. Consequently, the Committee did not exercise much control.'[70]

Different organizations are thus likely to have differential access to information about earnings elsewhere: their appreciation of pay inequity is likely to be patterned by the coverage of the groups and organizations to which they are party. Such wider organizations will have a considerable influence upon the pattern of wage determination, whether or not they themselves are party to collective bargaining. Patterns of group membership and affiliation such as this may be the organizational basis for the sorts of regulation in wage determination which Dunlop refers to as a 'wage contour', namely: 'A stable group of wage-determining units (bargaining units, plants or firms) which are so linked together by (1) similarity of product markets, (2) resort to similar sources for a labour force or (3) common labour market organization (custom), that they have common wage making characteristics.'[71] However, such regularities need not exist, and wage determination in a locale or particular set of firms may not display the regularity and order which Dunlop's conception seems to imply. The type of 'wage round' which Dunlop seems to envisage is that typified by Turner as a form of restraint,[72] but patterns of wage leadership may arise—as in 'competitive leap-frogging'—which do not develop into an observable regularity over time.[73] The 'key' bargains need not be the same in successive 'rounds' where:

(i) an area experiences influx or outflow of industry, for example where high-paying plants move into a low wage area, or where factory closure removes high-paying plants from an area;
(ii) technical change or the introduction of new machinery erodes the bargaining power of some groups and increases that of others, or alters the skill requirements of particular groups of jobs;
(iii) bargaining power shifts for some other reason, for example where the autonomy of a powerful shop-floor organization is curtailed by the imposition of a company agreement;
(iv) where incomes policy shifts the pay calendar: under the last Labour government, for example, settlements in August and September were salient as guides to interpretation of incomes policy, whereas previously the groups concerned may have been 'followers' rather than leaders.

In the medium term, then, there need be no stable pattern of wage settlements: the situation within a given area, product market, or company may be in a state of flux. The competitive pressures allegedly leading to equalization of rates need not operate, and the existence of any regularity in wage settlements will be an empirical question. One of the most important sets of variables to consider in this respect is the structure of collective bargaining arrangements in the industry or locale concerned. At one extreme, one might envisage one or two bargains of wide coverage which dominate the scene: alternatively, there may be dozens of small bargains in individual plants. It is evident that the former situation is more 'structured' in Robinson's sense of the term,[74] and that it is also closer to the situation envisaged by Ross where comparisons become coercive and equalization of wages or wage increases is likely to be sought.[75]

The presence or absence of elements of 'structure' in the distribution of wages within an area, industry or company will have severe repercussions upon the bargaining behaviour of shopfloor organizations. Where autonomous organizations pursue 'fragmented bargaining' independently of each other, the likelihood is that any pattern of wage-settlements will not be discerned across any broad area by participants. There may appear to be no 'prevailing' increase. Two likely consequences follow from this:

(1) individual bargaining units will wish to preserve their bargaining discretion (*a*) in the maintenance of bargaining autonomy, and (*b*) in the selection of comparisons:

(2) the size of the wage claim need in no way follow from events elsewhere, particularly if a wage-leadership role is assumed. Essentially, such a situation will generate bargaining uncertainty, which will be magnified where bargainers do not have information about events elsewhere: the standards of judgement of what is a 'fair rise' are eroded.

In short, I am essentially proposing two ideas: firstly, that comparisons tend to flow along 'organizational' lines, and, secondly, that where such lines do not exist, uncertainty in bargaining follows. The consequences of this uncertainty depend upon the bargaining context in which it occurs.

## CONCLUSION

This chapter has looked at fair pay in the context of collective bargaining. The bargaining model attempts an explanation of attitudes to fairness in collective bargaining in terms of the internal structure of the bargaining unit and the bargaining context in which it is set, while the latter two sections of the chapter seek to outline the variables which influence the precise way in which the model operates. The framework is depicted in Fig. 2.3. It is not possible to assert that all possible influences on the conduct of the bargaining unit have been included, nor that all possible relevant variables within the unit have been considered, since the framework must be deliberately selective. Nor is it possible to assess at this stage the relative strengths of different 'links', for example, between members' and stewards' 'outside' contacts. It is presented merely as an interpretive device.

FIG. 2.3. *The analytical model and major contingencies*

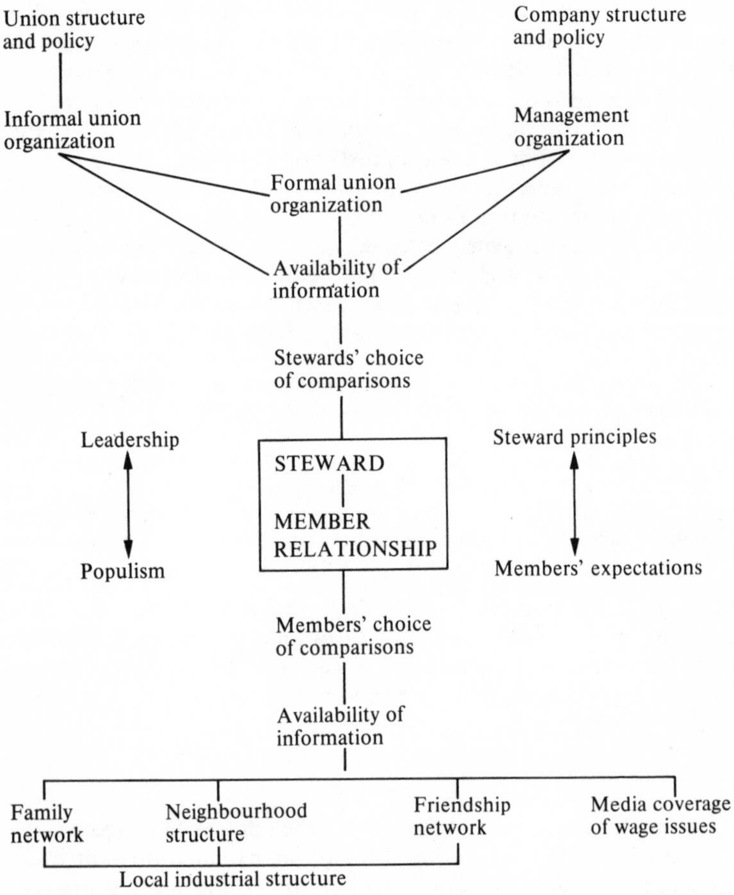

This distinction presented in the model between stewards and members is obviously overdrawn, and subject to the numerous empirical qualifications discussed above. All Fig. 2.3 does is to display the ways in which the contingencies of different industrial relations situations may interact with the structure of particular domestic organizations to affect the definition of an equitable pay structure.

In terms of the model, the main areas for analysis are:

(1) the substantive patterns of differentials experienced by bargaining units and reactions to them;
(2) the pattern of reactions to relativities external to the bargaining unit;
(3) the relationship between stewards and members on pay issues, with particular reference to the selection of wage comparisons.

Fig. 2.4. *Classification of wage differences*

**PLANT-INTERNAL**

Differentials Internal
to the Bargaining Unit

Relativities between
Manual Work Groups

Relativities between
Manual and Non-Manual
Groups

Income Differences
between Employers
and Employed

**PLANT-EXTERNAL**

Relativities Internal to
the Occupational Group

Relativities between Manual
Unions or Occupations

Relativities between Manual
and Non-Manual Groups

Income Differences between
Employers and Employed

*Notes:* (1) The plant-external category can be further divided; such comparisons may be internal to the company or external to it.
(2) Comparisons within any group mentioned may also be divided into 'vertical'—with a skill group above or below one's own—and 'horizontal' within one's own skill group.

The following chapters will seek to provide and evaluate data in an attempt to explore these areas. In these chapters, the classificatory basis of Fig. 2.4—which has been developed to avoid the terminological confusion which besets this type of work—will be adopted. 'Differentials'—referring to those wage differences which are in principle subject to a single administrative decision—will be considered separate from and prior to 'relativities'—which are not so defined. In practice, this means that the wage relations which shop stewards in my sample attempt to control will be considered separate from those to which they react.[76] For each type of wage relation, the industrial relations background will be presented first, then the attitudinal data will be evaluated in terms of it, and finally the implications for the model developed in the last chapter will be explained. The next chapter presents the background to the case studies. Chapter 4 discusses shop-steward organization and control over the rate structures (differentials), and Chapter 5 is concerned with wage comparisons (relativities). Chapter 6 evaluates the findings in light of the model presented here, and Chapter 7 focuses directly on the impact of incomes policies. Chapter 8 concludes with some policy recommendations.

## CHAPTER 3

# THE BACKGROUND TO THE CASE STUDIES

## INTRODUCTION

In this analysis, I have focused on two case-study plants, both branch-plants of the same multi-plant enterprise. Within those plants, I have concentrated on bargaining units composed of AUEW members. Clearly, such a narrow focus generates findings which are illustrative rather than conclusive: they may not be applicable to other situations, particularly since no attempt was made to isolate a 'representative' or 'crucial' sample. I shall discuss this below. The centrepiece of the research design was a structured interview schedule, but unstructured interviews, observation and documentary analysis were also used. Case Study A was completed in the summer of 1976, but due to difficulties of access Case Study B could not be undertaken until April 1977. An account of these difficulties, together with a description of the research design, is contained in Appendix 1. The interview schedule is reproduced as Appendix 2.

In this chapter, I want to detail the industrial relations background to the case studies, and to provide a description of the main features of the sample. In performing the latter task, I shall indicate the relevance for this sample of the theorizing about the 'parochial' nature of the problem of fair pay presented in Chapter 1. In both case studies, respondents selected wage comparisons which were 'vertically' limited, and there appeared to be a consensus over occupational ranking. However, before discussing these matters, something must be said about the significance of the sample.

## THE SIGNIFICANCE OF THE SAMPLE

Since I have not started out from any well-articulated theory of fair pay, with a view to testing specific hypotheses, there is no basis upon which a 'crucial' sample could be selected. Nevertheless, some samples are more interesting than others in that they may give insight into the mechanics of the processes under study. From this point of view, this sample is of considerable interest. It is composed of autonomous bargaining units, in an industry which has not been analysed to any great extent by those with similar concerns, in a company in which shopfloor bargaining is well developed, and it contains both skilled and unskilled workers.

The value of basing a case study on a particular domestic organization depends on the degree to which it can operationally be treated
as a closed system. As Batstone *et al.* note, the appropriate unit of
analysis will vary not only with the purposes of the study, but also
with the actual patterns of union behaviour. Studies focusing on
shopfloor bargaining ought to concentrate on areas where this is
well developed.[1] The sample was, as the following analysis will
show, sufficiently well organized and self-contained in this respect.

Much of the work on shop-steward activity has concentrated on
car work or related engineering industries and on production
workers within those industries. While there is no sound *a priori*
reason why car-work findings should not have wider applicability,
certain features of unofficial unionism in the motor industry may
not be general. In particular, the 'parallel unionism' which is apparently a feature of the motor industry, and which undoubtedly assists
the development of Joint Shop Stewards' Committees, may not be
replicated elsewhere. Certain other industries—including the one in
which the sample was located—are characterized by sectionalism
between bargaining units preventing such developments in unofficial unionism. Such 'fragmented' bargaining might be expected to
encourage the use of comparisons, particularly within the plant.

Following in part from this concentration on piecework and engineering, where payment by results is prevalent, it has often been
assumed that a pattern of 'primary drift'—due to the tendencies inherent in piecework systems—could be distinguished from a com-
pensatory pattern of 'secondary drift'.[2] Production workers on
piecework were characterized as a disruptive or at least motive
force, while timeworkers, usually employed on maintenance, were
seen to be chasing pay developments via the negotiation of lieu
bonuses. However, a number of points need to be made here. First,
in product markets other than that of motor vehicles, the primacy of
continued production might not be so pronounced, and the bargaining power of production workers may be less. Secondly, where production workers are not paid under piecework, autonomous drift
mechanisms may not be available to provide monetary advantage.
Thirdly, (and consequently) the 'followership' role of maintenance
workers in wage negotiation may not occur in other industries,
where the bargaining strength of maintenance workers in relation to
production is greater.

This sample is of maintenance or indirect workers and, as the
analysis below reveals, the situation is more complex than the
motor-industry model implies. Maintenance workers are an under-
investigated group. Yet, as maintenance work is performed across

the whole spectrum of manufacturing industry by workers who are broadly similar in skill, occupation, and trade-union membership (i.e. largely AUEW or EETPU skilled men) it is apparent that they occupy something of a key position, as an easily identifiable 'link' between otherwise diverse industries. For such workers, the selection of comparisons need not be limited by industrial boundaries, where these are frequently crossed by occupational links.

This sample is of considerable interest in other respects. Both subsamples contained skilled and unskilled workers. In the period up to the interviewing, similar differentials between engineering craftsmen and unskilled workers had undergone considerable convergence (to 1975) and then some slight expansion (under the Social Contract). This movement of differentials is associated elsewhere by Brown with the operation of definite norms of equity,[3] and this study can explore this assertion in more depth. Moreover, the sample is located in a multi-plant company where an unofficial combined committee has developed. Since little has been written about the impact of combined committees on pay bargaining, this too is of some interest, although much of the data is presented elsewhere.[4] Finally, the two subsamples are located in different geographical areas, thus avoiding the possibility that the findings might be distorted by any single regional effect on attitudes to equity.[5] Although the sample has several interesting aspects, sample selection was subject to powerful practical constraints. Only bargaining units up to a certain size could be included, and a time-rate payment system was preferred to a piecework one due to the problems of measuring earnings variance over time. These considerations should be borne in mind in the following discussion.

### INDUSTRIAL RELATIONS BACKGROUND

The company in which the analysis was undertaken is one of the largest producers of packaging and allied products in the world. It consists of an over-all holding company with three operating

### TABLE 3.1
### *Major Product Groups*

| | |
|---|---|
| Group 1 (metal products) | 8 plants |
| Group 2 (metal products) | 13 plants |
| Group 3 (paper packaging) | 11 plants |
| Research and Development | 3 plants |

*Source:* Company Accounts 1975–7. The original names are withheld in the interests of confidentiality.

companies. One company is concerned with overseas operations, another with the newer areas into which the group is diversifying and the third—with which I shall be concerned—with the bulk of packaging operations in the United Kingdom. This company has thirty five factories in the United Kingdom, divided into three major product groups, as shown in Table 3.1.

These groups are the main autonomous profit centres, although this is probably less true of Group 3 where product diversification between plants encourages a system of plant-level profit account-ability. Undoubtedly, Groups 1 and 2, the 'metal product' groups of the company, are the backbone of it, both in terms of size and profitability, and in the sense that the company has grown by acqui-sition out of an initial concern solely with these products. They are also the groups which, in technological terms, are the most homogeneous.

My main concern in this section is with the structure of collective bargaining within the Company. As might be imagined, where a concern has this number of plants in the United Kingdom in a vari-ety of different product markets, such a structure is complex. The Company has over two hundred agreements with seventeen dif-ferent trade unions, bargaining at different times during the year. In order to understand this structure, it is necessary to describe briefly its historical development.

For many years the Company was party to a Wages Council (sub-sequently a JIC) agreement covering the general workers in its employ; a national agreement covering basic rates and terms and conditions of employment provided a basis of common wage rates for the TGWU and GMWU workers who were concentrated in those two metal product groups. Subsequently, the company left the JIC and concluded, in 1971, an 'Independent Agreement' at na-tional level with the two general unions, which again provided common terms and conditions of employment for general workers throughout the company, but specified that wage negotiations should be at group level. The basis of the agreement was a job-evaluated five-grade structure (six-grade in certain Group 2 fac-tories) for all general workers. Thus, although the basis of grading and conditions of employment are common, there has been, since the agreement, a differential for Group 2 over similar grades in Group 1, which at the time of interviewing stood at approximately 3–4p per hour. The general worker agreements, which are signed in October of each year, remain the largest single agreements in the company, covering 6,000 (Group 1) and 5,000 (Group 2) workers each.

The level of terms and conditions established for general workers under the JIC and subsequently under the Independent Agreement was extended to all AUEW members (and other maintenance staff) until recently. In 1972 an Engineering Agreement was signed between national officers of the AUEW and management covering minimum rates to be paid within the company and basic terms and conditions of employment: the EETPU are also party to this agreement.[6] In Groups 1 and 3 and the capital goods group these minimum rates are supplemented by plant level wage bargaining producing a diversity of rates which will be discussed below. In Group 2 an agreement was signed in 1975 providing uniform rates for AUEW members within that group. It is management's intention to move towards similar agreements in other groups of the company. Group 1 does not have a great diversity of rates and may well adopt such an agreement in the near future; other groups, particularly Group 3, present more intractable problems. The company's aim is to have one set of terms and conditions of employment for all manual workers set at company level, but to separate off wage bargaining for the various grades at group level; the 'philosophy' is apparently the separation of wage bargaining from other issues at the level of the autonomous profit centre.

Given the product market diversity of Group 3, there may be problems associated with the implementation of group-level wage bargaining arrangements. In terms of 'good industrial relations', rather than cost-accountability, this exercise is further impeded by the contours of union organization within the group. In Groups 1 and 2 there is, generally speaking, a simple pattern of union organization; craftsmen are organized by the AUEW, and production workers wither by the TGWU or the GMWU. The latter are covered by group agreements already; they are on terms and conditions slightly inferior to those of craftsmen. In Group 3, however, production workers are organized by the print unions—mainly the NGA and the largely non-craft SOGAT. These unions are partly neither to the Engineering nor the Independent Agreement. Basic rates, and many of their terms and conditions of employment, are set by the BPIF agreement, the company being affiliated to the BPIF at local level. This agreement is supplemented in two different ways:

(a) it covers neither sick pay nor pension conditions, the terms for which are those of the Independent Agreement, and

(b) the rates of pay set by the BPIF agreement are national minima and are supplemented in a variety of ways at plant level.[7]

The organization of the production workforce in Group 3 by print unions poses several problems for any rationalization programme. Their patterns of organization and of bargaining, and their relations with other unions in the company are ill-suited to incorporation within the company bargaining structure preferred by management (see Chapter 5).

On the staff side, patterns of unionization are also complex, although movement proceeds towards common pay levels within groups. Common conditions of employment were set at national level prior to the unionization of staff in the early 1960s and have continued to be set on this basis throughout, most recently in negotiation with a Joint Staff Unions Consortium. Groups 1 and 2 have group staff pay agreements, and management hope to move towards similar agreements in other groups. The main staff union in Group 2 is ASTMS, who also organize extensively in the other groups; other unions with considerable numbers are TASS, the TGWU staff section (ACTS), the ATAES section of SOGAT and SLADE.

The Company's attempts to simplify collective bargaining arrangements has met with greatest success where general and staff unions are involved. By contrast, the craft unions preferred to bargain within the plants and moreover, to do so on a sectional basis. AUEW conveners were generally not party to Joint Shop Stewards' Committees, nor to plant-wide bargaining arrangements. They bargained autonomously for pay increases over the minima set by the engineering agreement. Only the non-monetary elements of this applied at plant level. There were thus problems of intra-plant comparability.

Furthermore, AUEW convenors from different plants did not act in an unco-ordinated manner. The process of plant bargaining was significantly influenced by the existence of a National Combined Committee embracing a proportion of maintenance staff in all of the production groups of the company. A brief description of the committee and some details of its operation have been included in Appendix 3. Here I shall simply note the influence the Combined Committee had on plant-level wage bargaining: there are two separable issues here—influence on plant-internal wage structures and influence on the selection of bargaining comparisons.

It was not the policy of the Combined Committee to interfere in any way with the convenor's conduct of bargaining within his own plant. Once the minimum level of wages had been established, the Combined Committee did not seek to encourage any further uniformity in the interplant wage structure: this was, in fact, discouraged as an erosion of bargaining 'leverage'. The Committee did not pressure convenors to conform to any particular pattern of differentials; its positive influence on the internal rate structure of either case-study plant was minimal. Not only did the Combined Committee encourage convenor autonomy, within the structure of the AUEW, it was powerless to prevent it. Its role in encouraging and directing company-internal wage comparisons was of much greater significance. The Combined Committee spread information about rates, premia and working arrangements between plants, and officers of the committee indicated that 'leapfrogging' was explicitly encouraged. Latterly, information bulletins had been circulated on a regular basis, detailing this sort of information.

In summary, then, company policy involved the simplification of bargaining structures in order to remove pressures towards competitive bargaining and establish control over labour costs at the appropriate sectors of accountability. The craft workers in the company were apparently one of the last major groups 'outside' this rationalization process. The AUEW and EETPU had established an unofficial organization which was to a large extent concerned to ensure that they remained so.

### THE CASE-STUDY PLANTS

Two plant-level case studies were conducted in the company: they will be termed Plant 'A' and Plant 'B' throughout. These two plants were in different product groups; as part of Group 3, Plant A was involved in the production of paper products including cartons, labels and other packaging goods, extending into cheque-book production for financial institutions, while Plant B in Group 1 was involved in the production of tinplate containers, from cans to aerosols and vacuum-sealed tubes. There were thus different production technologies employed on the two sites.

Factory A was situated on a large industrial estate in the Merseyside area, dominated by several large motor car manufacturers attracted to Merseyside in the early 1960s.[8] Other major factories in the area produced rubber products, paints, precision tools, surgical instruments and pharmaceutical products. There were also a number of smaller 'satellite' companies manufacturing components for the large assembly plants. Factory A was the only one on the estate, or indeed in that part of Merseyside, in the particular product market of paper cartons and packaging: it was one of only four factories in the Merseyside area which were designated 'carton' houses by the print unions. The company owned two other plants on Merseyside;

one in Group 2, the other in Group 3. Both were very different from A in terms of union organization, product markets, wage rates and, in some respects, terms and conditions of employment. Although the stewards at Factory A knew some of the AUEW representatives in these other plants, links with them at the time of the interview were no stronger than those with several other AUEW organizations in the area. At neither factory were engineers as well paid at that time as they were at Factory A.

Factory B was located in a coal-mining town in the East Midlands, on a small industrial estate which it dominated. There was no well developed engineering industry in the area, although it seems that engineering was a growth industry locally.[10] Another company plant, in Group 2, three miles away, was also one of the largest employers of labour in its own vicinity. Together, these made the company a significant influence on local employment, unlike the plants on Merseyside. Contacts between the convenor at B and representatives from this adjacent plant were good, since they too were members of the Combined Committee.

Both factories were approximately the same size (A approximately 1,300, B just over 1,000) and in both cases the AUEW bargaining unit on which I shall focus was one of the smaller ones on site. The major production unions at Factory A were SOGAT (826 members) and NGA (141): other smaller groups of TGWU, EETPU and UCATT workers were also employed on the manual side. At B, the largest production union was the TGWU with over 900 members on site: the AUEW was the next largest manual group, followed by the EETPU and UCATT. In both factories union membership was very high among manual workers. At A all manual societies operated some form of closed shop. At B all did so except the TGWU, which merely operated a closed shop on new entrants. There was a substantial number of female production workers at both plants: at A these were all union members, at B some were part-time and were the principal remaining group outside the union.[11] Industrial relations at both factories were harmonious. Apart from brief 'sit downs'—which were very rare—and the occasional nationally-sponsored protest—such as that against the Industrial Relations Act—the stewards of all societies at both plants could not recall any instance of strike action. The company appeared to adopt a conciliatory stance in industrial relations, at least in these two plants, and, although representatives were sceptical about managerial motives, both sets of stewards felt that the facilities offered to them were good, and the consultation machinery adequate.[12]

AUEW members were employed on maintenance or other 'indirect' work in both plants. At Plant A, on Merseyside, the target sample numbered 58 and at Plant B in the East Midlands, 61: the response rate achieved in Plant A was 69 per cent ($N = 40$) and in Plant B 82 per cent ($N = 50$). It is probable that this differential response rate was simply a function of the differential access achieved: not only were the facilities offered at A less suitable than those at B, but all workers at A were employed on shiftwork and were consequently more difficult to contact outside of working hours.[13]

The target sample included all grades and occupational titles, whether skilled or unskilled, within the two AUEW bargaining units. Consequently chargehands were included at both locations: foremen and other supervisory staff were, however, excluded.[14] In addition, any worker who was off sick for the whole period (approximately seven weeks at A and four weeks at B) was excluded from the sample on practical grounds.

In a number of respects, the subsamples at Factory A and Factory B were very similar. There were some occupational differences, principally because the AUEW organized more unskilled workers at Factory A, but in terms of educational attainment, work history and length of service with the firm, there were few differences between the two sets of respondents. Moreover, the average ages of the two subsamples were identical and there were no significant differences in family status. The relevant results are reproduced in detail in Appendix 4. This similarity is important since the remainder of this chapter will treat the sample as homogeneous for the purpose of discussing some general approaches to fairness.

## CONSENSUS AND COMPARISONS

The literature discussed in the first chapter indicated that there is some general consensus on relative occupational worth, and that most respondents tend to be unambitious in their selection of comparative reference groups. In combination, these two tendencies encouraged Hyman and Brough to define the problem of fair pay as 'parochial'. This section presents the evidence for ranking consensus and reference group limitation from the case studies. Such evidence is important both because it indicates the extent to which responses from this sample fall in line with trends which are apparently more general and because a number of policy proposals have sought support in it. The existence of an alleged consensus on the ranking of occupations has been seen as the basis for some form of national job evaluation, while the limitation of reference groups has been said to ease the problems of acceptability of incomes policy.[15] The data presented here encourage caution in both these respects, while indicating that respondents in the two plants followed more general attitudinal trends.

Respondents at the two case-study plants were asked to rank two groups of ten occupational titles each, in order specifically accord-

TABLE 3.2
*Whole Sample: Analysis of Rank Correlations Coefficients External Ranking*

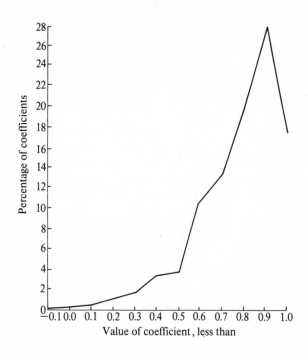

Total Number of Coefficients: 3486
Significance Levels are for a one-tailed test calculated for n = 10 using a student's t distribution.

    $\alpha = .005$        Value .7460
    $\alpha = .01$         Value .6989
    $\alpha = .05*$       Value .5390

Thus, 85% of coefficients are significant at $\alpha = .05$.

*The rankings of four individuals account for 47% of the non-significant correlations at this level.

ing to what they felt each was worth in monetary terms. The first group referred solely to jobs internal to each plant (Question 29). Since the plants were in different product markets and had different occupational structures, these lists could not be identical. But an attempt was made to preserve the same framework for each plant and, where changes were made, to use similar jobs for each: thus there are seven common job titles, and the same balance of non-manual–skilled manual–unskilled manual jobs in each list. The second list refers to jobs intended to be 'external' to both of the plants in question, and was the same for both (Question 59). The selection of the plant as the basis for such a dichotomy involved the making of certain suppositions about the familiarity of respondents

TABLE 3.3

*Factory A, Internal Ranking: Analysis of Rank Correlation Coefficients*

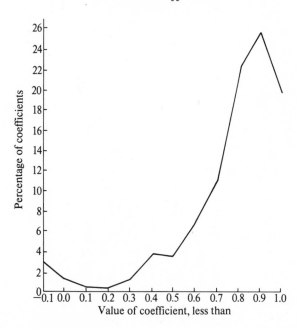

Total Number of Coefficients: 630
Significance Levels as for Table 3.2
Thus, 84% of coefficients are significant at $\alpha$ = .05*

*The rankings of three individuals account for 56% of the non-significant correlations at this level.

with plant-internal jobs, and about the utility of the plant as a unit within which a hierarchy of worth may be discerned. The 'plant-external' sets of occupations permit certain comparisons to be made with other work on occupational worth, and also permit inter-plant comparisons. The occupational titles used are reproduced in Appendix 2.

TABLE 3.4

*Factory B, Internal Ranking: Analysis of Rank Correlation Coefficients*

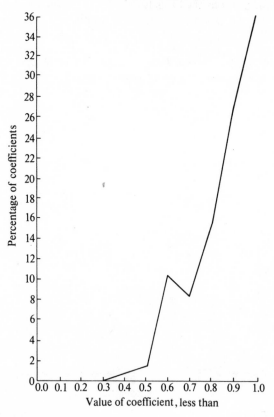

Total Number of Coefficients: 1225
Significance Levels as for Table 3.2
Thus, 93% of coefficients are significant at $\alpha = .05$*

    *The rankings of two individuals account for 77.5% of non-significant correlations at this level.

TABLE 3.5
*Mean Rank Orderings*

| 'External' Rankings | Plant A | Plant B |
|---|---|---|
| | Production Manager | Headmaster |
| | Headmaster | Underground Miner |
| | Underground Miner | Production Manager |
| | Foreman Fitter | Foreman Fitter |
| | Welder | Welder |
| | Machinist | Machinist |
| | Gas Fitter | Gas Fitter |
| | Car Assembly Worker | Car Assembly Worker |
| | Ticket Collector | Ticket Collector |
| | Insurance Collector | Insurance Collector |

| 'Internal' Rankings | Plant A | Plant B |
|---|---|---|
| | Factory Manager | Factory Manager |
| | Personnel Manager | Foreman |
| | Foreman | Personnel Manager |
| | Electrician | Electrician |
| | Printer | Turner |
| | Setter/Operator | Die Setter |
| | HGV Driver | HGV Driver |
| | Brakehand | Clerk |
| | Clerk | Semi-skilled Production Worker |
| | Labourer | Labourer |

Each respondent's ranking order (i.e. 1 to 10, corrected for ties) was correlated with every other, giving 35 x 36 and 49 x 50 matrices for factory-internal rankings, and an 82 x 83 matrix for external ones. This mass of information is summarized in the tables which follow, which are presented as frequency distributions of the correlation coefficients (Spearmans rho) derived, with the appropriate significance levels given. Clearly both in ranking jobs within the plants and external to them, there was a large degree of agreement: 84.9 per cent of correlation coefficients for the 'external' ranking were significant at $\alpha = .05$, while on the 'internal' ranking 83.7 per cent of coefficients at A and 92.8 per cent at B were significant at $\alpha = .05$. In all three tables the number of very high coefficients (i.e. above .75 and thus significant at $\alpha = .005$) is remarkable: in all cases over half of the coefficients were significant at this level (plant-external ranking 56.5 per cent, Plant A internal rankings 58.4 per cent, Plant B internal rankings 71.3 per cent). Moreover, these figures may in a sense *understate* the degree of consensus among the majority of respondents. As the notes to Tables 3.2 to 3.4 indicate, a high proportion of non-significant correlations can be accounted for in terms of the rankings provided by very few individuals. For example, the high number of correlations in the category 0.5–0.55 in Table 3.2 is generated by one individual giving the same rank to each job. Some individuals dissent consistently on both internal and external rankings, but in many cases there is no consistency, and the dissent is difficult to explain.

This evidence indicates very close agreement indeed. Table 3.5 indicates the mean rankings of named jobs within groups. Clearly, the consensus on occupational worth is a relatively 'orthodox' one: professional work is generally ranked above craft work which in turn is ranked above unskilled manual work. The results imply no radical dissent from the prevailing pattern of occupational inequality. Such a marked consensus has important implications for the regulation of pay and the creation of equitable pay structures. Walker has noted that some such consensus is the basic rationale underlying all job evaluation schemes, and both Phelps-Brown and Livy have stressed that a consensual basis is a *sine qua non* for the success of any job evaluation exercise.[16] The coverage of job evaluation schemes has recently grown to such an extent that several commentators have suggested the possibility of national job evaluation—possibly built up on the basis of 'key' comparisons between different schemes—which could be the basis for a long-term incomes policy.[17] If the appropriate consensus were general, this might explain the growth of job evaluation and provide encouragement to those who see in it the basis for the long-term planning of a rational and equitable structure of incomes.

On the face of it, the case study data seems to indicate that such a consensus exists. However, a closer inspection of the results reveals that particular pairings of jobs were subject to considerable disagreement, despite very high levels of agreement on the over-all ranking of occupations. Tables 3.6 to 3.9 indicate the number of times one job is ranked higher than another. So for example in Table 3.6, 'Personnel Manager' was ranked higher than 'Foreman' by 70 per cent of respondents, and the pairing reversed by 30 per cent.[18] In other instances, numerous 'ties' of rankings occurred. It is a feature of all four tables that a considerable amout of ranking disagreement occurs, which would not be evident from the analysis above, given the basis of calculation of Spearman's rho.[19] This disagreement is extremely significant. Job evaluation schemes tend to have a narrow 'vertical' coverage of occupations: very few schemes embrace both white-collar and manual occupations, for

*Pairings of All Occupational Titles*
*Percentage 'Higher Than' Next Occupation*

TABLE 3.6
*Internal: Factory A (%)*

|  | 1 | 2 | 3 | 4 | 5 | 6 | 7 | 8 | 9 | 10 |
|---|---|---|---|---|---|---|---|---|---|---|
| 1. Printer | — | 30 | 82 | 97 | 97 | 33 | 39 | 73 | 97 | 9 |
| 2. Maintenance Electrician | 25 | — | 85 | 97 | 97 | 33 | 39 | 70 | 97 | 9 |
| 3. HGV Driver | 6 | 3 | — | 73 | 85 | 9 | 15 | 36 | 67 | 3 |
| 4. Brakehand | 0 | 0 | 18 | — | 59 | 3 | 3 | 12 | 50 | 3 |
| 5. Labourer | 0 | 0 | 9 | 9 | — | 3 | 3 | 6 | 33 | 3 |
| 6. Personnel Manager | 55 | 58 | 85 | 94 | 94 | — | 70 | 76 | 94 | 6 |
| 7. Foreman | 58 | 58 | 85 | 97 | 97 | 30 | — | 79 | 97 | 6 |
| 8. Setter Operator | 18 | 15 | 46 | 85 | 88 | 21 | 21 | — | 76 | 9 |
| 9. Male Clerk | 0 | 0 | 21 | 41 | 55 | 3 | 3 | 15 | — | 3 |
| 10. Factory Manager | 91 | 91 | 97 | 97 | 97 | 94 | 94 | 91 | 97 | — |

*Notes:* (1) Where percentages in paired comparisons do not total 100 per cent, ties are indicated.
(2) This dissensus does not coalesce on a group level *within* bargaining units.
It reappears at different levels of aggregation.

TABLE 3.7
*Internal: Factory B (%)*

|  | 1 | 2 | 3 | 4 | 5 | 6 | 7 | 8 | 9 | 10 |
|---|---|---|---|---|---|---|---|---|---|---|
| 1. Turner | — | 24 | 96 | 88 | 98 | 30 | 8 | 96 | 96 | 2 |
| 2. Electrician | 24 | — | 92 | 88 | 98 | 30 | 12 | 96 | 94 | 0 |
| 3. HGV Driver | 0 | 2 | — | 24 | 92 | 10 | 0 | 66 | 56 | 0 |
| 4. Dye Setter | 4 | 0 | 50 | — | 96 | 14 | 6 | 62 | 64 | 0 |
| 5. Labourer | 0 | 0 | 4 | 0 | — | 4 | 0 | 6 | 4 | 0 |
| 6. Personnel Manager | 60 | 56 | 86 | 76 | 94 | — | 42 | 90 | 90 | 2 |
| 7. Foreman | 78 | 76 | 98 | 90 | 98 | 40 | — | 96 | 98 | 4 |
| 8. Semi-skilled Production Worker | 2 | 2 | 22 | 18 | 80 | 6 | 2 | — | 24 | 0 |
| 9. Male Clerk | 2 | 2 | 30 | 20 | 82 | 4 | 0 | 52 | — | 0 |
| 10. Factory Manager | 92 | 94 | 98 | 98 | 98 | 92 | 86 | 98 | 98 | — |

*Notes:* as Table 3.6.

TABLE 3.8
*External: Factory A (%)*

| | 1 | 2 | 3 | 4 | 5 | 6 | 7 | 8 | 9 | 10 |
|---|---|---|---|---|---|---|---|---|---|---|
| 1. Headmaster | — | 100 | 88 | 94 | 100 | 82 | 50 | 44 | 88 | 70 |
| 2. Ticket Collector | 0 | — | 0 | 3 | 18 | 3 | 0 | 3 | 3 | 0 |
| 3. Welder | 6 | 91 | — | 79 | 94 | 44 | 15 | 15 | 47 | 15 |
| 4. Car Worker | 3 | 83 | 9 | — | 70 | 15 | 0 | 9 | 6 | 6 |
| 5. Insurance Collector | 0 | 50 | 0 | 6 | — | 0 | 0 | 0 | 0 | 0 |
| 6. Machinist | 12 | 88 | 21 | 70 | 91 | — | 21 | 15 | 38 | 18 |
| 7. Miner | 44 | 97 | 76 | 94 | 97 | 76 | — | 44 | 79 | 62 |
| 8. Production Manager | 41 | 94 | 82 | 88 | 97 | 82 | 56 | — | 82 | 73 |
| 9. Gas Fitter | 6 | 91 | 18 | 76 | 94 | 30 | 9 | 15 | — | 18 |
| 10. Foreman Fitter | 24 | 100 | 74 | 94 | 100 | 76 | 32 | 21 | 79 | — |

*Notes:* as Table 3.6.

TABLE 3.9
*External: Factory B (%)*

| | 1 | 2 | 3 | 4 | 5 | 6 | 7 | 8 | 9 | 10 |
|---|---|---|---|---|---|---|---|---|---|---|
| 1. Headmaster | — | 96 | 82 | 90 | 98 | 76 | 56 | 32 | 86 | 68 |
| 2. Ticket Collector | 0 | — | 0 | 0 | 20 | 0 | 0 | 0 | 0 | 0 |
| 3. Welder | 10 | 94 | — | 62 | 90 | 12 | 6 | 10 | 40 | 10 |
| 4. Car Worker | 6 | 84 | 16 | — | 76 | 4 | 2 | 6 | 16 | 4 |
| 5. Insurance Collector | 0 | 44 | 2 | 4 | — | 0 | 0 | 0 | 0 | 0 |
| 6. Machinist | 14 | 94 | 54 | 78 | 92 | — | 12 | 12 | 60 | 10 |
| 7. Miner | 28 | 98 | 70 | 94 | 98 | 60 | — | 30 | 82 | 46 |
| 8. Production Manager | 34 | 98 | 80 | 88 | 98 | 74 | 54 | — | 84 | 58 |
| 9. Gas Fitter | 8 | 94 | 20 | 56 | 90 | 10 | 4 | 6 | — | 6 |
| 10. Foreman Fitter | 20 | 96 | 74 | 88 | 98 | 66 | 30 | 14 | 80 | — |

*Notes:* as Table 3.6.

example. The consensus which must be generated for the success of job evaluation concerns the ranking of *adjacent* occupations in the hierarchy: over-all agreement is less important. Clearly this sample did not possess the consensus necessary, and indeed the bargaining units of which they were members had both rejected job evaluation.[20] Despite a considerable degree of overall consensus about occupational worth, therefore, 'parochial dissensus' can jeopardise attempts to reform structures of income inequality.

This conclusion is reinforced by the findings on the selection of wage comparisons: those occupations on whose rankings respondents could not agree were those with whom they were most likely to compare their earnings. In the structured interviews, respondents were asked to identify jobs of equal monetary worth to their own, in two contexts: first, within the factory in which they worked (Question 21), secondly, external to the factory (Question 46). The responses are presented in Table 3.10. The vertically restricted pattern of comparison choice revealed here is entirely consistent with the findings of Runciman and Daniel, discussed in Chapter 1. Manual workers clearly limit their horizons in the selection of wage comparisons: the different propensities to select comparisons in class 'D' between the two subsamples is straightforwardly explicable in terms of the larger numbers of unskilled respondents at Factory A.

TABLE 3.10
*Selection of Wage Comparisons*

| | Factory A | | Factory B | |
|---|---|---|---|---|
| *Classification of Named Job** | *Internal per cent (Question 21)* | *External per cent (Question 46)* | *Internal per cent (Question 21)* | *External per cent (Question 46)*† |
| A | — | — | — | — |
| B | — | — | — | — |
| C1 | — | 5.0 | 14.0 | 8.0 |
| C2 | 57.5 | 40.0 | 74.0 | 71.0 |
| D | 27.5 | 25.0 | 2.0 | 5.0 |
| E | — | — | — | — |
| 'None' | 10.0 | 25.0 | 10.0 | 17.0 |
| 'Most jobs' | 5.0 | 5.0 | — | — |
| | 100.0 | 100.0 | 100.0 | 100.0 |
| | | N = 40 | | N = 50 |

*Source:* Structured Interview Schedule.

\* The classification adopted here is that used by the Market Research Society, itself adapted from the occupational categories of the 1971 census Classification of Occupations. It is one of several similar ones available, most of which would have been suitable to demonstrate the comparison limitation shown here. See I. Reid, *'Social Class Differences in Britain: A Sourcebook'* (1977), Ch. 2.

† Respondents at B tended to give more than one answer to this question.

TABLE 3.11

*Respondents' Selection of Dissonant Comparisons;*
*Questions 21 (46): 'Which jobs in the factory*
*(in other industries) should, in your opinion,*
*receive about the same amount of pay as your own?'*
*Questions 22 (47): 'Do you know how much*
*these jobs actually are paid?'*

|  | Equal Worth Jobs Paid | | | |
|---|---|---|---|---|
|  | More per cent | Same per cent | Less per cent | Don't know per cent |
| Factory A Internal (Questions 21–2) | 37.5 | 50 | 2.5 | 10 |
| External (Questions 46–7) | 25 | 10 | 10 | 55 |
| Factory B Internal (Questions 21–2) | 20 | 76 | 4 | 0 |
| External (Questions 46–7) | 38 | 26 | 14 | 22 |

*Source:* Structured Interview Schedule.

*Notes:* The high 'don't know' responses referring to external comparisons are perhaps what one would expect *a priori*. However, the higher 'don't know' rate at A is consistent with other aspects of bargaining behaviour there, and with other results to be documented below (Ch. 5).

Daniel's interpretation of the policy implications of vertically-restricted comparisons gives encouragement to those planning long-term incomes policies.[21] Given a focus on adjacent occupations, often within the same workplace, then the reform of plant wage structures through job evaluation will remove the anomalies and in-equities that thwart incomes policies. However, the data presented above indicate rejection of job evaluation: there is no agreed basis for reform. And it is clear that perceived inequities persist. Respondents were also asked about the pay of those jobs identified as being of equal worth in response to Question 21. The results are presented above in Table 3.11. Many respondents felt that jobs of equal worth to their own were receiving more pay. Given that the table is con-cerned with spontaneous comparisons, these inequities are likely to be strongly felt, and to act as an obstacle to successful income poli-cies. Manual workers restrict comparison choice, but there is no overwhelming tendency for them to choose 'consonant' compari-sons or to reduce perceived inequity, as would be expected by several social psychological theories of comparison selection. Patchen, for example, argues on the basis of cognitive dissonance theory that the worker will select wage comparisons in such a way as to balance his own ratio of contributions to earnings with that of significant others: in doing so, he clearly borrows ideas about cognitive balance from equity theory.[22] But the tendency to focus on consonant comparisons—equal worth jobs which are paid the same—is not particularly marked in Table 3.11. Significant numbers of respondents were prepared to highlight a disadvantage.[23]

Respondents' failure to make wide-ranging wage comparisons seems to be associated with an absence of information about the pay of non-manual jobs rather than with feelings of fairness: in response to an open-ended question about the equity of white-collar earnings within their plants, 50 per cent of all respondents failed to answer (Question 27) while a question about the *actual* pay of those occupations involved in the ranking exercise above achieved a response rate of only 17 per cent.

These results indicate that the existence of general consensus on occupational worth and a tendency to unambitious wage comparisons together provide no guarantee that a basis for the success of wage policies exists. The existence of 'parochial' dissensus on occupational ranking, the continuation of feelings of inequity where comparisons are restricted and the absence of information on white-collar earnings all imply a potential for grievances to be generated over pay differentials even where some wider agreement on the fairness of the occupational structure may be evident. A number of interesting questions about the generation and resolution of these grievances, and about the appropriate policy measures, cannot be answered by data of this sort.

CONCLUSION

This chapter has presented the background to the case studies, stressing the over-all similarities between the two sets of respondents; they are occupationally and demographically similar and bargain within a single multi-plant company. However, I have not simply been concerned to present background information here, and certain findings are crucial to the data that follow.

The sample as a whole displayed a very high level of consensus on relative occupational worth and a marked tendency to restrict horizons in the selection of reference groups. These tendencies have been seen as the basis for the rationalizing of the structure of income inequality; taken together, they imply the existence of a generally acceptable structure of earnings which could be put into effect simply by codifying the underlying consensus within a national incomes policy or job evaluation scheme.

However, further analysis of these tendencies reveals disagreement over the rankings of adjacent occupations and the combination of restriction of comparisons with feelings of unfairness; those jobs which are the subject of ranking disagreement are most salient as wage comparisons. Moreover, this pattern of views is underpinned by an absence of information about the relative earnings of groups outside the manual stratum. This 'parochial dissensus' implies certain obstacles to the simple operationalization of principles of equity in specific policy measures; such measures may founder even with a general consensus because they must be relatively precise and definitive about differentials and relativities.

Policy makers thus face an ambivalent set of views on which to base their measures; consensus and dissensus co-exist. Their uncertainty is impossible to resolve without looking at how this mixture affects the operation of wage-determining processes in collective bargaining; in particular, do these differing views have any influence on bargainers and, if so, does this pattern of influence have a positive or negative effect on the success of incomes policy?

I shall attempt to find some answers to these questions in the following chapters, which will present the bulk of the data from the case studies, and will seek to outline the reasons for the *differences* between bargaining units in the way they use moral arguments, rather than the similarities. Chapter 4 will look at matters internal to each bargaining unit, such as conceptions about the equity of pay structures, pay levels and pay rises and their relationship to shop steward behaviour, with the distinction between leadership and normatively central issues in mind. Chapter 5 will look at wage comparisons, both informal and bargaining.

## CHAPTER 4

# THE MANAGEMENT OF EQUITY

My central concern in this chapter is with the operation of conceptions of equity within the two bargaining units and, in particular, the extent to which shop stewards exerted control over rates and earnings in accordance with the principles of trade unionism discussed in Chapter 2. Initially, I shall outline the main features of shopfloor organization at the two plants, describe the negotiating strategies of stewards, and present some factual information about the rate structures. Subsequently, I shall analyse respondents' views on fairness within the bargaining unit, with particular reference to the distinction between 'leadership' and 'normatively central' issues. The main argument offered is that, while certain fair pay issues are normatively central, those which most concern shop stewards—such as the size of the next pay rise—are leadership issues. One may distinguish between the two case studies in terms of the success of shop-steward leadership on these issues.

## THE NATURE OF ORGANIZATION

### (a) Structure and Responsiveness

Both bargaining units were composed entirely of AUEW members. At A, respondents were divided among seven geographically separated departments, along functional rather than occupational lines: these were Central Services, Flex Pack, Machine Shop, Paper Group, Garage, Stores and Boilerhouse. The division was directly related to differences in the machinery to be maintained. At B, by contrast, the majority of respondents were in two adjacent occupationally distinct departments—Toolroom and Maintenance: there were two other departments, a small, contiguous Stores and a group of Line Engineers employed on the production lines themselves.

Both the organizations were relatively small. This obviously contributed to the high representation ratios observed: at Factory A, there were four AUEW stewards, including the convenor, i.e. one steward for every 14.5 members. They were located in the Machine Shop (Convenor), Flex Pack, Paper Group and Central Services. At Factory B, there were three stewards, including the convenor, and four shop committee members in the AUEW: i.e. one representative for every 8.7 members.[1] They were distributed (unevenly) between Toolroom and Maintenance. Members therefore had, in principle at least, easy access to representation on any grievance, particularly at B.

The background to this needs to be spelt out. Strong union organization at Factory A had, in the opinion of stewards and members, developed only in the previous five years, primarily due to the energies of the present convenor. He was an experienced representative, who tended to overshadow the other three stewards who were much younger than himself.[2] He had direct access to the factory manager in a strong personalized bargaining relationship;[3] other stewards accompanied him by rote, and deferred to him on many issues. There was no formal stewards' committee, and the other stewards felt that they could not have done the convenor's job themselves: as one of them put it, 'we'd be lost without Pat'. In so far as it was possible to monitor this through informal interviews and observation, it seemed that the convenor had considerable freedom of action: most of the initiatives originated with him, and he called meetings of the membership to report back 'as and when required'. However, despite his policy of involving unskilled men in the union, all the stewards at the time of interview were skilled.[4]

Factory B had more deeply rooted traditions of strong union organization, traceable back to the involvement of members of the workplace organization in the founding of the Combine in the early 1960s. The present convenor was less of a dominating influence because a number of previous convenors were still active: one representative in particular was a powerful influence on membership opinions and the 'theoretician' of the group. He once stood for District Secretary and was, at the time of interview, Secretary of the Combined Committee. The convenor consulted him on many issues, and they often negotiated as a pair. In addition, both were answerable to a formal shop committee of stewards and shop representatives, which exerted considerable influence on the activities of individual stewards; for example, it determined union policy on overtime and departmental differentials.

At both plants stewards were elected at mass meetings, to hold office for a maximum of one year without re-election. The amount of independence possible was thus limited. But the scope for independent action was obviously not defined solely by this 'constitutional' basis, and differed between plants.

Although there were differences in leadership style within the representative bodies, at both plants members appeared to be in tune with what stewards were trying to do. Not only was the representation ratio high, but in both plants large numbers of rank-and-file members had been stewards in the past: at A 35 per cent and at B 22 per cent had negotiating experience.[5] There was thus easy communication between members and stewards, and an apprecia-tion of the difficulties of the steward's job. This influenced mem-bers' evaluation of their trade-union organizations. The majority of members of both organizations were highly satisfied with their rep-resentation, and felt that the steward organizations were responsive to their needs. At A all respondents and at B 94 per cent felt that their shopfloor organization's policy on pay issues was one of which they approved (Question 63). Moreover 86 per cent of respon-dents at A and 82 per cent of those at B felt that stewards were effective in solving members' individual problems (Question 64) and 75 per cent of respondents at A and 100 per cent of those at B felt that the key decisions were taken by members, not stewards alone (Question 65). At A, only 5 per cent of respondents could cite an instance where a steward had refused to handle a grievance: at B there were no cited instances of this (Question 64). Members at both plants appeared well informed about shopsteward policies on differ-entials internal to the bargaining units (Question 67), and most felt that shop-steward policy on differentials was fair. At B, where the Toolroom—Maintenance relationship was a problem, 28 per cent of respondents, unevenly distributed between departments, felt that the policy on internal differentials was unfair (Question 68).

The sample is thus comprised of two small, fairly cohesive bar-gaining units. The small steward bodies showed some tendencies towards the formation of hierarchies, but these were not marked, and there was little evidence of any formalized division of labour between stewards, or sectional activity on pay. Such evidence as there was came from Factory A. Stewards appeared to keep in close contact with membership views, and members were generally satis-fied with this. However, at neither plant did the membership appear to be directly involved in developing strategies on pay negotiation.

## (b) Negotiating Strategies

It became clear that the main burden of pay negotiation at both plants fell on the two convenors when both sets of stewards were asked in informal interviews whether any systems of argument were used in pay negotiations on a consistent basis and, if so, what these were. Both convenors presented a comprehensive framework of arguments and indicated that there was a consistent basis for bargaining; stewards, by contrast, were less ready to describe the basis of argument or its supporting rationale.

At Factory A, the convenor's wage-bargaining strategy was to calculate the increase in the cost of living since his last settlement, and the wage-rise which would compensate for it, and add to this an amount which would fulfil his perceived duty to raise his members' living standards. The size of this amount would, he said, 'depend on the circumstances', by which he meant the profitability of the company as a whole, the state of the plant—gauged by the amount of work he could see going through—and the 'mood of the members'; he obviously saw wage increases in 'real' rather than monetary terms and did not see comparisons as important at the time. There are sound reasons for this, since the plant was then one of the highest paid in the company and the area. The convenor also emphasized that he would only compare earnings with others on 'the same terms and conditions—otherwise it's meaningless'. This severely limited the availability of local comparisons, as the next chapter will show.

At factory B, matters had become more formalized. Each year, the convenor presented management on behalf of the shop committee with a written claim which laid out the basis of the union case. Unfortunately, no copies of such claims had been preserved by the convenor, who destroyed his documents after negotiations ended in an agreement. However, interviews with stewards, shop committee members and the convenor himself revealed the basic elements. These were:

(1) Increases in the cost of living were to be compensated for in the claim: moreover, an attempt was made to work out regional variations in living costs, to facilitate comparison with a 'leading' rate in one of the company's London plants.[6]
(2) Rates in other toolrooms in the area were monitored: the rate in the toolroom was the 'key' one, other rates in other departments being defined in relation to this.
(3) Rates elsewhere in the Group 1 were monitored: however, as at A, this was the best-paid plant in its product group at the time of interview.

The sources of information for these claims were described as follows:

(a) at A, Labour Research publications (on movements in the Retail Prices Index) the annual accounts of the Company and management (on the state of business in the firm—though the convenor never used the profitability of the firm as an argument because 'in a bad year it would cut

the other way'), the Combined Committee (for rates elsewhere in the
company).[7]
(b) at B, Labour Research publications (again on movements in the Retail
    Prices Index) the Combined Committee (on rates in other factories) and
    face-to-face contacts with other convenors in the area (on local rates).

These arguments make interesting comparisons with those given
by the managers, who negotiated with AUEW stewards. At A, the
factory manager, who intervened personally in pay negotiations,
saw the AUEW as a strong, well organized group with whose internal differentials he would not interfere.[8] In negotiations, easily the
most important comparison was with the other AUEW workers in
the company: of less importance were plant-internal relativities and
of least importance local engineering rates. Factory A had no
recruitment problems, and paid a 'good rate' for the area. At B, the
personnel manager was the principal management negotiator: his
view on internal differentials was that there could be more and wider
merit rates to reward skill. The predominant comparison in negotiations was with other toolroom rates in the area: the personnel
manager acknowledged that this was disadvantageous and that
recruitment problems arose because of it. Both managers, however,
stressed that this pattern of comparisons was temporary: they had
experienced different ones in the past.[9] The differences between
union and management views of the important systems of argument
in negotiation were thus ones of emphasis rather than substance: not
surprisingly, managers appeared to lay more emphasis on the
recruitment and retention of staff, while stewards stressed 'equity'
arguments. But clearly, both are talking roughly the same
language.[10]

## (c) The Rate Structure

All respondents interviewed were paid on time-rates. Stewards were
thus involved in negotiations over pay primarily on the date of the
principal settlement, which was, at the time of interview, April at A
and July at B. This had, however, changed in the recent past, (see
Chapter 7). According to stewards at both plants, their main pay
problem was the regulation of the amount of overtime worked: this
was particularly acute at B, where a merit payment system—of a
type previously rejected by workers at A—operated to increase the
number of different individual rates. Apart from occupational differentials, the existence of two different shift systems at A created
differentials between departments: the Paper Group were on a
three-shift system, as were the Boilerhouse workers, while other

TABLE 4.1
*Percentage Differentials:*
*AUEW Factory A 1972–1977*

| | Sept. 1972 (£) | Sept. 1973 (£) | Sept. 1974 (£) | April 1975 (£) | April 1976 (£) | April 1977 (£) | July 1977 (£) |
|---|---|---|---|---|---|---|---|
| Per cent Differential | 80.41 | 80.19 | 79.94 | 81.64 | 83.14 | 83.14 | 82.74 |
| Year on year: | | | | | | | |
| Per cent Increase Skilled | 9.4 | 16.9 | 24.2 | 9.24 | 5 | 7.9 | |
| Per cent Increase Unskilled | 9.13 | 16.6 | 26.3 | 11.25 | 5 | 7.44 | |

*Source:* Company Records.

*Notes:* (1) The percentages quoted at A are based on two-shift gross hourly earnings i.e. they include all settlements, supplements and shift premia but *ignore the effects of overtime.* Those quoted for B represent the 'top' rate and unskilled rates respectively. The justification for selection of these rates—two-shift and 'top'—is that the largest groups of workers in each sample were paid according to them.

(2) Care should be taken in making direct comparisons *between* factories because of the different bargaining dates.

(3) It should be noted that, although there was a six-month delay between completion of interviews at A and those at B, in terms of the 'collective bargaining calendar' both sets of interviews fall after settlement under Phase I but before that under Phase II in the respective plants.

TABLE 4.2
*Percentage Differentials:*
*AUEW Factory B 1972–1977*

| | July 1972 (£) | July 1973 (£) | July 1974 (£) | July 1975 (£) | July 1976 (£) | July 1977 (£) | Sept. 1977 (£) |
|---|---|---|---|---|---|---|---|
| Per cent Differential | 72.02 | 78.45 | 84.11 | 81.3 | 83.12 | 83.12 | 84.3 |
| Year on year: | | | | | | | |
| Per cent Increase Skilled | 6.85 | 18.2 | 29.9 | 10.8 | 5 | 7.6 | |
| Per cent Increase Unskilled | 16.4 | 26.8 | 25.5 | 13.3 | 5 | 9.15 | |

*Source:* Company Records.
*Notes:* as Table 4.1.

departments operated a two-shift system. At B, no shift premia were paid: all respondents worked days.

The basic structure of rates at Plant A was the skilled–semi skilled–unskilled division common in much engineering work, though perhaps less frequently seen on maintenance than on production. At B, where respondents were, with one exception, craftsmen, the structure differed. In addition to the unskilled rate, there were four craft rates because of the merit payment system: much of the observed variance of earnings at B is thus strictly inter-personal. The basic and gross hourly and gross weekly earnings at both plants at the time of interview are reproduced in Appendix 5. Neither rate structure is particularly complex, although complexity increases where the effects of overtime working are included (see Table 4.8).

The differentials between skill groups at the time of interview are almost identical (on gross hourly earnings 83.14 per cent at A and 83.12 per cent at B). However this similarity masks a great difference in the 'trajectory' of change. Tables 4.1 and 4.2 show the change in differentials for the five years prior to interviewing. Over this period, differentials at A have been quite stable, whereas at B a marked convergence has occurred, particularly as a consequence of the July 1974 settlement, under free collective bargaining.[11] It was not possible to isolate any reason for such a convergence at B in the policy statements of stewards and management. In fact, at A the convenor *was* keen to cause differentials to converge: he wanted one rate throughout the unit.[12] But differentials remained stable. The convenor at B felt that wage relationships between skilled men were more of a problem. The two main departments at B—toolroom and maintenance—were, for explicitly political reasons to do with the unity of the bargaining group, formally on the same hourly rates. This caused considerable dissatisfaction in the toolroom, where respondents felt that the skills utilized in the department were of greater value than those required in maintenance. The main reason for the different pattern of change probably lies in occupational composition. At A the large number of unskilled men in the bargaining unit meant that skill differentials were an issue, whereas at B, where only two AUEW members were unskilled, stewards had more freedom to raise unskilled earnings disproportionately in times of high inflation, since the main 'issue' was the toolroom—maintenance differential. I shall offer more support for this line of argument below.

The attitudinal data thus refers to two small but well organized groups of engineering workers who were accustomed to bargaining on the basis of a well-developed negotiating strategy which had secured some measure of acceptability with their managerial opponents. The rate structure at Plant A was straightforward, having one rate per grade, and had been stable for some time. By contrast, the structure at Plant B was complicated by merit payments and had undergone some 'collapse'. These background features are extremely important in understanding the data which follow.

## VIEWS ON FAIRNESS

In interpreting the attitudinal data, I shall rely on the distinction elaborated in Chapter 2 between 'leadership' and 'normatively central' issues. Given this reliance it is worthwhile at the outset discussing how one might apply the distinction empirically.

The division was, in theory, between those issues on which most members are agreed, and on which the steward must follow the norms of the group, and those issues which are essentially open to leadership. In practice, this division is not an easy one to make. There may be some difficulty involved in distinguishing between those issues on which the membership is genuinely divided from those where a variance of response can be diagnosed as an absence of information, expertise or salience. Nevertheless, certain central issues which I have already discussed were governed by a consensus within the two organizations. The vast majority of respondents showed the same, or very similar, attitudes in both the selection of 'vertically limited' informal comparisons and the evaluation of relative occupational worth. This consensus may provide the basis for collective action and solidarity, but it may limit stewards' freedom of action where either their systems of argument violate members' conceptions of worth or where bargaining comparisons are used which are wholly unrelated to the informal comparisons used by members.

Alternatively, steward freedom to act may be limited by a division of interests between groups in the constituency. The conflict thus created may severely limit the ability of the steward to pursue a consistent pay policy, if such consistency runs counter to the requirements of maintaining some form of operational unity. A bimodal pattern of response may indicate such a division of interests: no straightforward pattern of action on the issue by the steward can satisfy the majority of members.

A third pattern of response—where inter-personal variance occurs which does not appear to coalesce on a group basis—seems to be the most amenable to steward leadership. Such a pattern indicates that the membership as a whole has not formed set ideas on a particular issue: in such circumstances, stewards will have freedom to develop and pursue courses of action with specific bargaining goals in mind. This pattern is likely to arise on issues where the possession of greater expertise or more information by the steward is important: for example, the model implies that pay-rise issues will be amenable to leadership. However, the issues falling into the three categories may vary between organizations.

TABLE 4.3

*Attitudes to Differentials: Factory A Engineers (Question 41)*

| Desired Structure | Stewards | Skilled | Unskilled | Total (per cent) |
|---|---|---|---|---|
| More than present 3 rates: | 0 | 4 | 1 | 5(12.5) |
| Present 3 rates: | 3 | 15 | 11 | 29(72.5) |
| 2 rates (Skilled & Unskilled) | 0 | 1 | 2 | 3(7.5) |
| 1 rate for all members | 1 | 1 | 1 | 3(7.5) |
| | 4 | 21 | 15 | N = 40 (100) |

*Notes:* (1) The table involves some simplification of responses, particularly in the first 'more than 3' category, where a number of desired structures were mentioned.
(2) The question was phrased so as to refer to all skill differentials, but not to those arising from the pattern of shiftworking. Chargehand rates were specifically excluded.

TABLE 4.4

*Attitudes to Differentials: Factory B Engineers (Question 41)*

| Desired Structure | Stewards | Skilled | Unskilled | Total (per cent) |
|---|---|---|---|---|
| More than present 3/4 rates | 0 | 0 | | 1(2) |
| Present 3/4 rates | 2 | 17 | | 19(38) |
| Present 3/4 rates (conditional) | 1 | 7 | | 8(16) |
| 2/3 rates | 2 | 8 | | 10(20) |
| 1 rate for all skilled | 1 | 10 | 1 | 12(24) |
| | 6 | 43 | 1 | N = 50 (100) |

*Notes:* (1) The complexity of this table results from the fact that there were a different number of rates in the two main departments, toolroom and maintenance. The 'starting rate' operated simply as such in the toolroom: everybody moved out of it on satisfactory completion of a probationary period. In maintenance, however, it acted as the bottom rate, on which members could remain for some time.
(2) The 'conditional' category contains respondents who felt that the structure of differentials should remain the same, but be administered differently: i.e. they felt that merit pay was unfairly distributed.
(3) The question was phrased so as to focus attention on the merit pay structure. Again on the grounds of low salience, both chargehand and unskilled rates are excluded.

## (a) Attitudes to Differentials

The data considered here cover respondents' attitudes to their own rate structures, omitting for the moment the distorting effects of overtime working. I am concerned here to establish the extent to which different groups of respondents in both plants felt these structures were 'equitable', and the scope this gives for stewards to negotiate changes in the rate structure. The data presented in Chapter 3 above imply the possibility of disagreement over the ranking of 'adjacent' occupations in the worth hierarchy, and it is of interest to examine this possibility *within* specific bargaining groups where the consequences for bargaining behaviour can be specified. In fact, the data indicate such disagreement at Plant B, and it clearly influenced shop-steward activity. Although it was possible to distinguish two separate membership reference groups at both plants, this did not generate as much difficulty for stewards at Plant A as at Plant B. Respondents' views on their respective rate structures are presented in Tables 4.3 and 4.4. Since one is dealing with skill differentials at Plant A and merit differentials at Plant B, it is perhaps best to discuss them separately.

It is apparent from Table 4.3 that the majority of stewards and of both skill categories were happy with the three-rate structure. Even the unskilled, at the base of the structure, were not particularly in favour of its reform, implying an acceptance of the equity of the skilled–unskilled differential. This can be compared with the consensus in the ranking of craft above non-craft jobs, evident in Tables 3.6 to 3.9. Whether because of the stability of the rate structure and the size of differential over time in the bargaining unit (Table 4.1), or because this type of stucture is common in engineering work, it clearly had acquired a certain legitimacy.

At Plant B, there was much less satisfaction with the existing structure. Although, as at Plant A, there is little relationship between a respondent's position in the rate structure and his attitude towards it, there was some feeling, particularly among the stewards, that fewer rates would be better. The background to this was a conscious effort on the part of stewards to decrease the number of rates allowed for in the merit pay system. Over the years, this had met with success, and the ultimate goal was a single craft rate.[13]

A further source of variance in past rate structures had been the existence of a differential between the two main departments— toolroom and maintenance. Although there was parity at the time of interview, the single top rate for craftsmen dated only from July

1975. Since inter-departmental pay differentials were the source of considerable conflict within the bargaining unit at the time of interview, I want to deal with this issue at some length.

The 'Maintenance' department at B were not, as their name might imply, solely engaged in attending production lines. Their principal function was the development of new production machinery, methods and techniques. As such, their job called—at least in their own eyes—for a more creative and problem-solving approach than would be in evidence on 'pure' maintenance work. Toolroom workers did not, in general, see things quite this way: in a comparison of their work with maintenance, they would point to the finer limits of toolroom work as evidence of their greater skill. Consequently, although stewards felt that inter-departmental parity was organizationally necessary, it was not universally acceptable.

This can be made clear by looking more closely at responses to questions about jobs of equal worth and pay, discussed above (Table 3.11). When respondents were asked to point to other jobs of equal monetary worth, 75 per cent of maintenance workers mentioned toolroom jobs, but only 7 per cent of toolroom workers felt that maintenance work was equally valuable (Question 21). Respondents were also asked to identify jobs of equal pay (Question 23) and whether this parity was fair (Question 24). Over 50 per cent of toolroom workers, 38 per cent of the whole sub-sample, pointed to maintenance workers, feeling that the relationship was unfair in that no differential existed. There was no corresponding pattern in the maintenance department, where respondents all felt that parity was fair. At A, no such uneven patterns of response were in evidence for Question 21; skilled and unskilled tended not to used each other as comparisons. At A, 50 per cent of respondents pointed to other members of the bargaining unit in response to Question 23, but all felt that parity was fair. The salience of this inter-departmental issue at Plant B is indicated by responses to a general question about the fairness of differentials between manual workers in the two plants. Sixty-three per cent of respondents at Factory A felt that manual differentials were fair, compared with only 28 per cent at B (Question 28). More than half of those who felt differentials were unfair were concerned with the toolroom-maintenance problem: this was far more salient than rates elsewhere in the plant.[14]

In terms of the distinction made at the outset, the scope for steward leadership in these areas seems limited. At neither plant did stewards have freedom to negotiate changes in the rate structure, since to do so would have generated dissatisfaction. The major difference is that at A this dissatisfaction would have been general, while at B change would have displeased one department or another. At A there was some kind of consensus on the rate structure, at B merely a compromise stewards would be unwilling to disturb. As the following sections will show, this 'bi-modal' pattern of response on pay issues is associated with a number of problems for stewards at Factory B.

If these results are taken in conjunction with those on a ranking consensus from Chapter 3, some pattern emerges. Each bargaining unit appeared to contain two distinct groups—skilled and unskilled at A, toolroom and maintenance at B. But whereas the pay expectations of these groups were compatible at A, at B conflict arose. The 'parochial dissensus' outlined above is important here since the difference in satisfaction between Plants A and B was in part due to occupational composition. The craft–non-craft difference was internalized by the majority of respondents and craft differentials were acceptable. But at B, where distinctions were more finely drawn, problems developed, since no consensus existed on the relationship between 'adjacent' occupations. This dissensus took the form of a tension between the principle of 'one craft rate' and the distinct conception of occupational identity held by toolroom workers. As Dunlop notes, toolrooms ordinarily constitute 'job clusters', distinct from other adjacent groups, unified by common patterns of work and training, and often covered by distinct forms of payment and wage rates.[15] In this instance, the failure to distinguish this group as they saw fit hindered the pursuit of the principles of unity and equity discussed in Chapter 2. The basis of collective action and steward leadership was thus undermined since the reference groups chosen by respondents were not consistent with concerted action at the level of the bargaining unit: for such action stewards would need to readjust the rank and file's focus of comparisons.

While there were clear-cut patterns of response to questions about the form of the rate structure, there was some variance in the way respondents defined and evaluated the size of differentials. This is of interest since the work of Behrend and Daniel discussed in Chapter 1 implies a general frame of reference for the evaluation of pay differences in absolute rather than percentage terms. Their results have clear implications for the design of incomes policies: if people generally see pay differences in absolute terms, then flat-rate incomes policies should be more acceptable than percentage-based ones. Yet at both case-study plants, a majority defined differentials in percentage terms (A 73 per cent, B 58 per cent), even though interviews took place during the £6 flat-rate incomes policy. Not only did

TABLE 4.5

*Responses to Question 57: Do you think that
a skilled craftsman should always be
paid more than a labourer? (What do you
think should be the size of the differential?)*

| Size of Differential (per cent) | Factory A (per cent) | Factory B (per cent) |
|---|---|---|
| None | 7.5 | 4 |
| 10 or less | 7.5 | 8 |
| 11–15 | 20 | 8 |
| 16–20 | 45 | 22 |
| 21–25 | 17.5 | 12 |
| 26–30 | | 2 |
| 31–35 | | 14 |
| 36–40 | | 16 |
| 41–50 | | 12 |
| Don't Know | 2.5 | 2 |
| | 100 | 100 |
| Actual size of this differential at the time of interview (per cent) | 16.77 | 16.88 |

*Note:* The question was open-ended as to whether the response should be in % or absolute terms. As noted above, a substantial minority of both sub-samples answered in absolute terms. These figures were converted as follows: at A the percentages are based on the skilled two-shift rate at the time of interview; at B on the basis of the top skilled rate: i.e. both include the £6 supplement but not the Phase II one. This is also the basis of calculation of the differential at the time of interview.

this sample not appear to follow the general trend, there appeared to be few pressures towards uniformity in the evaluation of differentials. Consequently, Table 4.5 which attempts to compare responses between the two locations, involves considerable simplification. It does serve to show, however, that there is greater consensus on the appropriate size of the skilled–unskilled differential at A than at B: the modal response category corresponds to the state of affairs at the time of interview in both plants, but the pattern of responses is more scattered at B.

Again, this difference is relateable to the fluctuating size of the skilled–unskilled differential at B and its low salience to respondents which permitted such fluctuation. An incomes policy with caused skill differentials to converge in percentage terms would not necessarily cause problems at Plant B. However, it might do so at Plant A, since it would interfere with the cohesion around the issue of differentials which was at the time beneficial for stewards.

The responses I have dealt with so far are relatively clear cut.
They indicate a certain division of interests over differentials at
Plant B, compared with the consensus at A. They also indicate that
certain general assumptions about the perception of differentials
and the consequences of their convergence may not always hold. In
the next section I want to assess the implications of these two sets
of responses for the stewards concerned, by focusing on those
issues where respondents do not have any clear cut ideas about
fairness; i.e. I shall focus on leadership issues. This involves a concern with earnings rather than rates and with pay rises rather than
pay differentials.

## (c) *Leadership and Equity in Pay*

The interview schedule included separate questions about the bases
respondents used for evaluating fair pay and fair pay rises. Both
questions revealed some broad degree of consensus. Question 45
asked respondents to evaluate in relative terms certain criteria upon
which their pay could be based: they were asked to 'score' each
criterion on a 1 to 5 scale, low scores indicating low importance and
high scores indicating that respondents felt this particular criterion
was important for their job. A list of the criteria is reproduced in
Appendix 2. At both plants respondents agreed that 'skill' and 'cost
of living' were the two most important criteria on which pay should
be based: as Table 4.6 reveals, the means on these criteria were very
high, indicating that most respondents had concurred on maximum
scores, and standard deviations were low on these two items.

TABLE 4.6
*Responses to Question 45: Criteria On Which
Pay Should Be Based*

| Item | Factory A | | | Factory B | | |
|---|---|---|---|---|---|---|
| | $\overline{X}$ | S.D. | Rank of Means | $\overline{X}$ | S.D. | Rank of Means |
| Skill | 4.76 | 1.47 | 1 | 4.78 | 1.61 | 2 |
| Cost of living | 4.73 | 1.58 | 2 | 4.80 | 1.49 | 1 |
| Profitability | 3.70 | 3.87 | 3 | 4.04 | 3.78 | 5 |
| Effort | 3.32 | 4.60 | 4 | 4.18 | 3.72 | 3 |
| Productivity | 3.11 | 3.92 | 5 | 4.08 | 2.96 | 4 |
| Family size | 2.35 | 3.72 | 6 | 1.94 | 4.07 | 7 |
| Seniority | 2.35 | 4.14 | 6 | 3.02 | 3.62 | 6 |

TABLE 4.7

*Responses to Question 19: 'How Would You Judge*
*if a Pay Award were Fair or Not?'*

|  | Factory A<br>per cent | Factory B<br>per cent |
|---|---|---|
| By looking at cost of living/<br>    purchasing power after tax | 57.9 | 58.6 |
| By effect on skill differentials | — | 10.4 |
| By looking at rises in the plant | 19.4 | 17.2 |
| By looking at rises in the area | 8.8 | 8.6 |
| Other | 13.9 | 5.2 |
|  | 100 | 100 |
|  | No. of responses = 57<br>N = 40 | No. of responses = 58<br>N = 50 |

Similarly, there was some consensus on the criteria according to which the equity of pay rises could be judged. As Table 4.7 shows, few respondents evaluated fair pay rises in terms of the effort bargain. In a later question about the fair basis for a pay rise 'at the present time' (Question 72), 72.5 per cent of respondents at A and 90 per cent of those at B suggested a cost-of-living basis.

There was a broad consensus within both groups on the criteria on which pay and pay rises were to be judged. But this consensus on principles did not prevent the issues of fair pay and fair pay rises being leadership issues. Agreement on principles of equity clearly did not point to any specific monetary amount: amounts quoted as fair pay and fair pay rises were extremely variable. At Factory A, felt fair pay (FFP) varied between £65 and £130 and at Factory B between £59 and £100. Responses about the felt-fair pay rise (FFPR) were even more variable. In the first place, respondents quoted both absolute amounts and percentages for FFPR, the majority at both plants favouring the former. Moreover the amounts quoted varied between £3 and £54 at A and £4 and £35 at B. As subsequent tables will show, such measures were far more variable than most measures of actual pay.

This variance raises two important questions. First, what gives rise to it: how is it the case that respondents may broadly agree on the basis of FFP and FFPR but disagree so markedly on the amounts? Secondly, how do stewards cope with it: clearly the potential for leadership is there, given the indecision of the membership, but what is the relationship between members' aspirations and stewards' bargaining goals, and what is the impact on steward control over earnings?

TABLE 4.8
*Variance on Earnings Measures*

|  | *APNOR* | *AP4* | *APLAST* | *FFP* | *FFPR* |
|---|---|---|---|---|---|
| Factory A |  |  |  |  |  |
| Skilled | 2.79 | 5.35 | 8.18 | 7.41 | 101.13 |
| Unskilled | 1.55 | 2.92 | 11.35 | 3.34 | 27.92 |
| Total | 7.68 | 9.05 | 13.72 | 12.87 | 123.87 |
| Factory B |  |  |  |  |  |
| Toolroom |  |  |  |  |  |
| (incl. line engineers) | 3.05 | 4.34 | 11.36 | 8.65 | 68.30 |
| Maintenance | 1.48 | 1.78 | 6.91 | 5.62 | 56.13 |
| Total | 3.38 | 4.77 | 13.37 | 10.34 | 90.77 |

*Notes:* (1) The variables are derived as follows:
   (*a*) APNOR—Gross earnings for a forty-hour week, including all shift premia and incomes policy supplements, but excluding overtime. This was derived from calculations involving known rates of pay.
   (*b*) APLAST—gross earnings, including all supplements and premia and all overtime earnings for the last pay week before interview. This was derived from Question 25 of the schedule.
   (*c*) AP4—Gross earnings, including all supplements, premia and overtime pay, for the 4 pay weeks prior to interview. This was derived from Question 26 of the schedule.
   (*d*) FFP—gross weekly amounts seen by respondents as fair pay. Where gross hourly amounts were given they were converted by multiplying by 40 and adding £6. Where respondents gave a range, its arithmetic mean was used. This was derived from Question 17 of the schedule.
   (*e*) FFPR—Gross amounts seen as a fair pay rise by respondents. Where respondents replied in percentage terms, this was converted to an absolute amount by applying the percentage to APNOR. This was derived from Question 18 of the schedule.
(2) The variance measure is the coefficient of variation i.e. the standard deviation divided by the mean, expressed as a percentage.

The variance of FFP and FFPR, together with the variance on several measures of actual pay, is presented in Table 4.8. At the level of each bargaining unit and at that of each reference group within bargaining units, the following pattern of increasing variance can be observed: negotiated rates (APNOR), gross earnings in the four week prior to interview (AP4), felt-fair pay (FFP), gross earnings in the week before interview (APLAST) and the size of the felt-fair pay rise (FFPR).

One would expect APNOR to be the least variable measure. Stewards attempt to minimize variance on negotiated rates in the interests of unity and equity, but residual variance is likely to be higher where the organization contains different skill grades as at A, because views on the appropriateness of a skill differential are 'normatively central'. Similarly, one might expect that overtime working would increase variance (APLAST) but that stewards would seek to regulate this over the longer time period (AP4). One can thus provide a plausible explanation for the differential variance of actual pay measures. But it is more difficult to suggest reasons for the variance of FFP and, particularly, FFPR, and to suggest why this variance is greater in relation to that on APNOR in Plant B than in Plant A.

There is a considerable body of literature seeking to explain perceptions of fair pay in terms of individual income or work content, or in terms of life or work history. Much of it has its basis in cognitive dissonance theory. For example many studies explicitly borrow from equity theory, assuming that fair pay (the 'outcome') will be related to measures of the individual's contribution (the 'input') because individuals will themselves seek some balance between contribution and rewards: consequently such studies test for correlations between measures of FFP and variables such as performance, age, or seniority.[16] Perhaps the most famous variant is the time-span of discretion theory of Eliot Jaques (TSD), which assumes a dissonance-reducing mechanism causing individuals to relate fair pay to job content measured by the single variable of time-span of responsibility.[17] Other studies have simply stressed the strong empirical correlation between measures of actual pay and felt-fair pay, often without articulating dissonance assumptions.[18] This literature is important for a number of reasons. Firstly it implies that one can explain FFP without reference to the operation of group processes or collective bargaining mechanisms: this obviously runs counter to the arguments offered in Chapter 1 which provide the rationale for this study. Secondly, it implies that a diffuse pattern of responses is in fact the determinate result of the operation of individual cognitive balance mechanisms which are likely to prove impervious to pressure or influence from other group members or group representatives: this runs counter to the logic of the distinction between leadership and normatively central issues, and suggests that a diffuse pattern of response does not provide scope for leadership by stewards. The individualistic approach is thus an alternative to my own, and it is crucial to the present study that it be shown to have low explanatory power.

I have presented evidence above which implies that dissonance-reduction assumptions do not apply to this sample (Table 3.11) but

TABLE 4.9
*Correlation Analysis: Factory A*

|  | APNOR | AP4 | APLAST | FFP | FFPR | Age | L.S. |
|---|---|---|---|---|---|---|---|
| APNOR | .7471** | .2230 | .7057** | .1877 | −.1136 | .3754† |
| AP4 |  | .1133 | .6726** | .0068 | −.3874† | .1251 |
| APLAST |  |  | .0517 | −.0189 | −.0371 | .1295 |
| FFP |  |  |  | .2298 | −.3218 | .0646 |
| FFPR |  |  |  |  | .0987 | .0421 |
| Age |  |  |  |  |  | .6512** |
| Length of Service |  |  |  |  |  |  |

*Notes:* (1) The statistic presented is Pearson's coefficient. Significance levels are marked as follows: ** .001; * .01; † .05.
(2) Data for Age and Length of Service are from Questions 12 and 3 of the schedule. Other variables are as in Table 4.8.

TABLE 4.10
*Correlation Analysis: Factory B*

|  | APNOR | AP4 | APLAST | FFP | FFPR | Age | L.S. |
|---|---|---|---|---|---|---|---|
| APNOR | .6888** | .2669 | .2524 | −.1286 | .0918 | −.0272 |
| AP4 |  | .2104 | .2040 | −.3164† | .0285 | .0322 |
| APLAST |  |  | .1738 | −.1759 | −.4020* | −.1917 |
| FFP |  |  |  | .2644 | .0319 | .1637 |
| FFPR |  |  |  |  | −.0505 | .0870 |
| Age |  |  |  |  |  | .7721** |
| Length of Service |  |  |  |  |  |  |

*Notes:* as Table 4.9.

it remains to be shown that there is no empirical relationship between these types of variables and FFP and FFPR. Consequently an attempt was made to explain the variance in perceptions of fair pay in terms of three measures of actual pay and two 'input' measures—age and length of service.[19] The results are presented in Tables 4.9 and 4.10. Generally, they indicate that this form of analysis of felt-fair pay has low explanatory power; the majority of relationships between FFP, FFPR and predictor variables are not significant. A number of more detailed points can be made.

First, the relationship between the actual pay measures and FFP does not suggest the operation of a general frame of reference for estimating FFP: those relationships are strong at A but largely absent at B. I shall attempt to explain this difference in terms of different levels of wage satisfaction at the two plants. Secondly, aside from the relationship between AP4 and FFPR at B, there is generally no significant relationship between the actual pay measures and FFPR. Thirdly, there is no significant relationship between FFP and FFPR at either location.

The third feature is most easily dealt with. It appears from Tables 4.6 and 4.7 that the frames of references for judging FFP and FFPR differ somewhat. In this respect it is interesting to note that for both samples it was generally true that

$$AP40 + FFPR \neq FFP \text{ and}$$
$$APLAST + FFPR \neq FFP,$$

i.e. FFP did not appear to be derived by respondents making this addition themselves, and there was no consistent tendency for this addition to be greater or less than FFP.

Similarly FFPR does not in the main appear related to actual pay measures. The AP4–FFPR relationship at B is an exception, but is less significant than several of the other relationships. Table 4.8 shows FFPR to be by far the most variable measure and this variance is greater relative to the variance on APNOR at B than at A. FFPR seems to be definitely a 'leadership' issue, at both plants. As Ross notes, the size of the appropriate pay rise will be decided by the stewards on the basis of greater bargaining expertise and access to information, and the counterpart to this is that members will not independently form any cohesive ideas about it. This is important, since collective bargaining is more often concerned with the negotiation of pay rises than with the revamping of pay structures, and the success of incomes policy depends largely on the acceptibility of the pay rise norm. If steward leadership has wide scope in deciding on the size of fair pay rises then the role of the steward is crucial to the success of any policy measure. I shall return to this in Chapter 8.

However, a necessary condition for the exercise of leadership is some basis in negotiating success: members must be relatively satisfied with the earnings achieved by stewards. In concluding this chapter, I want to argue that stewards at A could lead on the basis of such success, but that at B earnings dissatisfaction was so great that they could not. Consequently, at A satisfactory earnings were used as the basis of calculation of FFP but, as indicated in Table 4.9, at B respondents dissociated the calculation of FFP from unsatisfactory levels of actual pay. The basis of FFP in some actual pay measure is thus contingent upon pay satisfaction.

TABLE 4.11
*Responses to Question 16: 'Do You Think
that Your Abilities are Fairly Rewarded
in Your Job by the Pay you Get?'*

|  | Factory A<br>per cent | Factory B<br>per cent |
|---|---|---|
| Yes | 47.5 | 12 |
| No | 42.5 | 88 |
| Don't know | 10 | — |
|  | 100 | 100 |
|  | N = 40 | N = 50 |

*Notes:* (1) A follow up question ('why/why not') was asked to elicit the basis of these feelings. At A respondents were satisfied in relation to local area rates (27.7 per cent), their effort bargains (13.8 per cent) and the cost of living (16.6 per cent): they were dissatisfied in relation to SOGAT/NGA rates (25 per cent) and the craft differential over SOGAT (19.4 per cent). At B, where most respondents were dissatisfied, the focuses were other craft work (38.6 per cent), other engineering work in the area (31.8 per cent) and average manual earnings (15.9 per cent). Respondents tended to give more than one answer.

TABLE 4.12
*Wage Aspirations: Total Sample*

|  | $\bar{X}$ APNOR<br>(£) | $\bar{X}$ FFP<br>(£) | $\bar{X}$ FFPR<br>(£) | $\dfrac{\bar{X}\,FFP}{\bar{X}\,APNOR}$<br>(£) | $\dfrac{\bar{X}\,FFPR}{\bar{X}\,APNOR}$<br>(£) |
|---|---|---|---|---|---|
| Factory A |  |  |  |  |  |
| Skilled | 74.13 | 88.26 | 13.31 | 119.42 | 17.46 |
| Unskilled | 61.11 | 67.58 | 8.56 | 110.59 | 14.00 |
| Over-all | 69.25 | 80.36 | 11.90 | 116.04 | 17.18 |
| Factory B |  |  |  |  |  |
| Toolroom | 60.60 | 77.15 | 13.03 | 127.94 | 21.63 |
| Maintenance | 60.25 | 78.13 | 14.02 | 129.68 | 23.27 |
| Over-all | 60.33 | 77.40 | 13.23 | 128.29 | 21.93 |

Qs 16 askéd respondents if they thought they were fairly rewarded in their jobs. The results are tabulated in Table 4.11, which shows considerably more wage dissatisfaction at B than A, and the impression is corroborated by two other sets of results. The first, shown in Table 4.12, uses the FFP and FFPR data. The table indicates clearly that the discrepancy between felt-fair and actual pay measures is greater at Plant B than at A. This pattern is consistent despite the

lack of relationship between FFP and FFPR. The table com-
plements 4.11 which indicates the *frequency* of expressions of pay
dissatisfaction. Here, on the assumption that the shortfall of actual
from equitable pay is proportionate to the intensity of feeling, the
table shows greater depth of dissatisfaction at B than at A.

The second set of responses, to Question 52, elicited feelings
about minimum wages. The vast majority of respondents at both
plants favoured legislation on minimum wages: at A 92.5 per cent
and at B 80 per cent did so. A further indicator of the wage dissatisfaction at B is that the modal figure quoted equalled or exceeded
top-rate 40 hour earnings in the toolroom, at £60–64 per week (the
average is only slightly lower). At A the modal amount quoted was,
at £50–54, equal to or less than the two-shift unskilled rate.

TABLE 4.13
*Variance on Earnings Measures*

|  | *Factory A* | *Factory B* |
|---|---|---|
| Variance APLAST<br>──────────── %<br>Variance APNOR | 178.65 | 395.56 |
| Variance AP4<br>──────────── %<br>Variance APNOR | 117.84 | 141.12 |

One can develop this picture further by looking more closely at
the pattern of overtime working. In a time-rate situation such as
this, one would expect that stewards would be concerned to control
the amount and distribution of overtime working, while members
might see overtime as an important means of increasing their earnings in the short term. At both plants, APLAST was the most
variable actual pay measure, but some equalization of the distribution of overtime is implied by the lower variance of AP4. One might
assume that stewards would seek to reduce any earnings variance in
excess of that given by the normatively central APNOR, in order to
reduce individual conflict over earnings: Table 4.13 indicates the
extent to which they were successful. The results above demonstrate
that while overtime working increases earnings variance in any one
week, the effect is reversed over the four week period. Table 4.13
indicates that overtime working in a given week introduces much
more earnings variance at B than at A, and that the 'reversed' effect
reducing variance over the four week period is weaker. There is a

clear relationship between wage satisfaction and membership commitment to the rate structure on the one hand, and steward control of overtime on the other. The lower variance of AP4 than APLAST indicates some steward control over overtime working at both plants, but stewards at B had a considerable overtime problem, as the table indicates.

The level of overtime working was high at both plants. At A, Saturday morning overtime was almost continually available during 1976 and 1977. In addition, 'covering' for absence generated considerable overtime: in the boilerhouse particularly, a large number of overtime hours were worked in the summer of 1976. At B, the convenor was under some pressure from management to approach the District Committee with a view to gaining exemption from the limit of 30 hours per man per month imposed by that body at the time: this pressure continued—and was resisted—throughout Spring and into Summer 1977, as management wished to fill export orders and members wished to increase earnings. The crisis which resulted is documented in Chapter 7 below.

Despite this, both convenors were extremely critical of high levels of overtime working: they pointed to the high levels of unemployment in their respective areas as justifying a limitation on overtime, but they and their members were not always in agreement on this. Indeed at A, the convenor had repeatedly to rebuke a steward who worked all the overtime available ('he practically lives here') for not providing a 'lead', while at B the Shop Committee felt compelled to instruct stewards not to work excessive overtime and to encourage members not to do so.

## CONCLUSION

The first part of this chapter established that both case studies were of well organized bargaining units which were seen as responsive to members' needs, yet which allowed convenors some freedom of action to frame a policy on pay. Both units contained two membership reference groups—skilled and unskilled at A, toolroom and maintenance at B. But those groups stood in very different relations at the two plants: differentials were a problem at B but not at A. This difference was due mainly to occupational composition: in terms of the hierarchy of worth to which most respondents adhered, the two groups at A were clearly distinguished, but at B opposing principles were involved where the differences were finely drawn. The idea of a single craft rate was in conflict with the occupational identity of the toolroom. The rate structure at Plant A had been more stable over time, which may have invested it with greater legitimacy.

Respondents at B were considerably more dissatisfied with pay than those at A, and this dissatisfaction encouraged members into an individualistic solution to wage problems—overtime working—which the stewards could not control. Subsequently, a crisis of steward control over earnings developed at Factory B.

Such differences have clear implications for the problem of steward leadership. Both fair pay and pay-rise issues were open to steward leadership, but stewards at B were under greater pressure from a dissatisfied membership than those at A. At B, because of the composition of the bargaining unit, the skilled-unskilled differential was a leadership issue: it was not so at A. But, at B, intergroup relations were more of a problem. Nevertheless, steward leadership on pay issues is important in both cases.

The variance on FFPR and FFP, and the scatter of responses on the size of the fair differential clearly indicate that in the negotiation of wage rises stewards have some scope to decide on the *size* and *form* of claims. As a consequence, they may have an important influence on the size of the wage round under free collective bargaining or the acceptability of the norm under incomes policy. But this influence will depend on the degree of wage dissatisfaction in the bargaining unit. Under free collective bargaining high wage dissatisfaction may simply lead to higher steward claims: under incomes policy it may generate very different bargaining behaviour. The principal influences encouraging wage dissatisfaction must therefore be understood: the pattern of wage comparisons chosen is amongst the most important of these influences, and I shall discuss such comparisons in the next chapter.

## CHAPTER 5

# THE PATTERN OF WAGE COMPARISONS

## INTRODUCTION

This chapter will focus directly on the impact of external wage comparisons on feelings about wage equity. Just as the previous chapter focused on the distinction between leadership and normatively central issues, this one will be concerned with the relationship between bargaining and informal comparisons and the implications of this relationship for shop-steward pay leadership. It was argued in Chapter 2 that bargaining and informal comparisons were distinct in that the latter, having no specific collective bargaining function, would be more varied and inconsistent. In fact, the data bear this out; although the data presented in Chapter 3 indicate a focus on other manual groups, within this vertically restricted band there was considerable variance in the way respondents selected comparisons. One of the main conclusions to be drawn from this chapter is that individuals in similar work situations are so idiosyncratic in their choice of wage comparisons that it is almost impossible for policy makers to take the process of reference group selection into account in the drawing up of incomes policies.

Nevertheless, some distinct patterns of comparison selection were evident at the two plants, with very different consequences for steward leadership. Respondents at Plant A were concerned with print rates within the plant, those at B with toolroom rates in the local area. I shall discuss these in turn, but first I want to discuss bargaining comparisons.

## STEWARDS' BARGAINING COMPARISONS

At the time of interview, there were no current bargaining comparisons at Factory A. At Factory B, stewards focused on local toolroom rates, which they felt were moving away from their own. However, this simple statement of affairs at one point in time does not illustrate the full range of comparisons available to stewards, from which they had drawn in the past. This range depended on the wage information available, and it is useful to discuss the institutional arrangements through which such information was transmitted. These arrangements were of two main types: the Combined Committee, which was company-wide, and the formal union, which in this case (the AUEW) was area-based. Within the two plants, there were no institutional arrangements for transmitting wage information between different unions, but, given the likely importance of informal transfers of wage information, I will close this section with a discussion of inter-union relations in the two plants.

## (a)  The Combined Committee

I have discussed the functions of the Combine above (Chapter 3). The information provided by membership was not used by the two convenors at the time of interview, since they tended to focus on other rates within their product group and, within their respective groups, both plants were at the top of the wages leagues. But both managers and stewards at both plants pointed out that comparisons with other engineering workers in the company had been powerful in the past: the usefulness of such comparisons was clear, since both sets of management acknowledged their power as bargaining levers. I shall discuss the management role in more detail in Chapter 6, but given the power of these comparisons it is of interest to note how unaware the membership at both plants were of their use. At Factory A only 25 per cent of respondents recognized that such comparisons had been used: at B only 6 per cent did so (Question 35). Such comparisons were pure bargaining arguments without any informal counterparts.

## (b)  The AUEW

The engineering section of the AUEW has a predominantly area-based structure. Members in the workshops are organized into local branches which in turn elect members of a district committee. The shop stewards are the district committee's representatives in the plants. The first-level full time official is the district secretary, also elected by members in the branches.[1] Shop stewards in the workshops may gain wages information about the local area in a number of ways: from the results of the quarterly earnings survey disseminated by the district secretary or from informal contacts at branch or district committee or quarterly shop-stewards' meetings. But the point about the AUEW is that involvement with any of these is an empirical question.

For example, neither set of stewards attended the quarterly meetings: they did not consider them to be of any use. Nor were they in close contact with the district committee or the full time official (FTO). These latter relationships can be discussed in terms of the isolation and independence measures used by Batstone et al., discussed in Chapter 2. Isolation is measured in terms of the number of issues raised at branch or district committee concerning the workplace organization: independence is measured in terms of the involvement of the FTO in workshop affairs.

At A, the FTO had not been involved in the factory for some years, and the convenor could not recall asking advice from the local office: this state of affairs was confirmed by the local district secretary who felt that the workers at Plant A were exceptionally well organized, and typical of a number of plants within his jurisdiction characterized by 100 per cent organization and coverage by a company agreement; all such plants 'give me little trouble'.[2]

The degree of isolation/integration is difficult to measure given that stewards were dispersed among a number of branches: they exerted little influence at this level. The 1975 District Committee minutes reveal that, in that year, only the annual wage agreement came before the Committee from Factory A, and it was passed;[3] no issues concerning the organization at A were raised via the branches. At Factory B it had again been some years at the time of interview since the full-time official had been called into the factory, although in both plants the company's grievance procedure would involve him at the second stage. Measurement of the isolation/integration continuum is far more difficult on the basis of Batstone *et al.*'s dichotomy of issues raised at branch level or District Committee. Certainly the convenor referred annual wage agreements and over-time problems to the District Committee; he was required by the rule book to do so,[4] but again few issues reached the Committee via the branch in 1975.

Both small organizations were thus isolated and independent. The institutions of the formal union were unlikely to provide a great deal of information. But these measures overlook major differences in the influence of the branch in the two case studies: this influence is related to local industrial structure.

The local area around Factory A was dominated by car-work; there were no other plants either in the company or in the industry in the immediate vicinity: local trade-union structure was not orientated towards the concerns of stewards, whose members were dispersed among a dozen branches, both in the local area and on adjacent 'overspill' estates. Only the convenor attended the branch at all regularly, and this from 'a sense of duty'.[5] Other stewards, who had no involvement with the union outside of the plant, felt that their branch affairs were dominated by the concerns of larger bargaining units, particularly the car plants. The convenor felt that his branch involvement had been useful in establishing contacts and finding out what the 'going rate' in the area was, but professed to make such contacts and find out such information through political contacts in any event.[6]

The situation at the other case-study plant was very different. For many years before the interviewing took place, Factory B had been the largest toolroom in the local area: its workforce had been the largest single body of union members, and had consequently exercised considerable influence on local branch affairs. There were only two branches in the locale, and they were apparently dominated by the concerns of Factory B and the adjacent company plant. All of the stewards indicated that they attended the branch regularly. Moreover, the domestic organization contained a branch president, both of the branch secretaries from the two branches in the locality, and two other branch committee members. Stewards at B were asked if branch attendance assisted them in discovering information about rates elsewhere in the area: all replied that face-to-face contacts with other stewards—particularly before and after meetings—were the principal means by which earnings information was transmitted. The convenor stressed, moreover, that each year he systematically compiled a list of rates and earnings from such contacts for use in negotiation. There was thus a considerable orientation towards the branch and the branch area, which can be contrasted with relations with the district. In informal interviews the stewards stressed that they were 'nothing to do with Nottingham', i.e. they had no contact with the District, and the District Secretary emphasized that the town containing the case-study plant had for many years been 'a little community on its own': the domestic organization at B had been very strong for about fifteen years and, despite good individual involvement at branch and district committee level, it had always 'done its own organization' and so was left largely to itself. There had been in the past a move to make the local area around Factory B a 'district' in itself, the backbone of which would have been the two domestic organizations in the Company and area: once this had been vetoed, the organization at B had achieved almost complete independence of the district committee by greater involvement in the Combined Committee: the local officer professed to have no direct contact with the latter body.[7]

## (c) Inside the Plants

In both plants, there were several independent manual bargaining units. In neither case were these units co-ordinated by a Joint Shop Stewards' Committee; the necessary ingredients for competitive bargaining were present. In outlining relations between unions at this level, it is of considerable interest to discuss the reasons why no

JSSC had developed, particularly since there had been several attempts to establish one.

At Factory A, the four major manual bargaining units—the EETPU, AUEW, NGA and SOGAT—were not covered by the same terms and conditions of employment. The separate national agreements to which they variously referred have been outlined above, but there are certain factory-specific complications. Within the factory, the NGA had only recently combined into a single chapel, having previously been in separate 'gravure' and 'lithographical' chapels which, although both referring to the BPIF agreement ultimately, were on slightly different 'in-house' conditions. Moreover, in 1974, the EETPU moved off the JIC agreement on which they had previously negotiated, onto the terms of the Company's national agreement for engineers and electricians. In general, the print conditions covering the NGA and SOGAT yielded better holiday pay and overtime arrangements than the Company craft agreement: this was a cause of some discontent.[8] These basic divisions reflected the different styles of bargaining over pay which the different societies employed, and were perpetuated by disaffection between skilled and unskilled workers, particularly on the print side.

When contact was first made with the AUEW convenor at A, in early 1976, he was active in the promotion of a JSSC: his model was another of the Company's plants in the South-West of England, also in Group 3 and with a similar occupational structure to Factory A, which had developed a JSSC when widespread redundancies threatened in the early 1970s.[9] The convenor had learned of this through the Combined Committee. Seeing the problems of union organization within Factory A largely in terms of divisions among the workforce, he felt the advantages of a united front would be considerable. There had been earlier attempts by him to put together a JSSC and a subsequent attempt took place at the turn of the year, 1976–7.

Other trade-union representatives on the site were less enthusiastic. The EETPU steward felt that his own members would oppose any change which decreased their bargaining autonomy: he also felt that SOGAT representatives would oppose a JSSC, professing bewilderment at SOGAT's internal organization and bargaining policies, and a complete absence of knowledge of their rate structure. SOGAT had, he said, always been 'out on a limb' and would wish to retain their negotiating power intact. The NGA, moreover, were guilty of 'print elitism' in their past dealings with other unions.

For the two NGA representatives (FOCs) the major obstacle to a

JSSC was also the 'attitudes of SOGAT officials' (by which they meant representatives in the plant).[10] They criticized SOGAT's structure of differentials on the grounds that the classification of a job ought not to be negotiable on a plant-by-plant basis. They welcomed any development which would extend their organizational basis (the AUEW Combined Committee had impressed them considerably) and they were pursuing the idea of a similar structure to cover the NGA in the company.[11] However, their ideas about the role of a JSSC differed somewhat from those of the AUEW convenor. He had envisaged a body with negotiating powers having set policies on redundancy, overtime working, and the like, and centralizing the pattern of representation in the factory. The NGA FOCs however envisaged a less formal arrangement, pooling information and discussing general issues such as safety at work and physical conditions and amenities in the factory. They saw its role as an extension of the existing consultative arrangements which could not have any jurisdiction over pay or any other issue affecting the rules of member societies.[12] Inclusion of the former issue would lead to an unacceptable convergence of pay differentials between themselves and SOGAT.

The SOGAT representatives naturally enough pointed the finger elsewhere. The 'old brigade elitism' of the NGA was attacked by the FOC, who felt that 'across the board' bargaining within a JSSC would be an unacceptable restraint on the bargaining power of his 'stronger' departments. The SOGAT MOC, representing over four hundred women in the plant, felt that a JSSC would be a welcome addition to bargaining arrangements within the plant but there would have to be some assurance that 'the women's voice could be heard on it'. She too was doubtful that the NGA would co-operate fully.

The background to this inter-union antipathy lies both in the rate structure itself, which is reproduced in Appendix 5, and in the styles of bargaining which render it opaque, and encourage officers, particularly in the print societies, to be secretive about the earnings of their members. The EETPU and AUEW representatives both preferred a simple rate structure with a small number of job categories: they were opposed to any differentials which did not arise out of skill or shift-premia considerations. But both the NGA and SOGAT operated under a system whereby the basic rates of the BPIF agreement—which operated nationally—were supplemented at *departmental* level by merit payments and at the *individual* level by machine extras.[13] These items require some explanation.

'Merit Pay' did not, as in Factory B, apply on an individual level to print workers at A: it was a 'productivity' earnings supplement built up on the basis of departmental agreements on work practices and manning levels. An example was supplied by the FOC: a department of, say, ten men might, on the retirement of one of their number, approach the FOC with a view to negotiating a reduction in manning, and the sharing out of the retiring member's wages among the remaining nine. Thus, said the FOC, the wage bill remained undiminished. (The attitudes of the EETPU and AUEW stewards to this was that it represented unacceptable 'selling of jobs'.)[14]

'Machine extras' were further supplements on an individual basis paid to machine operators which changed when technical innovation occurred. Their rate of increase was thus unpredictable but, at the time of interview, the Company's capital investment programme within Group 3 resulted in considerable increases in this supplement in certain departments. Because the technology was on such a scale that the factory would seldom contain two machines of the same type, because the amount of payment depended on the negotiating strength of the department[15] and because such payments were pro-rata according to grade, they encouraged further diversity of earnings.

The opacity of the structure is increased by one practice peculiar to SOGAT, that of job-grade negotiability. No SOGAT job had a 'fixed' grading within the nationally-negotiated three-grade structure, but all could be upgraded by local bargaining. This could lead to peculiar developments, such as the upgrading of fork-lift truck drivers from Grade III to Grade 1, during the period after one of their number was elected FOC.

The complexity of print rate structures in the factory is considerable (see Appendix 5).[16] Merit pay and machine extras constitute a considerable percentage of print earnings: they are extremely variable, and the amounts involved are a closely guarded secret, since the competitive bargaining which might develop on the basis of full information would, in the opinion of the SOGAT FOC, be uncontrollable. Management and NGA representatives colluded to conceal NGA rates from other societies. In summary, the basis of trust for an 'opening of the books' which a JSSC would require did not exist. As a whole, the plant manual rate distribution remained 'unstructured' and the different styles of bargaining prevented any structure being applied.

At Factory B, the rate structure was much simpler, but no more conducive to the formation of a JSSC. The main manual bargaining groups were the TGWU and the AUEW/EETPU. The rate structures of each were easy to comprehend (see Appendix 5) but based on completely different principles and bargaining arrangements. Plant representatives of all three manual unions saw the failure of past attempts to form a JSSC as lying, not in a lack of good feeling or any open factionalism between the two unions, but on the issue of, in the words of the TGWU Secretary, 'the values of different skills'. The way in which the AUEW evaluated different skills has been outlined above. The TGWU were, on the other hand, covered by an explicit skill-evaluation process—the company-wide job evaluation system for general workers which had been introduced with the 'Independent Agreement'. From the point of view of the AUEW stewards, there would be a number of 'practical' difficulties to be overcome in forming a JSSC—such as the apathy of members and the difficulty of fitting meetings in after working hours—but the major obstacle was seen to be the job evaluation system.

They felt that job evaluation 'sets one man off against another' on pay issues, and they were opposed to any move towards the group-level pay bargaining in which the TGWU were involved. Whereas the AUEW/EETPU shop committee compiled its own pay claims and negotiated over them, the TGWU claim was settled by national officers of the TGWU and GMWU at group level. The TGWU at B could not move away from the scheme: group level bargaining was union policy, and full-time officers favoured it. Although B had been one of the plants to vote against job evaluation in 1971, it had been out-voted: in the words of the TGWU Secretary: 'We never wanted it, but we're stuck with it'.[17]

As at A, the workforce at B appears to be effectively divided by bargaining arrangements, if not skill divisions. This disunity was important for the patterns of wage determination in the two plants. No overarching structure of organization encompassed manual bargaining units at the two locations. Yet competitive bargaining had not developed at either plant: in bargaining, the maintenance workers did not tend to 'follow' production. Neither group of stewards was prepared to accept the implications of comparisons with production workers, because in both cases the bargaining arrangements which generated production wage rises were looked on unfavourably. Stewards at A did not want to negotiate merit pay or machine extras: those at B did not want involvement in group-level bargaining.

Stewards at both plants thus had a range of options in the selection of wage comparisons. The principal difference appeared to be that Factory B stewards had a much better developed local information network based on the branch. But these options will only be exercised where the comparisons they make available are disadvan-

tageous. Given the style of print bargaining at Plant A, there are
thus possibilities for intra-plant comparisons which are unlikely at
Plant B.

In both plants, the comparisons used by stewards had been communicated to the membership. At A 46 per cent of respondents
recognized a recent comparison with electricians, while 30 per cent
recognized that no comparisons were being made at the time of
interview. At B, 60 per cent identified involvement with local engineering rates in bargaining comparisons (Question 31). Moreover,
75 per cent of members at A and 92 per cent at B expected stewards
to support the informal comparison they made (Question 34(b)).[18]
Some convergence of bargaining and informal comparisons is
implied here, as one would expect within small bargaining units. But
such convergence is limited by the principal feature of the data to
follow: the extremely *diffuse* nature of informal comparisons.

TABLE 5.1

*Responses to Question 34(a): 'Sometimes pay claims
are justified by the claim that some workers'
pay has fallen "seriously out of line" with the pay
of another group. In your own case, whose pay would
you look at to see whether your own was out of line?'*

| Group Named | Factory A per cent | Factory B per cent |
|---|---|---|
| (a) Factory-internal | | |
| Non-manual | 2.5 | 2.0 |
| Other skilled engineers | 0.0 | 10.0 |
| Other skilled manual | 50.0 | 0.0 |
| Semi-skilled manual | 12.5 | 10.0 |
| Sub-total | (65) | (22) |
| (b) Factory external | | |
| Non-manual | | 4.0 |
| Skilled engineers (manual) | 7.5 | 56.0 |
| Other skilled manual | 5.0 | 12.0 |
| Semi-skilled manual | 2.5 | 0.0 |
| Sub-total | (15) | (72) |
| Past standard of living | 7.5 | 4.0 |
| No reference | 12.5 | 2.0 |
| Total | 100 | 100 |
| | N = 40 | N = 50 |

*Note:* In interpreting this pattern of response, it should be borne in mind that another group
could be 'out of line' because its wages were *too close* to the respondents' group, not because they
were *equal*. But respondents appeared more concerned with parity.

INFORMAL COMPARISONS

Aside from this diffuseness, the main feature of informal comparisons is a concern with intra-plant issues at A and local issues at B.
This is clear from Table 5.1: 65 per cent at A focused inside the
plant, 72 per cent at B focused outside. The sections which follow,
which deal with these areas in turn, will attempt to explain why this
was the case.

### (a)  Plant-Internal Comparisons

It should be stressed at the outset that I am concerned here with
intra-plant relativities, not differentials internal to the bargaining
unit. As the previous chapter shows, the latter were a source of
dissatisfaction at B, and could influence responses to questions
about internal relativities (e.g. Question 28). Here I shall focus
solely on external comparisons. There are three sets of data; that
relating to wage leadership and relativities, to occupational worth
and to perceived under-pay and over-pay.

TABLE 5.2

*Responses to Question 56: 'Do you think that,*
*in the period before pay policy came into operation,*
*any group within the factory was setting the pace*
*for pay increases. If yes: which group?*
*If no: what did set the pace for pay increases?'*

|  | Factory A per cent | Factory B per cent |
|---|---|---|
| (a)  No |  |  |
| Cost-of-living | 51.2 | 54 |
| (b)  Yes |  |  |
| NGA | 27.9 | — |
| SOGAT | 16.3 | — |
| AUEW | 2.3 | 38 |
| Foremen | — | 4 |
| Other | 2.3 | 4 |
|  | 100 | 100 |
|  | No. Responses = 43 | No. Responses = 50 |
|  | N = 40 | N = 50 |

Table 5.2 concerns the identification of wage leadership in the
period up to the application of pay policy. Given the rate structure
of Factory B the response pattern is hardly surprising (Appendix 5).
But Factory A is more interesting because, while NGA rates were
unknown, SOGAT rates were generally lower. Yet they were seen by

a minority to set the pace for pay increases. It could be argued that AUEW members were concerned with converging relativities, but responses to Question 58 indicate that they felt the situation was much worse than that. Whereas at B all respondents felt that skilled workers in the factory were always paid more than unskilled, only 50 per cent did so at A; 40 per cent felt that there was considerable overlap between AUEW skilled and SOGAT *rates*, and a further 10 per cent felt that differential overtime working caused overlap in *earnings*. Finally, a general question on the fairness of manual relativities produced similar results. At A, 20 per cent felt that print rates were too high: surprisingly at B, 26 per cent, mainly line engineers, were unhappy with the differential over the TGWU. I will suggest reasons for this in the remainder of this section.

The second set of data involve further discussion of the data presented in Table 3.9. I have already used this to indicate dissatisfaction internal to the bargaining unit at B. Only 6 per cent at B identified equal pay jobs and only 14 per cent equal worth jobs outside the bargaining unit. Most felt that these were fairly paid. The concern here is with responses at Factory A, where 55 per cent of respondents saw other AUEW or maintenance workers as being paid the same (Question 23) and felt that the relationship was fair (Question 24), but 32.5 per cent looked at SOGAT workers and felt that the relationship was unfair. In responses to Questions 21 and 22, a further 32.5 per cent felt that they could identify print jobs of equal worth which were in fact paid more. There is some consistency between these responses and those to Questions 30 and 32, which asked respondents to identify underpaid and overpaid jobs within the factory. At A, 32.5 per cent pointed to unskilled workers in the plant, and 25 per cent to the bargaining unit itself as underpaid: at B, these categories included 18 per cent and 38 per cent of the sample respectively: there was greater concern at B, as the last chapter noted, with pay dissatisfaction internal to the unit.[19] At A, the overpaid jobs in the plant were identified as NGA (20 per cent) and SOGAT (22.5 per cent), at B only 4 per cent pointed to another manual group in the factory as overpaid.[20]

These three sets of results do not point to any clear-cut conclusions, but the following points emerge:

(1) there appears to be a consistent 'groundswell' of opinion pointing to unfavourable comparisons with print workers at Factory A: 44.2 per cent identified their wage leadership, 42.5 per cent thought they were overpaid, and 32.5 per cent identified an unfair parity relationship. In response to Question 28, 20 per cent felt that comparisons with print workers were unfavourable;

(2) very few respondents at B showed a parallel concern with TGWU production rates: none identified their wage leadership, none thought they,
were overpaid, only 6 per cent identified an unfair parity relationship.
In response to Question 28, however, 26 per cent felt that the difference
between TGWU and AUEW rates was insufficient.

Although respondents consistently restricted wage comparisons
to those with other groups of manual workers in a number of contexts—under-pay and over-pay, parity, wage leadership and the size
of differentials—there was no marked tendency to focus on one
group. There appear to be few pressures towards uniformity in
comparison choice. However, some plausible explanation for the
principal patterns of intra-plant informal comparison can be offered in terms of simple contiguity: those respondents who worked
close to members of other societies were more likely to use them
as comparisons than those who did not. At A, departments such
as the boilerhouse or garage, where contact with print-workers was
likely to be less, were unlikely to point to such workers in comparison or as overpaid. At B, line engineers dominated the small minority who were prepared to highlight some aspect of TGWU rates
as unfair, for example, of the 26 per cent who felt that the differential over the TGWU should be greater (Question 28) 10 per
cent were line engineers, who constituted only 14 per cent of the
whole sample. The basis of this contiguity theory can be seen in
Figure 5.1.

However, comparisons with print workers by respondents at A
are more likely than those with production workers by respondents
at B for other reasons. Although AUEW rates were better than
those of SOGAT, the SOGAT structure of bargaining and basis of
conditions of employment meant that it was difficult for respondents to establish exactly what SOGAT rates were—there was no
single 'rate for the job'. The consequent opacity of the rate structure
fostered suspicion rather than apathy. There appear to have been
two reasons for this. Firstly, SOGAT representatives negotiated on
pay more or less continuously throughout the year: the combination
of departmental bargaining and two irregularly-negotiable earnings supplements meant that there was seldom a time when some
SOGAT rise could not be discussed. The AUEW, by contrast,
typically negotiated only once a year. Secondly, while rates were
unclear, AUEW respondents knew that SOGAT shift and overtime
premia were slightly better than their own: there existed the possibility that, despite inferior rates, SOGAT earnings might exceed
those of AUEW craftsmen. This suspicion put stewards under a
certain amount of pressure.

FIG. 5.1. *Layout of engineering departments: Factories A and B*

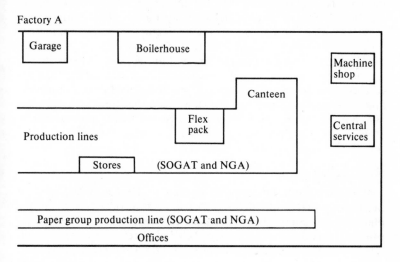

Factory A

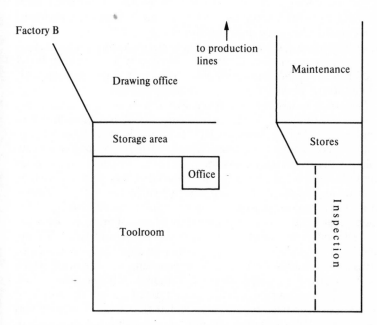

Factory B

The scatter of responses on the selection of plant internal comparisons is similar to that on FFP and FFPR. Although there are
identifiable foci of interest, notably a groundswell of opinion dissatisfied with print rates or earnings at Factory A, it does not look as
though either set of stewards were confronted by a single normatively central informal comparison within the plant. This is clearly
important: if informal comparisons are leadership issues, then acceptable policies of wage restraint or reform need to pay considerable attention to the role of the steward, rather than make general
assumptions about the scope and form of wage comparisons.[21]
However, the situation is not so clear cut: when comparisons outside the plant are considered, the picture alters.

### (b) Area Relativities

Just as there are certain features internal to the plant which make it
more likely that respondents at A will refer to other groups in the
plant as wage comparisons, there are certain aspects of the relationship of the two organizations to their local areas which may facilitate or impede the making of 'local' comparisons. I have described
above the concern of shop stewards at Factory B with the local
branch structure. A similar local concern on the part of respondents
at B generally has been indicated in Table 5.1. In this section, I want
to argue that these comparisons were particularly salient because
they consistently showed Factory B to be poorly paid for its industry
and area. At A the absence of concern is equally straightforwardly
related to the plant's high-wage status.

The gross hourly earnings (exclusive of overtime) at A and B are
compared in Tables 5.3 and 5.4 with earnings figures calculated on a
similar basis derived from the New Earnings Survey: this comparison is carried back to 1972, which is the earliest that data was available for the two plants concerned. Only the roughest comparisons
can be made from such a table, since the NES data are at a very high
level of aggregation: the details are given in the notes to tables.
Moreover, the comparison at B is less reliable because the bargaining date does not equate with the date of compilation of the NES.
More specific figures exist, but their relevance and reliability are
equally suspect. The EEF regional returns apply only to federated
firms which would exclude the company and several firms which
were important comparisons for respondents. On the other hand,
the AUEW shop stewards returns might be of use but the Assistant
Divisional Organizer on Merseyside felt that their reliability was
very suspect because of the low rate of return of questionnaires. In
any case, neither set of figures was made available.

TABLE 5.3
Gross Hourly Earnings: Factory A and Selected NES Figures,
Exclusive and (Inclusive) of Overtime Effects

| Occupational Title | Date of Statistics | | | | | | | |
|---|---|---|---|---|---|---|---|---|
| | Sept. 72 (p) | April 73 (p) | Sept. 73 (p) | April 74 (p) | Sept. 74 (p) | April 75 (p) | April 76 (p) | April 77 (p) |
| Factory A | | | | | | | | |
| Maintenance Fitter | 102.8(108.6) | | 112.5(118.2) | | 131.6(138.3) | 163.5(171.6) | 178.5(185.1) | 187.4(194.1) |
| Pipe-fitter | 102.8(108.6) | | 112.5(118.2) | | 131.6(138.3) | 163.5(171.6) | 178.5(185.1) | 187.4(194.1) |
| Labourer | 82.66(86.8) | | 90.2(94.8) | | 105.2(110.5) | 133.4(140.1) | 148.4(153.6) | 155.8(161.3) |
| Nationally | | | | | | | | |
| Maintenance Fitter | | 85.0(89.5) | | 98.0(102.9) | | 131.4(136.6) | 152.7(158.1) | 165.4(170.6) |
| Pipe-fitter | | 83.0(85.3) | | 94.8(97.5) | | 126.1(129.4) | 144.7(148.3) | 158.6(162.1) |
| Labourer | | 65.8(68.7) | | 76.4(79.2) | | 101.4(104.6) | 120.9(124.2) | 131.5(134.0) |
| Merseyside M.C. | | | | | | | | |
| Average manual earnings | | 87.1 | | 95.0 | | 125.3 | 145.9 | 155.8 |
| Occ. Cat. 14 North-West Region | | | | | | | | |
| Average earnings | | (87.8) | | (99.8) | | (129.4) | (152.0) | (166.0) |
| SIC Category 18 North-West Region | | | | | | | | |
| Average manual earnings | | (89.0) | | (101.1) | | (133.5) | (158.5) | (167.2) |

For notes see p. 96

Table 5.3 Notes

Source: Company Records, New Earnings Survey, Tables 86, 108, 118, 122.

Notes: (1) The geographical basis for certain regional figures is inconsistent. The over-all manual mean is for the Merseyside M.C. but the occupational and industrial data refer to the entire North-West Region.

(2) The industrial figures are for 'paper and packaging' which is a sub-category of Standard Industrial Classification 18. The occupational category 14 is much more diffuse: it contains sixty-nine occupational headings, some supervisory, of which only eleven are definitely represented in the sample *as a whole*. As an estimate of pay for comparable work in the region, they are likely to be a slight overestimate because of the inclusion of supervisory categories. Moreover, they include the effects of overtime.

(3) The figures quoted for Factory A are gross hourly earnings excluding overtime, for two-shift workers, being 77.5 per cent of the sample.

(4) The basis of calculation of the bracketed overtime-inclusive figures is as follows: 4.5 hours at time + ½ on two-shift rates are added to 40-hour gross earnings, and the resultant figure divided by 44.5. At the time of interview, this addition was worth £11 (approximately) to skilled and £9 (approximately) to unskilled men, on top of gross weekly earnings. The 4.5 hours represents routine overtime working on Saturday morning, which all respondents had worked in the week before interview. The only other overtime allowed at the time was covering for absence (in the boilerhouse).

Table 5.4 Notes

Source: Company Records: New Earnings Survey, Tables 86, 108, 118, 122.

Notes: (1), (2) and (3) for Table 5.3 apply here also. In addition:

(1) The figures quoted for Factory B are gross hourly earnings excluding overtime, for workers earning the top rate in their respective departments. 36 per cent of workers, the largest single category, did so.

(2) The basis of calculation of the gross overtime-inclusive figures is as follows. The assumption is made that the rate of overtime working in the week prior to interview, average 3.74 hours per week, was worked throughout the period. This is slightly less than the 10 per cent average quoted by the personnel manager. It is an arbitrary assumption, but as useful as any other. The limitation of 30 hours per month, which was invoked after the interviewing, yields an average of 7.5 overtime hours per week, making earnings comparable with quoted indices.

TABLE 5.4
Gross Hourly Earnings: Factory B and Selected NES Figures,
Exclusive and (Inclusive) of Overtime Effects

| Occupational Title | Date of Factory B Statistics | | | | | | |
|---|---|---|---|---|---|---|---|
| | July 72 (p) | July 73 (p) | July 74 (p) | July 75 (p) | July 76 (p) | July 77 (p) | July 78 (p) |
| Factory B | | | | | | | |
| Toolmaker | 84.7(88.3) | 90.5(94.4) | 107.0(111.6) | 139.0(144.9) | 154.0(158.7) | 161.7(166.6) | |
| Maintenance Fitter | 84.7(88.3) | 89.3(93.1) | 104.0(108.4) | 139.0(144.9) | 154.0(158.7) | 161.7(166.6) | |
| Labourer | 61.0(63.6) | 71.0(74.0) | 90.0(93.8) | 117.5(122.5) | 132.5(136.2) | 139.1(143.0) | |

| Occupational Title | Date of New Earnings Survey Statistics | | | | | | |
|---|---|---|---|---|---|---|---|
| | April 72 (p) | April 73 (p) | April 74 (p) | April 75 (p) | April 76 (p) | April 77 (p) | April 78 (p) |
| Nationally | | | | | | | |
| Toolmaker | 83.7(86.1) | 92.7(96.1) | 106.4(109.3) | 132.5(136.2) | 154.3(157.8) | 167.7(171.8) | 193.6(198.5) |
| Maintenance Fitter | 76.9(80.2) | 85.0(89.5) | 98.0(102.9) | 131.4(136.6) | 152.7(158.1) | 165.4(170.6) | 188.1(194.0) |
| Labourer | 52.8(59.8) | 65.8(68.7) | 76.4(79.2) | 101.4(104.6) | 120.9(124.3) | 131.5(134.0) | 146.4(149.6) |
| Notts Average Manual Earnings | 69.8 | 79.5 | 91.5 | 124.8 | 143.3 | 154.6 | 181.4 |
| Occ. Cat. 14, E. Midlands Average Earnings | (71.6) | (85.1) | (98.5) | (129.8) | (150.4) | (166.1) | (188.0) |
| SIC 12, E. Midlands Average Earnings | (70.6) | (82.6) | (92.3) | (118.9) | (144.0) | (158.4) | (181.1) |

TABLE 5.5
Gross Hourly Earnings: Factory B and Engineering Earnings
Exclusive and (Inclusive) of Overtime

|  | 1972 (p) | 1973 (p) | 1974 (p) | 1975 (p) | 1976 (p) | 1977 (p) |
|---|---|---|---|---|---|---|
| Factory B Toolroom earnings | 84.7(88.3) | 90.5(94.4) | 107.0(111.6) | 139.0(144.9) | 154.0(158.7) | 161.7(116.6) |
| East Midlands Skilled Timeworkers | 78.3(81.7) | 87.0(91.0) | 100.6(105.1) | 131.8(136.7) | 150.1(155.5) | 158.8(165.5) |
| National toolroom fitters (timerates) | 86.5(89.3) | 95.5(99.5) | 108.8(113.7) | 135.9(140.4) | 156.1(161.8) | 167.8(174.8) |

Notes: Factory B earnings are as in Table 5.6. The East Midlands and National toolroom figures are from the Department of Employment June Survey of Engineering, Shipbuilding and Chemicals (published in the Department of Employment Gazette, October annually, Tables 4 and 7 to 1975, Tables 7 and 10 thereafter). The June survey does not include earnings in Minimum List Heading 395 'can and box-making'.

Despite these shortcomings, it seems clear that Factory A fares better in comparison with available indices than does Factory B. This is true of gross hourly earnings excluding overtime, and of the more inclusive figure, the basis of which is given in the notes to the tables. Factory A is well above the NES figures for all years, and particularly at the time of interview. By contrast, Factory B has no such pronounced advantage. This may not be too clear from Table 5.4, since bargaining dates differ from the dates of NES data collection. A better idea of the picture at B can be gained from Table 5.5, in which earnings at Factory B are compared with data from the annual June survey of engineering earnings. Throughout most of the period 1972–7, earnings at Factory B lagged behind national toolroom earnings, and this discrepancy increased in 1976–7. Moreover, while earnings at B were generally higher than those of East Midlands skilled timeworkers over the period 1972–7, this differential collapsed over the latter part of the period, particularly if overtime working is considered: in 1974 factory B earnings were 106.1 per cent of the East Midlands figures, but by 1977, they were only 100.7 per cent of skilled earnings for the region. This slump in performance against earnings for comparable work outside Factory B was perceived clearly by respondents, as the emphasis on external comparisons in responses to Question 34 (above) indicates. This impression is further confirmed by responses to Question 37, which are shown in Table 5.6.

TABLE 5.6

*Responses to Question 37: How does your pay
in this factory relate to the pay for similar work
in other factories in the area?*

|  | Factory A per cent | Factory B per cent |
| --- | --- | --- |
| Above average/Specified comparisons | 17.5 | 14 |
| About average/Specified comparisons | 37.5 | 40 |
| Below average/Specified comparisons | 15 | 46 |
| Don't know | 30 | — |
|  | 100 | 100 |
|  | N = 40 | N = 50 |

Table 5.6 is simplified. Only 42.5 per cent of respondents at A actually discussed earnings in terms of an area average: all of them felt that AUEW earnings were good in comparison. A further 27.5 per

cent compared their wages with other specific factories locally—
some in the car industry—while a surprising 30 per cent could not
assess the relationship between their own rates and specific factory-
external rates or an average thereof. By contrast, all respondents at
B referred to an area average, and the largest response category
thought that the rate at B was poor for the area. The data presented
here are, in conjunction with the previous sections on negotiating
strategies, consistent with the contention that area rates were far
more salient for respondents at B than for those at A: some reasons
for this can be presented.

The first thing is the shortfall itself: from 1975 onwards, earnings
at Factory B had increased less than those locally and nationally for
similar work. Secondly, the occupational specificity of toolroom
workers and the industrial structure of the area were such as to
facilitate focus on a particular wage contour outside the factory at
B, but inimical to such a focus at A. Whereas at A respondents
could focus on a variety of different plants in the area, all of whom
employed maintenance workers, at B, the structure of local engineering encouraged focus on a single contour: at A, 35 per cent of
respondents pointed to named other factories employing people in
similar jobs, but at B respondents all answered in the occupation
specific terms of 'other toolrooms'—they perceived a general contour, (Question 36). Thirdly, and perhaps most importantly for informal comparisons, the negotiating strategies of stewards involved
the use of local comparisons in bargaining.

At A, stewards and management felt few pressures on bargaining
from the local labour market: those at B, as noted above, felt that
the pressures both of comparisons and of labour supply which ema-
nated from the area were considerable. This had communicated
itself to the workforce: whereas at A, 40 per cent attributed inter-
plant differentials to differential trade-union strength and 20 per
cent to profit or productivity differences, at B 40 per cent pointed to
competition for labour, 15 per cent to different patterns of fringe
benefits and 14 per cent to profit or productivity differences (Question 38(a)). One of the main reasons why stewards and members at
Factory B were in close agreement on the importance of local issues
has to do with the involvement of the latter in branch activity: 24 per
cent of respondents at B claimed to attend branch meetings regularly, and 18 per cent occasionally. In addition, it will be recalled
that the workshop contained a number of branch officers: alto-
gether a surprising 52 per cent of respondents had some contact with
the branches.[22] A large number of members thus had access to the

stewards' most important source of earnings information. By contrast, only 10 per cent of members at A attended branch meetings regularly, and 5 per cent occasionally.

The idea of a 'competitive' rate for skilled men had become quite salient at B during the incomes policy period. Factory B was experiencing recruitment difficulties, which encouraged a high level of overtime working. The reason for this was that, in a 'tight' labour market situation,[23] a number of small engineering firms had moved into the area and were apparently ignoring incomes policy to pay very high rates, with low fringe benefits, which were a cause of some concern to respondents at B.[24] Respondents felt unfairly constrained by an unevenly-applied incomes policy: the area rate, which had apparently always been a focus for negotiations in the past, was moving out of reach.[25]

This clearly is a normatively central informal comparison: i.e. a disadvantageous comparison which is the object of strong feelings on the part of the membership, and which stewards consequently could not ignore. The incomes policy which sought to cope with *this* would need to have greater reference to the equalization of earnings within occupations than to the requirements of shop-stewards' roles. In practice, the Social Contract did not concern itself with such matters, and caused considerable problems within the plant. I shall return to this in Chapter 7.

### (c) Other relativities

A number of questions included in the interview schedule sought comparisons made by respondents *outside* their company and industry. The intention was to find out whether respondents were encouraged to compare with those groups most prominent in media reporting of settlements and disputes. But the results were in a sense disappointing: those sorts of comparisons were seldom made. Forty-five per cent of respondents at A and 36 per cent at B indicated that they would not make comparisons outside the industry. A further 10 per cent at A and 26 per cent at B indicated that such an external comparison would involve movements in the general pattern of wages, not any specific groups of workers (Question 60).[26]

Even where respondents were directly asked about such wide relativities, the failure to respond rate was very high. But some interesting findings did emerge, which are worth a brief summary. First, the tendency to consider craft jobs as of equal worth was as evident outside as inside the industry: 40 per cent at A and 55 per cent at B named such jobs as of equal worth. Secondly, relatively few respondents were prepared to name any other manual job as overpaid (25 per cent at both plants), but when asked about pay leadership, both sets of answers focused on manual jobs: principally miners (A, 45 per cent; B, 50 per cent), car workers (A, 21 per cent; B, 11 per cent) and dockers (A, 9 per cent; B, 9 per cent). Thirdly, there appeared to be a focus on those groups which have received considerable media attention; miners and car workers as wage leaders, health workers and farmworkers as underpaid. (Question 50).

These wider comparisons are likely to have very little impact on bargaining behaviour. The diffuse pattern of response indicates scope for leadership, but such comparisons are clearly useless as bargaining arguments.

## CONCLUSION

Although not current at the time of interview, bargaining comparisons had featured in negotiations at both plants: at A, comparisons had been made with engineering workers throughout the company, at B the focus was on local toolroom rates. These comparisons can be considered as items from a range of options provided by the stewards contacts in the Combine and the AUEW. Surprisingly, neither set of negotiators found intra-plant comparisons popular, although unco-ordinated bargaining took place. Differences of interest and of bargaining power separated bargaining units at both plants.

The main difference between the case studies was the balance of intra-plant and extra-plant informal comparisons. At Plant A, an opaque wage structure and the pay bargaining tactics of print unions contributed to a feeling of dissatisfaction among members of the AUEW. At B, awareness of local rates fostered by branch involvement and the influx of higher-paying plants into the area led to a feeling of being 'left behind' in pay matters. But informal comparisons at A were not focused on print rates to such an extent that bargaining comparisons were influenced: at B, the principal bargaining argument was heavily influenced by informal comparisons.

This influences the pattern of steward leadership and the arguments used in negotiations. The convergence of unfavourable informal and bargaining comparisons at Factory B caused problems for stewards: it was the main influence on the high levels of wage dissatisfaction discussed in the last chapter, and hindered control over overtime working. Because of this comparison, stewards were seen to be unsuccessful. At Plant A, earnings were 'up' on available indices, to the extent that unfavourable comparisons of earnings were hard to find: focus switched to the pay *rises* achieved by print workers.

The findings indicate the crucial role played by stewards in the 'management of discontent' generated by informal comparisons. Such comparisons do generate wage dissatisfaction: it clearly is not the case, as both Patchen and Goodman appear to assume, that informal comparisons are naturally consonant, and only bargaining comparisons 'deliberately' dissonant.[27] But this dissatisfaction is often diffuse: members often focus on different comparisons and it is difficult to identify their origins. In such circumstances, steward strategies are much more influential for bargaining arguments than membership sentiments. But circumstances can arise where the contingencies of informal comparison selection influence collective bargaining: as Chapter 7 will demonstrate, bargaining relationships may break down completely if negotiators cannot accommodate powerful informal pressures.

Thus, where stewards can lead, their acceptance of incomes policy is clearly crucial to its success. Where they cannot lead, incomes policy is severly jeopardized. Policy makers cannot hope to cope with the range of possible contingencies which could generate the types of informal pressures evident at Plant B, nor to predict the focus of informal comparisons in a range of different bargaining units. Steward leadership is thus the *sine qua non* for the acceptability and success of incomes policy just as it is the prerequisite for stable bargaining relationships, principally because in both instances it ensures predictability in bargaining arguments. I shall return to this theme in the final chapter, after discussing specific examples of the sorts of problems which loss of leadership by stewards can generate. However, in the next chapter, the usefulness of the model presented in Chapter 2 is reassessed in light of the findings so far.

## CHAPTER 6

# STEWARDS AND MEMBERS

## INTRODUCTION

At the outset, I emphasized that argument about 'fair pay' in collective bargaining were best seen as products of specific social processes operating within the bargaining context: if one wishes to understand why trade-union representatives use particular ethical arguments in negotiation, one needs to study the relationship between their bargaining goals and membership wishes. The leadership model developed in Chapter 2 sought to analyse this relationship on pay issues, and it has been used to structure the presentation of the data so far.

In this chapter, I want to look more closely into the steward–member relationship and at the tension between steward policy and membership views on fair pay. In doing so, I shall follow the divisions of the previous chapters, and deal with matters within the bargaining units and external to them separately. Subsequently I shall analyse the coherence of steward policy at the two case-study plants, and suggest that the differing bargaining relationships at A and B explain much of the difference in the use of ethical arguments between the two plants. However, since the empirical findings are complex, it is perhaps useful at this point to summarize them before proceeding: they may usefully be divided between those which established over-all similarity between the two groups and those in terms of which they may be contrasted.

Some similarities were ensured by the selection of two case studies similar in size, demographic and occupational structure, in plants owned by the same company and covered by the same bargaining arrangements. Given their size, it is not surprising that both shopfloor organizations were seen as democratic by members. Nor is it surprising that there was a general consensus on relative occupational worth, and that respondents tended to compare their wages with others in the same or similar social categories: there is considerable evidence that both of these tendencies are widespread. But more unexpected was the extreme variance of felt-fair pay and felt-fair pay rises: a number of psychological theories would lead one to expect some uniformity within groups such as these, and the variance has clear policy implications.

The major differences between the case studies became apparent in trying to explain this variance in terms of actual pay. At neither plant was variance on FFPR explicable in this manner. But FFP could be explained in terms of actual pay variance at Plant A: at Plant B, it could not. The crucial difference here appeared to be high wage dissatisfaction at Plant B, which encouraged respondents not to use actual pay in equity calculations. The combination of dissension within the bargaining unit over departmental differentials and an extremely powerful informal comparison with local toolroom earnings generated wage dissatisfaction to such an extent that the stewards' position became untenable. At Plant A, neither internal dissension nor informal comparisons were so potent: stewards controlled overtime working and manipulated comparisons with greater ease. A closer look at the basis of the leadership model helps to show how they did so.

TRADE UNION PRINCIPLES

Although Chapter 2 suggested that certain parallels could be drawn between custom and practice rules and fair pay arguments in bargaining, it is clear that there are limits to this analogy. First of all, while shops stewards in different situations might pursue broadly similar sets of effort controls, the principles which govern the 'reward' side of the bargain seem much more variable. Secondly, it is clear from the case studies that leadership and normatively central pay issues may vary between locations.

The first point may be illustrated by Table 6.1 which presents a checklist of the principles which stewards in the case studies might pursue, under the assumptions of Chapter 2, and the extent to which the organizations studied were disposed to pursue them, and were successful in that pursuit. Following the model, one might expect that stewards would wish to remove personal and departmental differentials and control occupational differentials and overtime working. One might also expect that stewards would attempt to exert control over the process of work in several respects.

Table 6.1 shows that dissimilar patterns of differentials, and indeed different organizational policies on differentials, coexisted with broadly similar policies on effort control; these organizations were not simply at different stages on some road to equity, they were on different roads. In particular, the print unions appeared to have a completely different approach to differentials and to overtime. A table such as this can give only the crudest indication of the issues involved and there are, as noted, certain 'scoring' problems; nevertheless, it is a useful guide to bargaining practice in the two plants.

TABLE 6.1

*Trade-union Pay Principles, Factories A and B*

| Principle | Factory A | | | Factory B | |
|---|---|---|---|---|---|
| | AUEW | NGA | SOGAT | AUEW | TGWU |
| Differentials | | | | | |
| removal of personal differentials | 2 | 0 | 0 | 0 | 2 |
| removal of departmental differentials | 2 | 0 | 0 | 1 | 2 |
| removal of occupational differentials | 0 | 2 | 0 | 1 | 0 |
| Overtime | | | | | |
| control over distribution | 2 | 2 | 2 | 2 | 1 |
| control over amount | 2 | 2 | 0 | 1 | 1 |
| Job Control | | | | | |
| control over internal mobility | 1 | 2 | 2 | 1 | 1 |
| control over redundancy | 2 | 2 | 0 | 1 | 1 |
| control over hiring (closed shop) | 2 | 2 | 2 | 2 | 1 |
| 100% membership | 2 | 2 | 2 | 2 | 1 |
| control over; | | | | | |
| speed of work | 2 | 2 | 2 | 2 | 1 |
| tools/machinery | 2 | 2 | 2 | 2 | 1 |
| actual methods | 2 | 2 | 2 | 2 | 1 |

*Sources:* Observation, unstructured interviews, documentary sources.

*Notes:* (1) Scoring is on the following basis: achieved policy of the domestic organization, 2; policy of the organization, 1; not organizational policy, 0.

(2) The criteria for policy identification were, given the variety of methods, intuitive. Where no written policy statement on the item existed, it was identified as policy only if the convenor and a majority of the stewards felt that it was policy. Similarly 'achievement' and 'non-achievement' are matters of degree; certain items, such as 100 per cent membership, are much easier to be sure about than others, e.g. control over the distribution of overtime.

In such broad terms, it is possible to relate the differences highlighted in Table 6.1 to wider issues of craft values and definitions of skill, as well as to 'historical' factors. For example, the print unions at A had traditionally negotiated on a jobbing basis, where, over and above basic pay levels, individuals were paid for exactly what they did, by 'merit' and 'machine' supplements. This related to a wider tradition of pay negotiations which has been discussed

elsewhere.[1] The TGWU members at B—lacking any such firm traditions—had their own evaluative criteria dictated by the job evaluation scheme.

The table revealed certain similarities between the two case study
plants. At both, stewards held to the idea that the craft qualification
should carry a certain rate of pay irrespective of the exact nature of
the work upon which the craftsman was directly involved. In all
respects, their *policies* on job control were similar. However, their
pay policies differed in two respects; it was the policy of organization A to remove personal differentials, but not of B, and it was the
policy of B to remove some occupational differentials, but not of A.
In both cases the decision to control these issues was, apparently,
made in the interests of unity. According to the convenor at A, merit
awards had been used in the past to divide the men; they had been
administered on particularistic criteria, and he had negotiated their
removal. According to the convenor at B, management had in the
past attempted to 'play one department off against another' by
altering differentials; he had consequently sought parity in the interests of organizational unity. In both cases only the problematic
differentials had been removed, the others being allowed to persist.

Both steward organizations had sought solutions to problems
of divisive differentials: but the strategy pursued at Plant A had
proved more acceptable to members. This acceptability is due to the
fact that, on those principles which *were* pursued by both organizations, stewards at Plant A were more successful.[2] This raises a
number of points about pay leadership at the case study plants. If
one attempts to look at empirical instances of leadership behaviour,
the evidence is equivocal. At A, the convenor instigated industrial
action without prior consultation with his constituents and was
supported, he initiated action by telephone while absent from work
and manipulated members' access to information about other wage
rates and rises; his position had not been contested in an election for
five years. On the other hand, there were instances where members
overruled him on the nature of industrial action and vetoed his
affiliation of the organization to an outside unofficial body; he experienced great difficulty in increasing the trade-union involvement
of unskilled members, particularly as stewards. At B, the convenor
was similarly free from electoral opposition over a long period, was
able to limit overtime with considerable success until the summer of
1977, and was able to initiate action in support of the claim for staff
status which he devised himself. On the other hand, he could not
succeed, as had the convenor at A, in resolving difficulties between

departments nor in eliciting support among his constituents for the Leyland toolroom strike. Moreover, he lost control over overtime working during the summer of 1977 (see Chapter 7).

The immediate conclusion to be drawn is apparently that leadership is both issue-specific and transient. One can, however, be more exact than this. On the basis of the empirical evidence it seems reasonable to make a threefold division of issues:

(a) those issues on which the steward is almost certain never to take a lead, because they are complete 'non-starters' with either management or members or both;
(b) those issues on which the steward is generally likely to lead because he has more expertise than the membership, including a knowledge of what management might see as a 'fair argument'; these issues would include the size of the next pay rise, the level of overtime to be worked, and the nature of industrial action;
(c) those issues which are indeterminate; whether they are leadership issues or not is an empirical question.

Table 6.2 attempts to classify the latter two sets of issues for the two case studies. Clearly, there are differences; one might summarize them in the statement that pay issues seem to be more amenable to leadership at Plant A than at Plant B. The single most important difference between the two units was the level of wage dissatisfaction within each. To adopt Ross's approach, the stewards' ability to lead on pay issues depended on the level of wage satisfaction and the avoidance of any invidious comparison with other groups of workers. The latter will be discussed in the next section; it is with the former that I am concerned here, and Table 6.3 demonstrates the important differences between Plants A and B in the relationship between stewards' and members' conceptions. At A, steward aspirations—measured by the difference between actual and felt-fair pay and by the size of the felt-fair pay rise—were considerably in excess of those of their members. By the same measures, the reverse was the case at B. The necessary precondition for pay leadership—substantial wage aspirations—was thus absent; stewards will find it particularly difficult to exercise their initiative where the amounts they quote as aspirations are lower than those desired by their members. The repercussions of this failure to lead can be gauged by recalling Table 4.8. At B, variance of earnings produced by overtime working was consistently higher than at A (i.e. on gross earnings the week before interview and the gross earnings in the four weeks prior to interview). Although one needs to be cautious about the use of the model, it does seem clear that stewards at B were overall less able to lead than those at A: members at Plant B

### TABLE 6.2
*Issued-specificity of Shop-steward Leadership:*
*Comparison of Leadership-prone Issues, Plants A and B*

| Plant A | Plant B |
|---|---|
| | Stewards totally free from membership constraint |
| FFPR (Pay-rise issues) | |
| FFP (Fair Pay Issues) | FFPR (Pay-rise issues) |
| Control over distribution of overtime | |
| Control over amount of overtime | FFP (Fair Pay Issues) |
| Comparisons with print workers on site in bargaining | Control over distribution of overtime |
| | Control over amount of overtime |
| | Size of skilled–unskilled differential |
| | Comparisons with local toolroom rates in bargaining |
| Maintenance of time-rate payment system | |
| | Size/existence of toolroom–maintenance differential |
| Size of skilled–unskilled differential | |
| | Maintenance of time-rate payment system |
| | Steward decision totally constrained by membership |

were extremely dissatisfied with their pay, and this led to individualistic projects to increase earnings, such as high levels of overtime working. This had clear implications for the use of bargaining comparisons.

## TABLE 6.3
### Wage Aspirations; Steward–Member Differences (Total Sample)

| | $XFFP$ $(£)$ | $XFFPR$ $(£)$ | $\dfrac{XFFP}{XAPNOR}\%$ | $\dfrac{XFFPR}{XAPNOR}\%$ |
|---|---|---|---|---|
| Factory A | | | | |
| skilled | 88.26 | 13.31 | 119.06 | 17.96 |
| unskilled | 67.58 | 8.56 | 110.59 | 14.01 |
| stewards | 95.23 | 23.77 | 131.01 | 32.71 |
| Factory B | | | | |
| all members | 77.89 | 13.55 | 128.0 | 30.0 |
| stewards | 73.32 | 11.57 | 119.0 | 18.78 |

*Notes:* (1) Sources for measures on variables as shown in Table 4.8 above.
(2) Attempts to explain this pattern of difference in terms of the earnings position of the individuals concerned breaks down given the absence of any APNOR–FFPR relationship at both plants and of any APNOR–FFP relationship at B.

### BARGAINING AND INFORMAL COMPARISONS

Table 6.1 effectively codifies the discussion in Chapter 5 about the difficulties involved in forming a JSSC at either factory. But these differences of bargaining 'style' had further implications: at both factories, there was a considerable disincentive to AUEW shop-stewards to compare with production unions.

The convenor at A indicated why wage comparisons with SOGAT would not be encouraged. He felt that such a comparison might imply acquiescence in the sort of job change and manning reduction which was typically a feature of such negotiations.[3] He simply did not want to implement merit pay or machine extras, and so would only compare with SOGAT in the event of an annual cost-of-living settlement. When a comparison was provoked its impact was carefully controlled and its force diverted to 'safer' ground; although the membership was incited by SOGAT rises, the convenor bargained on a different basis. The convenor at B, and several of the stewards there, noted that comparisons with the TGWU—on the basis that differentials were being eroded—typically elicited the response from management that a solution to this situation could be found in job evaluation; the AUEW were encouraged to join the group-based evaluation scheme, but they were not receptive to this idea.

The discrepancy between, on the one hand, AUEW and SOGAT earnings and, on the other AUEW and TGWU earnings was not, then, the principal reason for the stewards' failure to use them as comparisons in negotiation; rather, such membership discontent with these comparisons as developed at either plant and which had its basis in collapsing differentials was not encouraged because, as bargaining comparisons, they were of little use in negotiation.

In addition, there were pressures towards the use of certain other groups as wage comparisons. At Factory B, three related sets of pressures combined to ensure that the comparison with toolroom rates elsewhere in the area was used in negotiation. First, this tied in with managerial concerns with recruitment and retention;[4] secondly, it was supported by the contours of local union organization and involvement in the branches; and, thirdly, there was considerable 'informal' pressure from the membership. At A, by contrast, both management and stewards agreed that comparisons with engineering workers elsewhere in the company were the most important and that comparisons drawn with print workers on site would be—for different reasons—unwelcome. The membership pressure to compare with SOGAT was thus resisted. At the time of interview, membership pressure did not have a great impact on the selection of bargaining comparisons; when pressure subsequently increased, it was not reinforced by any pressures arising from the contours of local union organization.

The fact that comparisons were not being used in bargaining at the time of interview in Factory A, and that wages were being negotiated, where possible, on a cost plus basis implies that the convenor could be independent of the comparisons used in negotiations, i.e. he could use them tactically as 'systems of argument'. A number of different comparisons appeared to be available at A—with other company plants, with the electricians on site, or with other engineering firms in the area—all of which had apparently been used in the past without jeopardizing either the bargaining relationship with management or the wage satisfaction of the membership. On the other hand, it is difficult to see how stewards at B could use any comparison other than with local engineering rates once this had become 'out of control' in the sense that members were focusing on it independent of steward wishes, since all pressures appeared to reinforce it. In practice, if not in the terms of any agreement, stewards were 'tied' to the use of this comparison. They were not free to use systems of argument manipulatively within the bargaining relationship, but were constrained by the impact of external circumstances on the bargaining unit. The over all picture—of a greater independence of action for stewards on pay matters at Plant A—remains the same.

These conclusions can be presented schematically, as in Figure 6.1

below. Despite all the similarities between the two organizations, the substantive use of fairness arguments in bargaining differed in each case, and the diagram indicates the important external influences which caused this difference; the most important single set of variables are those which define the relationship between the organization and its environment, and the features of the environment which influence the use of fairness arguments at A differ from those which do so at B.

The pattern of environmental constraints strongly influenced the level of wage satisfaction within the two case studies. Given that wage satisfaction appeared to be the most important influence on steward leadership and thus on the use of 'fair pay' arguments, it is worth noting that the success of stewards at Plant A which kept levels of dissatisfaction down did not depend only on bargaining achievements. It was a pure 'windfall' in that, although earnings were higher at A than at B for workers of roughly comparable skill, the skilled rates at A were lower than the top rates at B; higher earnings at A were purely a consequence of shift premia payment, and the working of shifts tends to be dictated less by the course of negotiations than by the demands of the production system. In fact, these important premia had not been the subject of negotiations at A during the term of office of the convenor. However the trend of earnings movements, rather than the state of earnings against other reference points at any given time, was important. Undoubtedly, the memory of past local wage leadership had contributed much to dissatisfaction at B. Echoing the feelings of the District Secretary, several members remarked in interview that rates at B were relatively much poorer than they used to be (Question 37). In less formal interviews, stewards also noted this relative decline. At A, by contrast, much of the dissatisfaction with print rates was defused by the feeling, particularly among long-service workers, that AUEW earnings had improved relative to print rates 'since we got organized'—i.e. since the present convenor took over.[5]


Wage satisfaction was thus influenced by two contingent features of payment system and industrial history. This in turn had repercussions on the use of comparisons; while it is not clear that a diminishing of the membership pressure on stewards at B, which arose from wage dissatisfaction, would have altered the use of bargaining comparisons by stewards, given the other pressures to maintain present usage, it is apparent that the independence of steward selection of comparisons at A could have been challenged by pressure from the

FIG. 6.1. *Adaptation of model of comparison choice (Fig. 2.3)
to results from the case studies: major influences on the choice
of bargaining comparisons*

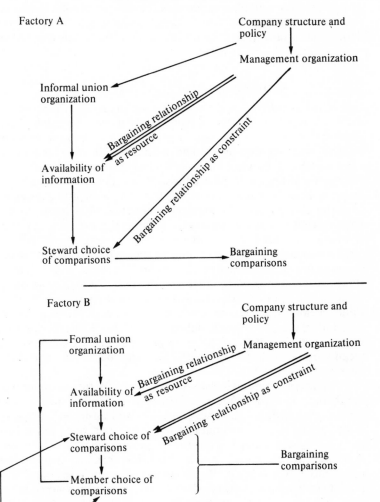

*Notes:* This is in some ways a complementary summary of findings to that of Table 6.1, which
covered 'internal' matters. It is in fact a selective presentation of the more comprehensive Fig. 2.3,
and there have been some changes to the 'paths' of the original model.

membership to move in another direction. Bargaining and informal comparisons thus stood in very different relationships in different organizations; the distinction between them must not be overdrawn in practice. Bargaining comparisons are not simply developed by stewards acting in concert to influence and direct members' ideas about what is fair. In fact, as the next section will demonstrate, such comparisons, like many other aspects of shopfloor policy on pay, need not represent the views even of the majority of stewards.

### 4. THE COHESION OF STEWARDS' VIEWS

One of the pitfalls of using the two dichotomies—between 'leadership' and 'normatively central' issues, and between 'bargaining' and 'informal' comparisons—is that the contrast between the views of stewards and members tends to be overstated. However, one of the most striking findings of the case studies was the extent to which there did not appear to be a consistent 'shop-steward' pattern of response in either organization which could be directly contrasted with those views held by members. Variance of opinion on apparently central issues was observed in both organizations, and very few issues appeared to unite stewards.

This was true for both FFP and FFPR. What is masked by the presentation of mean scores in Table 6.3 is that, in some cases, stewards mentioned vastly different amounts. At A, the amounts mentioned for FFP varied from 113 per cent to 103 per cent of skilled mean FFP; at B, the variance was greater at between 109 per cent and 78 per cent of the members' mean. On FFPR, the variance was much greater; between 403 per cent and 58 per cent of the skilled mean score at A, and between 185 per cent and 37 per cent of the members' mean at B.

The pattern is repeated elsewhere. At A, only the convenor was not happy with the three rate structure which the membership generally backed, but there was no policy consensus on the appropriate size of skill differential internal to the unit, or as to whether this should be expressed in flat-rate or percentage terms. This was, moreover, against a background of considerable consensus on this issue among members. At B, while three officers were happy with the rate structure at the time of interview, two others wanted fewer rates and one wanted a single rate for all craft workers. Moreover, as might be expected on a committee composed of representatives from both toolroom and maintenance, there was no consensus on the issue of pay parity between these departments; two officers from the toolroom wanted a differential to be established, but others were concerned with relativities elsewhere.

This variable pattern is confirmed by responses to the open-ended questions on the selection of comparisons. In response to Question 34, two of the three stewards at A pointed to other print workers on site, despite the rejection of such comparisons by the convenor himself. At B, representatives pointed to production workers and draughtsmen in the plant, as well as to the 'dominant' comparison, that with other toolroom workers in the local area.

Even within small shop-steward bodies, then, there may be no single view on issues of considerable importance such as differentials, wage aspirations, and the selection of comparisons. It is not true, for example, that bargaining comparisons simply reflect steward views as opposed to those of their members; on the contrary, it may be difficult to distinguish steward and member responses in any meaningful way. This ought to be considered in light of the evidence on the openness of organization in both plants, presented in Chapter 4, and on the relationship between stewards' and members' comparisons in Chapter 5.

On normatively central issues, there is consensus as there is among the membership and on leadership issues there is a similarly variable pattern of response. How, then, do steward views contribute to a bargaining policy which *can* be distinguished in a number of respects from the views of members? The answer lies in the fact that there are issues upon which an identifiably separate steward response pattern can be isolated; these issues tend to be broader than the specific, substantive points discussed above; the two most important sets are those related to incomes policy, and to broader 'ideological' issues.

I shall not anticipate here the analysis of attitudes to incomes policy presented in the next chapter. It is sufficient to note that, in general, shop stewards at both factories were more likely than their constituents to oppose the idea of an incomes policy, specific examples of such policy, and the co-operative relationship between government and trade unions on which such policies have been based. Conversely, stewards were more likely than constituents to favour an immediate return to free collective bargaining, and more likely to feel that the major cause of the country's economic problems was something other than the rate of wage increases.

Stewards also tended to be ideologically further 'left' than members. The scoring on four items—two 'left' and two 'right'— derived from Blackburn and Mann's analysis and presented in Table 6.4 reveals that, while members of both organizations tended to be more 'left' than 'right', stewards tended to be more 'left' than their respective constituents. It also appears that, measured by the

TABLE 6.4
Total Sample: Ideology Scores, Responses to Question 83

| | Members' $\overline{X}$ at A | Stewards' $\overline{X}$ at A | Members' $\overline{X}$ at B | Stewards' $\overline{X}$ at B |
|---|---|---|---|---|
| 'Left' | | | | |
| 1. 'management and workers are really on opposite sides' | 3.45 | 4.25 | 3.58 | 3.83 |
| 2. 'industry should pay its profits to workers, not to shareholders' | 3.52 | 4.00 | 3.65 | 4.00 |
| 'Right' | | | | |
| 3. 'most management have the welfare of their workers at heart' | 2.63 | 1.75 | 2.88 | 2.50 |
| 4. 'worker participation in management could only do the firm harm' | 2.18 | 2.75 | 2.70 | 2.50 |
| (Total 'left' score)— | 2.16 | 4.25 | 1.65 | 2.83 |
| (Total 'right' score) | | | | |

*Notes:* (1) Scoring was, on all items, as follows: strongly agree, 5; agree, 4; don't know, 3; disagree, 2; strongly disagree, 1.
(2) There was low inter-item correlation; this may indicate that respondents actually are ambivalent in their imagery, holding both 'left' and 'right' views. The only strong correlation was a high negative relationship between 'welfare' and 'opposition' items which was, at sample level, significant at 0.001.
(3) Standard deviations on all items were as follows: Item 1, A, 1.1082, B, 0.9916; Item 2, A, 0.8912, B, 0.8646; Item 3, A, 1.2545, B, 1.0622; Item 4, A, 0.7121, B, 1.0351.
(4) Steward numbers—the basis of columns 2 and 4—were small: only 11 in total.

discrepancy between total 'left' and total 'right' scores, stewards at A were more 'left' than those at B.[6]

These findings have wider implications. The issues on which stewards differ as a body from their members do not concern specific substantive points such as the size of the next pay rise, they concern general orientations to bargaining. The two general bases of agreement acknowledged here seem to imply that stewards wish to preserve the freedom to bargain over pay (and so oppose incomes policy), because they see a basic opposition of interests in industry (and so score high 'left' on ideology). This does not necessarily mean that they will always strive to succeed as leaders, since this depends on a variety of circumstances, but it does mean that stewards appear committed to broad sets of principles where members need not be. On the one hand, there is no agreement on the felt-fair pay for an occupation, on the size of the next pay rise, or on the ways in which different jobs should be compared. On the other hand, there is a commitment among workers' representatives to certain definite principles of independent action and organized opposition. This seems to confirm Daniel's conclusion that, 'union negotiators might have a different social perspective from workers generally, derived both from their different roles and possibly from a different ideology which enabled them to make judgements less constrained by their particular socio-occupational positions.'[7] The implications of this on a larger scale will be explored in the final chapter. Here I wish to examine the implications of this finding for the behaviour of shop-floor organizations.

Stewards are not committed to any set of arguments or figures, yet such arguments and figures become important in bargaining. Moreover, it may be the case that the same arguments and figures derived from the same sources are used repeatedly in bargaining. Since this consistency in bargaining can still be contrasted with the variability of both stewards' and members' views in important respects, the question remains—what imparts uniformity to the variable feelings of members within the organization so that consistent arguments can be presented in negotiation?

### STEWARDS AND THE BARGAINING RELATIONSHIP

In Chapter 2, it was suggested that shop-steward behaviour could be understood in terms of the operation of four principles—the pursuit of unity and equity, the reduction of uncertainty in relations with management and the cementing of a useful bargaining relationship. Clearly the pursuit of unity and equity among the membership do not imply consistency of argument in bargaining: what is unifying or equitable may depend on transient, 'spontaneous' views. But the latter two principles clearly do imply consistency: the arguments used by stewards in bargaining are affected by the requirements of stabilizing and improving a relationship with managers who may themselves be subjected to various forms of uncertainty. The acceptability of stewards' arguments depends on their usefulness in solving essentially managerial problems: the relationship between stewards' arguments and managerial goals is important. Management too are constrained. To recall the analysis of Chapter 2; if managers accept an argument in wage bargaining then—on the custom and practice analogy—it becomes very difficult to reject if used again, perhaps in changed circumstances where its use is unwelcome.

At the time of interview, neither management appeared to be concerned to interfere with the patterns of differentials internal to the units: they both acknowledged the skilled–unskilled distinction and had convinced stewards at both plants that they had no intention of narrowing it in the short term. Nevertheless, both managements appeared to have long-term aims which the stewards saw as divisive and which were linked specifically to merit pay and job evaluation. Both managements undoubtedly placed a certain priority on the efficient operation of merit payments and upon the implementation of group-level bargaining with which job evaluation was linked: stewards saw this as an attempt to divide the bargaining unit and to shift control away from the shop floor.

These considerations exercised greater pressure on stewards at B than at A. In the first place, merit pay schemes were in operation at B, but not at A: Secondly, group level bargaining was much more of a live issue in Group 2; the problem of division was thus more immediate than in Group 3, where the presence of print unions and the profit-autonomy of plants were both obstacles to the effective implementation of group level bargaining. There was thus a potential for stewards' problems to arise out of managerial policy. This pressure appeared to be less at A, where the bargaining relationship was more permissive. Management also had identifiable priorities in the use of wage comparisons; there were three main types—company-internal, plant-internal and local. I shall deal with each in turn.

(a) Company-internal comparisons, though not advantageous to stewards at the time, were 'valid' at both plants for both parties. They had been used where relevant in the past, and were something of a lifeline, particularly at Factory B, for stewards and managers in the summer of 1977. (See Chapter 7).

(b) Plant-internal comparisons were not used at either plant in negotiations. At A, the management wished to avoid competitive bargaining inside the plant largely because wage stability on the print side was premised on the secrecy of relative earnings. Stewards also discouraged their use by members, because of their implications for the rate structure. At B, they were largely irrelevant given that the occupational structure of the plant was such that AUEW members were likely to retain the wage leadership they had always held in the past.

(c) Local comparisons had never been very salient at A, since the plant had always paid well for the area. At B, they were the most salient for all concerned. For both stewards and managers, they caused considerable problems: the former were concerned with wage dissatisfaction, the latter with the recruitment and retention of staff where the uneven impact of incomes policy put them at a disadvantage.

The importance of management preference in steward use of comparisons is clear; where the use of a comparison parallels management concerns, it is salient in bargaining, but where there is no such parallel, or where the use of a comparison has unwelcome implications for management, it tends not to be used. So, plant internal comparisons are peripheral at A, local comparisons dominant at B and company-internal comparisons—which are reasonable for managers to use where group-level wage bargaining is the goal—are acceptable at both plants. This 'institutionalization' of wage comparisons supports the findings of Ross and of Brown and Sisson, discussed in Chapters 1 and 2.

It seems clear that the convenor at A was able to use comparisons manipulatively—or not at all. The bargaining relationship between himself and the factory manager was acknowledged as important by both parties; it appeared to flourish at the expense of a succession of personnel managers.[8] At B, restricted use of comparisons and a more limited bargaining relationship coincided. Consequently, the convenor and stewards had less independence of action. Whereas at A the convenor's own contacts, involvement and substantive bargaining success enabled him to become a major link between the group and the outside world, at B the convenor was not able to achieve this because of his members' wage dissatisfaction and their involvement in external union affairs: his members were in a position to evaluate his expertise, since they had access to similar information.

Broadly speaking, it seems that the convenor at Plant A had achieved much more independence and exercised more leadership than his counterpart at Plant B, and the implications of this for the use of moral arguments are clear. At Plant B, negotiations appeared to rely on the single comparison with local rates; to the extent that stewards could not succeed against this comparison, their tenure was threatened. At Plant A, a range of moral arguments and comparisons were used in a manipulative fashion, ultimately leading to a compromise acceptable to both sides.

Clear-cut conclusions are difficult to achieve. Because leadership is issue-specific, there may be—and indeed in the case-studies there were—differences between organizations in the extent to which stewards can lead on a given issue which cannot wholly be correlated with any over-all impressions of the extent of leadership in the two organizations. In the short term, leadership on single issues may be critical. Secondly, and as a corollary, leadership may represent a purely temporary state of affairs to be altered by some external, contingent set of events. Thirdly, it may be the case that incomes policy—an instance of one such external influence—has a consistently supportive or depressive impact on steward leadership. Since the empirical study could not include a situation where incomes policy did not operate, this must remain conjectural, but the next chapter focuses directly on bargaining under incomes policy.

## CONCLUSION

What is in practice a 'fair argument' for groups of workers in wage bargaining depends on specific organizational variables; the views of the members of the group on fair pay or relative occupational worth may in practice have little bearing on the way the group acts in collective bargaining. In many respects, the requirements of a stable bargaining relationship may be more important. Where stewards are able to arrive at a unifying policy on wages, satisfy their members' wage aspirations and manipulate information sources, the chances are that a stable 'vocabulary' will be developed in bargaining with management which limits the range of admissable arguments, i.e. what is a 'fair point'. The steward's ability to do this depends on a number of contingencies in the bargaining situation which are effectively outside his control. The two which appear to be most important are the scope of the bargaining unit and its relationship to its local environment, both inside and outside the plant. Where the steward cannot lead, i.e. where the arguments he can deploy do not go beyond the myriad arguments and comparisons his members may produce, or where he fails to 'keep up with' an argument he has used in the past, then his control over bargaining in the unit will probably be eroded.

One casualty of this may be consistency of argument in the bargaining relationship; if stewards fail in their handling of pay grievances, membership pressure might lead to claims of a sort unwelcome to both management and stewards. Alternatively, it may simply be the case that, where stewards are seen to use the correct arguments, but to do so ineffectually, their influence also diminishes. Reliance on single arguments may be predictable in the short term, but it is a fragile basis for a bargaining relationship.

Fairness in collective bargaining thus has to do with the balancing of opposing interests rather than a straightforward appeal to a set of principles. Shop stewards must, to use Mills's phrase, 'manage discontent' on the shop floor in such a way as to fulfil the institutional requirements of a bargaining relationship with management. It appears that flexible, manipulative use of 'fair pay' arguments is paradoxically associated with stability and predictability in bargaining, since it implies that stewards have the independence to pursue a definite policy on pay.

This has clear implications for incomes policies—whether such policies are designed simply as short-term wage restraint or as longer-term attempts to 'restructure' occupational and industrial relativities. The central purpose of the next chapter is thus an assessment of the impact of incomes policies on the case-study plants.

## CHAPTER 7

# BARGAINING UNDER INCOMES POLICY

## INTRODUCTION

Incomes policies cannot easily be dissociated from ideas about equity and fairness. Either they promote such ideas directly, in seeking to alter established wage differences in the interests of 'rationality' or 'equity', and so involve reasonably coherent principles of fairness and some diagnosis of the inequity of existing patterns of inequality. Or they are presented solely as devices to restrain wages and control inflation—without any implication that they will encourage a 'fairer' pattern of inequality—in which case it is still crucial that they be fair in the sense of being evenly applied. In either case the problem of acceptability is a normative one. But evenhandedness in administration does not necessarily ensure acceptability: it does not exclude the diminution of established differentials and relativities, the erosion of living standards, and interference with the relationship between stewards and members in its impact on the role of the former.

The model presented in Chapter 2 stresses the relevance of the patterns of differentials and relativities—and of steward influence— to an understanding of fairness in collective bargaining, and in the last three chapters I have presented data on the two case-study plants covering these areas. In this chapter I want to assess the impact of incomes policy on respondents' perceptions of equity and inequity. I shall look both at the way respondents as individuals evaluate incomes policies—as the instruments of equity, as 'evenhanded' restraint or as inequitable—and the way they bargain as groups in situations where incomes policies restrict the role of wage bargaining. I shall, therefore, be explicitly concerned with the way incomes policies restrict the scope of wage negotiations and I shall subsequently be arguing that their acceptability depends on the extent to which they are in practice permissive in this respect, rather than on the principles of fairness which they may seem to contain *in abstracto*. Initially, however, I want to assess the impact of pay policy on differentials internal to the two bargaining units.

In the five years prior to the interviewing period Brown identifies 'a compression of skill differentials without precedent in peacetime this century'.[1] This compression occurred particularly under the free collective bargaining of the voluntary stage of the Social Contract (1974–5) although Equal Pay legislation had some impact. Subsequently, under the 'redistributive' phases of 1975–7, negotiators seemed keen to maintain or widen skill differentials as inflation slackened. His results from a sample of West Midlands' engineering factories seem to be typical of more general trends evident in data from the New Earnings Survey.[2]

TABLE 7.1

*Earnings Movements under Incomes Policy: Factory A*

|  | Conservative | | | Labour | | | |
|  |  | | | Social | | | |
|  | *1* | *2* | *3* | *Contract* | | *'£6'* | *'5%'* |
|  | *Sept.* | *April* | *Sept.* | *April* | *Sept.* | *April* | *April* | *April* |
| *Incomes policy stage* | *1972* | *1973* | *1973* | *1974* | *1974* | *1975* | *1976* | *1977* |
| New Earnings Survey: Fitter's Earnings / Labourer's Earnings % |  | 130.3 | | 129.2 | | 130.6 | 127.3 | 127.3 |
| Factory A Skilled Earnings / Unskilled Earnings % | 124.4 | | 124.5 | | 125.2 | 122.5 | 120.5 | 120.3 |

*Notes:* (1) The NES figures are based on gross hourly earnings including the effects of overtime (Table 86).
(2) The Factory A figures are based on gross hourly earnings including the effects of overtime, based on the assumptions of Table 5.6.

It seems clear that some of the forces Brown identifies have parallels within the two case studies, but there are some important differences. Table 7.1 shows the change in differentials over the period in Factory A, as compared with more general figures from the New Earnings Survey.

The table shows that skill differentials at Factory A converged markedly during the Social Contract, but because of the Company's close adherence to the policy norms in the next two phases, there was no expansion of differentials subsequently. In fact differentials converged once more as a consequence of the '£6' policy. Table 7.2, for Factory B, again reveals marked convergence, though this appears to be associated with Conservative incomes policies rather than with free collective bargaining. But, again, there is continued convergence due to close observance of the Labour government's incomes policy. Since skilled–unskilled differentials were not particularly salient at Factory B, Table 7.2 includes a comparison with

TABLE 7.2
Earnings Movements under Incomes Policy: Factory B

| Incomes Policy Stage | Conservative | | | | | Social Contract | | Labour '£6' | | '5%' | |
|---|---|---|---|---|---|---|---|---|---|---|---|
| | July 1972 [1] | April 1973 | July 1973 [2] | April 1974 | July 1974 [3] | April 1975 | July 1975 | April 1976 | July 1976 | April 1977 | July 1977 |
| New Earnings Survey $\frac{\text{Toolroom Workers' Earnings}}{\text{Labourers' Earnings}}$ % | | 139.9 | | 138.0 | | 130.2 | | 127.0 | | 128.0 | |
| Factory B $\frac{\text{Skilled Earnings}}{\text{Unskilled Earnings}}$ % | 138.8 | | 127.6 | | 119.0 | | 118.3 | | 116.5 | | 116.5 |
| $\frac{\text{Factory B Skilled Earnings}}{\text{National Toolroom Fitters earnings (timerates)}}$ % | 98.9 | | 94.9 | | 98.15 | | 103.2 | | 98.1 | | 95.3 |

Notes: (1) The NES figures are based on gross hourly earnings including the effects of overtime (Table 86).
(2) The Factory B figures are based on gross hourly earnings including the effects of overtime, based on the assumptions of Table 5.7 above.
(3) The national toolroom figures are from the June Survey as in Table 5.7 (inclusive of overtime effects).

national toolroom earnings in June of each year, from the Department of Employment Survey. Factory B earnings clearly fall relative to national indices during the incomes policy periods of the Social Contract: this may be because the Company has adhered closely to incomes policy norms whereas others have not.[3] The most successful period of negotiations for stewards at B was clearly the free collective bargaining of 1974–5.

At both plants, then, skill differentials converged over the five year period, and this was more pronounced at Factory B than Factory A. This convergence continued over the period 1975–7 when the Company adhered strictly to incomes policy norms—of £6 and 5 per cent between cut off points of £2.50 and £4.00—when elsewhere these norms were treated more flexibly.

Although subject to broadly similar effects within similar bargaining structures, the two case-study groups tended to react differently to the Labour government's incomes policy: respondents at Plant B were much less ready to accept specific policies or the general idea of incomes policy. The following sections will seek to present reasons for this and to assess the impact on subsequent bargaining behaviour.

TABLE 7.3
*Responses to Question 75:*
*'What do you see as the general reason for government pay policies?*
*Do you think that such policies work?'*

| Response | Factory A (per cent) | Factory B (per cent) | Total (per cent) |
|---|---|---|---|
| To curb inflation/'get the country back on its feet'/halt price rises | | | |
| (a) successful (i) | 17(42.5) | 8(16) | 25(28) |
| (b) unsuccessful (ii) | 7(17.5) | 19(38) | 26(29) |
| To help cut the balance of payments deficit (i) | 3(7.5) | — | 3(7.5) |
| As assault on wages/living standards (iii) | 3(7.5) | 8(16) | 11(12) |
| To counter public sector deficits/bad economic management (iii) | 2(5) | 5(10) | 7(8) |
| To stabilise capitalism (iii) | 1(2.5) | 2(4) | 3(3) |
| To keep profits high (iii) | 1(2.5) | 6(12) | 7(8) |
| Others | 2(5) | 2(4) | 4(5) |
| Don't know | 4(10) | — | 4(5) |
| | N = 40  100 | N = 50  100 | N = 90  100 |

ATTITUDES TO INCOMES POLICY

## (a) General Principles

Table 7.3 indicates respondents' reactions to a very general question about the aims and efficacy of government pay policy. It appears that factory A tended to be less critical of policies in general. The diffuse pattern of responses may be collapsed into three categories as follows:

(i)   those who interpreted pay policies in an 'orthodox' fashion—i.e. technically as measures of economic policy, and who felt, in addition, that such policies worked;
(ii)  those who interpreted policy similarly, in a 'technical' sense, but felt that they did not work;
(iii) those who were opposed to the whole idea of incomes policy, preferring to interpet it in different terms.

TABLE 7.4
*Reclassified Responses to Question 75*

| Definition | Factory A | Factory B | Total |
|---|---|---|---|
| (i)   'Orthodox' | 20 | 8 | 28 |
| (ii)  'Orthodox—critical' | 7 | 19 | 26 |
| (iii) 'Oppositional' | 7 | 21 | 28 |
| Total | 34 | 48 | 82 |

*Notes:* A chi-square test revealed that the two distributions were significantly different. The value of chi-square obtained (chi-square = 15.749, d.f = 2) is significant beyond the .001 level of probability.

These categories are indicated in the table. With this change, the response pattern is that of Table 7.4. Categorized in these terms, the distributions are significantly different. Factory B respondents were much more likely to be critical of the idea of incomes policy, or reject it totally.

This may be related to responses to Question 77, which asked: 'Some people say the main cause of the country's economic problems is high wage settlements. Would you agree?' At A 67.5 per cent of respondents and at B 88 per cent (79 per cent over all) felt that causes other than high wage settlements were paramount. There was a strong feeling at both plants that there were other important identifiable problem areas. In identifying issues which were detrimental to the performance of the national economy, 26 per cent of the whole sample mentioned monetary speculation or high profits, a further 18 per cent bad industrial management and consequent low performance, and 16 per cent the absence of price control. Furthermore, 35 per cent of the sample felt that the wage-push diagnosis was forwarded because wages were a scapegoat or merely the easiest cost element to control: another 20 per cent went further by saying that wage settlements were the object of a propaganda campaign conducted by the media or the 'middle class'. In summary, then, although there are differences between samples A and B in the extent to which they reject the idea of incomes policy, they are largely similar in their failure to line up behind a cost-push theory of inflation which accords wage settlements an important initiatory role.

Both convenors and the majority of stewards at both plants were at least critical of incomes policy, but felt constrained by union and management policies, which were convergent in this instance. For a number of reasons (to be documented below) the pressure for rejection of incomes policy was greater on stewards at B than at A.[4]

*(b) The three phases*

In addition to this general question, others were included in the schedule about the individual phases of the *'Attack on Inflation'*. At the time of interview, it was possible to be specific about only two phases: both organizations had received the '£6' and were expecting to receive the '5 per cent' at the next settlement date. The idea of a third phase was only a live issue at Factory B in April 1977: even here it was not possible to be specific, since details of the policy were not generally known.

TABLE 7.5
*'What do you think of the £6 policy?' (Prompt: Was it necessary and fair? Did it lead to an erosion of differentials?)*

| Items | Factory A (per cent) | Factory B (per cent) | Total (per cent) |
|---|---|---|---|
| Necessary anti-inflation policy | 24(48) | 26(33) | 50(39) |
| Unnecessary/Opposed to it | 4(8) | 8(10) | 12(9.3) |
| Decreased differentials | 12(24) | 28(35) | 40(31) |
| No differentials decreased | 8(16) | 9(11) | 17(13) |
| Fair if there had been price control | 0(—) | 8(10) | 8(6.2) |
| Don't know | 2(4) | 0(—) | 2(1.5) |
| No. Responses | 50(100) | 79(99) | 129(100) |
| No. Respondents | 40 | 50 | 90 |

TABLE 7.6
Responses to Question 80:
'What is your opinion of the Phase II policy?'

| Items | Factory A (per cent) | Factory B (per cent) | Total (per cent) |
|---|---|---|---|
| Necessary anti-inflation policy | 7(16.7) | 3(5.2) | 10(10) |
| Other favourable comments | 6(14.3) | 0(—) | 6(6) |
| Simply not enough money | 9(21.4) | 36(62) | 45(45) |
| Will erode differentials further | 3(7.1) | 3(5.2) | 6(6) |
| Need price control instead | 5(11.9) | 6(10.4) | 11(11) |
| Opposed to all wage restraint | 3(7.1) | 0(—) | 3(3) |
| Will reject phase II | 0(—) | 7(12.1) | 7(7) |
| Other unfavourable comments | 4(9.5) | 3(5.2) | 7(7) |
| Don't know | 5(11.9) | 0(—) | 5(5) |
| | | | |
| No. Responses | 42(99.9) | 58(100.1) | 100(100) |
| No. Respondents | 40 | 50 | 90 |

Table 7.5 presents respondents' views of the '£6' policy phase. Its necessity was mentioned in 39 per cent of responses over all. The erosion of differentials which the policy involved was mentioned in 31 per cent of responses: this was more common at A than B. Tables 7.1 and 7.2 indicate that this convergence was not simply a feature of the £6 policy, but given the greater convergence of differentials at B, and the shortfall on indicators of toolroom earnings nationally under the £6 policy, this response is understandable. When the pattern of Tables 7.5 and 7.6 are compared, three things are evident: first, the £6 policy was more acceptable in both plants; secondly, Factory B respondents were less satisfied with Phase II than Factory A; thirdly, the emphasis has shifted from a concern with the collapse of differentials to a concern with the cost of living.

One can evaluate the differences between Tables 7.5 and 7.6 by again 'collapsing' the response pattern. There are, however, certain limitations: in the first place, because the two sub-samples are not identical, any testing for shifts in attitudes to the different phases must be *within* subsamples; secondly, it must be remembered that in both cases answers to questions about Phase II are prospective. Nevertheless, responses may be dichotomized as 'favourable' or 'unfavourable' with respect to each policy, as in Table 7.7.[5] A number of chi-square tests were performed on the data dichotomized in this fashion, with the following results.

TABLE 7.7

*Dichotomized responses to Questions 79 and 80*

| | Phase I | | Phase II | |
|---|---|---|---|---|
| | *Factory A* | *Factory B* | *Factory A* | *Factory B* |
| Favourable | 32 | 35 | 13 | 3 |
| Unfavourable | 16 | 44 | 24 | 55 |
| Total | 48 | 79 | 37 | 58 |

(1) Opposition to Phase II was considerably greater than that to Phase I in both subsamples (Factory A, chi-square = 7.121, significant at $\alpha$ = .01, Factory B, chi-square = 23.77, significant beyond $\alpha$ = .001).
(2) Opposition to both phases was greater at Factory B than Factory A (Phase I: chi-square = 5.13, significant beyond $\alpha$ = .05, Phase II, chi-square = 20.53 significant beyond $\alpha$ = .001).

Respondents are thus dissatisfied with pay policy and more dissatisfied with later phases than earlier one: throughout, this trend is more pronounced at Factory B than at Factory A. However, respondents did not necessarily favour a return to free collective bargaining, as Table 7.8 reveals.

TABLE 7.8

*Response to Question 82: 'Would you like to see a return to free collective bargaining?'*

| Response | Factory A (per cent) | Factory B (per cent) | Total (per cent) |
|---|---|---|---|
| Yes | 13(32.5) | 26(52) | 39(43) |
| Eventually: when the crisis is past/inflation rate down | 16(40) | 6(12) | 22(25) |
| No | 10(25) | 17(34) | 27(30) |
| Don't know | 1(2.5) | 1(2) | 2(2) |
| | $N = 40$ (100) | $N = 50$ (100) | $N = 90$ (100) |

Although discontent with pay policy—manifest here as a desire to return immediately to free collective bargaining—was again greater at B than at A, the pattern of response is consistent with the idea that respondents were unhappy with the particular forms of policy which have been adopted rather than the idea of an incomes policy *per se*. The

TABLE 7.9

*Responses to Question 76: 'Do you think that union leaders should continue in the next phase to co-operate with the government to formulate an incomes policy or would you prefer that they do not get involved?'*

| Response | Factory A (per cent) | Factory B (per cent) | Total (per cent) |
|---|---|---|---|
| Yes | 27(67.5) | 17(34) | 44(49) |
| Conditional: depending on the type of settlement | 9(22.5) | 11(22) | 20(22) |
| No | 4(10) | 21(42) | 25(28) |
| Don't know | 0(—) | 1(2) | 1(1) |
|  | N = 40 (100) | N = 50 (100) | N = 90 (100) |

essence of the Social Contract was voluntary co-operation between the Labour government and trade unions and, as Table 7.9 shows, there was considerable enthusiasm for such co-operation. Overall, then, the pattern of response displays considerably more dissatisfaction with incomes policy at B than A, which parallels the more general dissatisfaction revealed above. It is possible to outline the reasons for this.

Incomes policy was clearly not seen as evenhanded at Factory B. Wage dissatisfaction and the disturbance of relativities were seen in terms of the evasion of policy by other toolroom workers in the area. The timing of interviews is also clearly important, given the difference in settlement dates of the two groups. Interviews at Factory A took place as Phase II was being publicized nationally: the £6 payment had been made three months previously, and Phase II was, from the workers' point of view, eight months away. Factory B interviews took place in April 1977, just before the Phase II settlement was implemented (this group bargained 'late'): the prospect of another year of wage restraint faced respondents. Both sets of stewards monitored movements in the Retail Price Index: as inflation continued at high rates through late 1976 and 1977 the '5 per cent' settlement appeared less adequate. This was particularly the case in Factory B. Both convenors took to quoting the rise in the Retail Price Index since the last settlement as some general indicator of the appropriate size of the next claim. At Factory A, in August 1976 this was 3.3 per cent: at B it was 15.5 per cent in April 1977. Against this background the 5 per cent settlement assumed a rather different significance.

It may well be that, as Corina notes,[6] incomes policy itself is a perishable device, useful only in the short term. It should be administered with this transience in mind since, as simple restraint, it solves none of the problems of relativities which the collective bargaining system itself throws up. Certainly in the results described here there appears to be a strong 'temporal' effect, so that successive phases were less popular in each plant, and all questions revealed greater dissatisfaction with incomes policy at plant B.[7]

However, in addition to this temporal effect, two other differences combined to increase dissatisfaction at B. First, the different bargaining dates of the two major manual groups at B—AUEW in July and TGWU in October—were affected in such a way that the TGWU 'bargained first' in the wage round after incomes policy was implemented on an August to August basis. Consequently, because of the August to August scheduling of each phase, the TGWU in the plant were, so to speak, always one step ahead. Secondly, as noted above, respondents at B felt that pay policy was being ignored by small toolrooms in the local area: consequently they felt unfairly restrained in comparison to other groups of workers engaged on similar work elsewhere. It appeared to them that the impact of incomes policy was arbitrary and thus unfair.

Stewards' responses to these questions at both plants tended to be slightly more 'extreme' than those of their members; although the numbers here are very small, it appears that stewards were more likely to oppose both phases at both plants (at B they were generally opposed to the idea of a third phase), more likely to want an immediate return to free collective bargaining, and less likely to want co-operation with the government to continue. Daniel feels that the basis for this more 'extreme' position lies in the impact of wage restraint on the shop steward's role: 'It seems probable that the feelings which plant-level union representatives have about incomes policy largely result from the fact that it undermines their position, status and influence, if it does not threaten their whole reason for being.'[8] However, as the remainder of this chapter will show, this is to make unwarranted assumptions about · the impact of incomes policy on shopfloor bargaining.

### THE IMPACT OF PAY POLICY ON BARGAINING

After the interviewing had been completed, bargaining behaviour at the two case-study plants was monitored for a period, by means of frequent unstructured interviews with stewards and members and analysis of relevant documents.[9] This behaviour will be described in the remainder of this chapter. I shall be concerned to show that incomes policy circumscribed but did not terminate the bargaining role of stewards, and that loopholes in the policy were exploited pragmatically in a manner consistent with shop-steward strategy.

The restrictive set of voluntary measures adopted from July 1975 apparently left little room for bargaining in the case-study plants, particularly as the £6 limit became established as an entitlement. The exception clauses in the White Paper allowed for the implementation of measures designed to establish equal pay, of Wage Council proposals, or the result of arbitration references made prior to the White Paper and, in certain cases, of payments to individuals on incremental salary scales. Existing piecework schemes could continue to pass on to the worker the rewards for productivity increases.[10] None of these provisions applied to the case-study plants, but both received amounts in excess of incomes policy norms in the two years after the *Attack on Inflation*: Factory A gained an award under the transitional arrangements in force in 1975, and both factories exploited the 'new work' loophole introduced under Phase II of the policy.[11]

The transitional arrangements for Phase I allowed that 'settlements may . . . be implemented for groups which, before the date of publication of this White Paper, have reached agreements for annual settlement dates not later than 1st September provided that they have had no principal increase under the existing TUC guidelines during the last twelve months.'[12] Principal settlements could be paid up to 1 September 1975, but, if in excess of £6, had to be renegotiated if they fell after this date. Interim payments to be paid after 1 August 1975 had to be offset against the £6 limit. Up to 1 September 1975 in the first case and 1 August 1975 in the second, settlements did not have to be offset.[13] Such forward pay arrangements had, in the opinion of the Department of Employment, to be specific as to the amount and type of payment agreed. Vague commitments to review pay in light of cost-of-living changes or the 'state of the company' were insufficient: 're-opener' clauses in agreements were ruled out.[14]

In order to understand the significance of these arrangements for the pay dispute which developed at Plant A in November 1976, one needs to go back as far as April 1975, the date of the last pre-policy wage settlement. I shall discuss in turn the background to the dispute, its origins and progress as briefly as possible, before turning to assess its significance.

Up to and including 1974, the AUEW at Plant A had settled pay annually in September. In 1975, the date was brought forward to April 28th, which solved problems for managers and for stewards. An 'anomalous' pay relationship with electricians was resolved, and the AUEW were brought onto the same settlement date as the print unions: two strong pressures towards competitive bargaining in the plant were removed. However, this change cut across wider developments. A re-opener clause in the September 1974 Group 2 agreement was invoked in April: engineers in the group were awarded 6p per hour on basic rates to compensate for the rising cost of living. Subsequently, in May and June this rise was generalized—under pressure from AUEW stewards—to Group 1 and the Capital Goods Group and to general workers and staff in Plant A whose remuneration was either directly determined by, or in practice related to, the Independent Agreement (see Chapter 3). The AUEW convenor at A, having followed these events via his contacts in the Combined Committee, claimed this 6p award, but was unsuccessful. Management refusal was based on the argument that re-opener clauses could only be invoked after six months of an agreement and that, because of the change of settlement date, the issue could not be discussed until November. The convenor reluctantly agreed to this: 'As things had been rather dicey during the protracted dispute with the electricians, we reluctantly agreed, but we were confident that we would receive 6p in November, enhanceable for all purposes.'[15]

In July, however, the *Attack on Inflation* was implemented, and the re-opening of negotiations did not take place: the issue was not raised again until resurrected in very different circumstances in November 1976. On the 10th of that month, a deputation of members and stewards from the Flexible Packaging department approached the AUEW convenor with the information that SOGAT members working on machinery maintained by AUEW members had, within the Phase II 'new work' guidelines, negotiated an agreement for machine extras on top of the £6 supplement which they received in April of that year at the same time as the AUEW.[16] Under considerable membership pressure the convenor submitted a parity claim. But this was not a claim for machine extras, it was a resurrection of the 6p per hour claim, which was more consistent with the wages structure in the AUEW bargaining unit than were machine extras.

SOGAT styles of bargaining tolerated individual pay supplements creating differentials within grades: as the data presented above demonstrate, the AUEW members and stewards would not tolerate this. A machine extras claim would have given a supplement only to those who worked on the new machines. The membership opposed unconsolidated additions to hourly rates, and differentials within skill groups. Nevertheless, the company's ability to pay and the unexpected flexibility of the pay policy had both been demonstrated. The convenor was under considerable pressure to produce substantive results, and he found a solution in the '6p' issue.

Initially, management rejected outright attempts to revive this claim, but when the convenor then claimed 'machine extras' (with the intention of dividing such payments across the whole bargaining unit, *pro rata* by grade) they agreed to discuss the '6p' claim. The direct claim for machine extras was a much more explosive issue for management, because of the implications for comparability. Most other plants in the company (though not in Group 3) had already received the 6p award, but a successful claim for machine extras would open doors through which other AUEW groups might follow, escaping the incomes policy. Eventually, when the claim was backed by a work-to-rule and an overtime ban, management advised the convenor of their intention to make a joint approach to the Department of Employment.

Given that the existence of a forward commitment was questionable, and that the date of payment was too late to avoid offsetting, it is surprising that the joint approach yielded as much as it did.[17] The agreed settlement was a curious one. It consisted of a lump sum back payment based on the amount resulting from adding 6p per hour to hourly basic rates for the period 28 October 1975 (the 're-opener' date) to 28 April 1976 (the date of the £6 settlement) plus a further amount in lieu of enhanced shift and overtime payments for the same period. The settlement yielded nothing after 28 April 1976, since it was deemed to have been offset against the £6 settlement from that date. The 'old' and 'new' rate schedules are reproduced in Table 7.10: it is apparent that all the settlement does is effectively bring part of the £6 settlement forward to October 1975.

TABLE 7.10

|  | Old sequence (£) | New sequence (£) |
|---|---|---|
| April 1975 | 1.348 | 1.348 |
| October 1975 | 1.348 | 1.408 |
| April 1976 | 1.348 + £6 p.w. | 1.348 + £6 p.w. |

*Source:* Convenor's records.
*Note:* The figures are hourly basic rates for skilled workers.

The stewards were dissatisfied with this settlement: it yielded much less than the SOGAT machine extras. Since the 'forward commitment' argument had failed, stewards continued to argue on the basis that the 6p payment should have operated from 1 April 1975—prior to the policy, and thus unaffected by it. They argued that the basic skilled rate should have been £1.408 before the start of wage restraint. The issue went all the way through the company's disputes procedure, reaching the final stages only in August 1977.[18] The only further benefits to members were a payment of £25 per man for the period 1–28 April 1975—from the date of the cost of living award in Group 2 to the actual date of settlement in Plant A. In fact, this award is inconsistent with that agreed by the Department of Employment, but this fact is only of marginal concern here.[19]

The second 'line of attack'—which was pursued by stewards at both plants—concentrated on the 'new work' clause introduced under Phase II of incomes policy. This clause allowed individuals who had taken on work of increased responsibility—for example, on new machinery—to be paid in excess of the 5 per cent norm. There were a number of strings attached to this: the Department of Employment distinguished between individual 'new work' and group 'regrading', the latter having to be offset against the norm, suggested that the changes involved should be both necessary and distinguishable, and stipulated that the new rates ought to be in line with payments for similar work elsewhere.[20] The guidelines issued by the Department of Employment which were in the possession of the Combined Committee Secretary, emphasized these points. They stressed that any rise was intended to operate on an individual basis: 'This principle is necessary to ensure that individuals who are promoted or move to completely new work can be paid the rate for the job. It is not, however, intended to enable groups of workers to obtain increases outside of the central figure simply because methods of work organization or particular details of their work have changed.' Moreover, a significant difference in job content was necessary to justify a new rate which had to be 'reasonable to all other groups whose position in the wages structure is frozen despite odd differences in their own jobs which may have occurred.'[21] These two conditions would seem to rule out, on the one hand, the generalization of increases via 'flexibility' retraining and favour, on the other, the use of comparisons to establish an equitable and acceptable size of pay rise. This might serve to weaken the 'direct' relationship between the size of the change and of the accompanying monetary increase: this should be borne in mind in the evaluation of events at Factory A. The 'new work' claim, like the '6p' one, started in Group 2. New can-making technologies had been introduced, and the electrical and engineering departments had claimed an increase on the basis of them. The initial settlements were for less than 12.3p per hour—the amount ultimately paid at A—but after two disputes which resulted in the achievement of this figure there was 'a free for all with all factories in (Group 2) and (Capital Equipment) pursuing the 12.3p claim with back pay and others claiming parity with factories which had negotiated more'.[22] The Combined Committee was undoubtedly important in the transmission of information about the claim. The figure of 12.3p when transferred between factories in this way, became a 'norm' beyond which management would not go rather than an amount repeatedly justified by a series of changes in job content.[23]

The 'new work' clause was thus used to justify group, rather than individual rises, and the amounts involved were largely determined by interplant comparability. This process can be documented in Plant A. The validity of the new work was not directly established in terms of the guidelines: a cue was taken from other company plants, the concern being with what should be 'surrendered' for 12.3p, rather than what any necessary changes were 'worth'. Rival proposals for changes in work organization were forwarded. The management report included proposals for staggered meal breaks and departmental reorganization, which were rejected. The final report focused on flexibility and retraining, and on restrictions to be placed on managements' use of outside contractors.[24] On its acceptance, in June 1977, a 12.3p per hour increase was paid to skilled men, *pro rata* to unskilled. In addition a lump sum back payment, based on the earnings of those men directly concerned with the new machinery at the enhanced rate, was distributed among all AUEW members.

'Flexibility' was thus the key to generalizing the increase to all AUEW members. The 'new work' was generated by the machinery which had caused the previous dispute about SOGAT machine extras, and only sixteen men worked on it: under the flexibility agreement, all fitters were to be trained to do so. While there was undoubtedly some basis for the new work deal, there were jobs within the bargaining unit which needed to be 'revalued' to maintain parity for reasons of equity rather than to reward increased work. The re-evaluation exercise extended to the garage and to the boilerhouse as well as to the stores, so that unskilled men could be included. Fitters' mates were awarded the increase on the basis that 'Fitters' mates will carry out certain routine maintenance jobs, previously done by skilled fitters.' The vagueness is deliberate, since both mates and fitters indicated in interview that mates already performed certain routine skilled tasks.

The two central points—that changes were often notional and that the amounts involved were determined by comparability—can be emphasized. The schedule of changes for certain of the fitters was as follows: 'Maintain current flexibility, inventiveness and co-operation.' Moreover, when SOGAT officers were putting together 'new work' claims, rigid adherence to work rules and manning levels was implemented, even when this involved extra effort for workers, so that co-operation could be 'sold'. As the MOC said, about one such practice (a re-establishment of old manning levels) 'I had to get it back again before I could sell it'. Once such claims were devised, they were discovered to be 'worth' 12.3p per hour to electricians, printers and SOGAT members—from machine minders to security guards.

The two disputes quoted reveal the operation of identifiable equity concerns in collective bargaining. Stewards, even under considerable membership pressure, strove to maintain pay rise equity in the bargaining group, to the extent of decreasing the absolute amount of increase available to individuals. They appeared to share with management a concern to avoid plant-internal competition in bargaining, and both sides recognized the power of inter-plant comparisons within the company. In particular, the 'new work' claim revealed how equality of pay rises was maintained within bargaining groups (the flexibility agreements) between bargaining groups in the same plant (e.g. SOGAT and the AUEW) and between groups in different plants (those covered by the Combined Committee). The equity concerns of stewards structured the conduct of collective bargaining, but the exercise of leadership was required for them to become influential: the basis for such leadership did not always exist, as the example of case-study B indicates.

Events subsequent to interviewing at Plant B can be described more briefly; their background has to some extent been covered already. However, they differ from those at A in that a crisis of steward control developed which was apparently far more disruptive.

Despite attempts to delay the Phase II settlement until August, in order to settle at the higher Phase III rate, the Phase II deal was signed as an orthodox settlement on 19 July 1977. Following this, wage dissatisfaction heightened and, during the summer when overtime was increasingly available, the stewards lost control over the levels of overtime working. Considerable opposition developed to the steward policy of limitation of the number of hours worked by individuals which culminated in the rejection, at a site meeting in August 1977, of this policy and the subsequent resignation of a number of the stewards. As the convenor described it, 'We got some very right-wing committee members on, and they were classed as overtime kings. The overtime limit was being exceeded, so I put a stop to it on the instructions of the District Secretary. A terrific row blew up and I resigned as convenor after a lot of shouting on the shopfloor.'

After his resignation, there was a brief 'interregnum' during which very high levels of overtime were worked. However, at a site meeting shortly afterwards, the convenor was re-established in his post; he held new elections for the steward positions to get 'the right people' on the committee, and acknowledged credentials for another toolroom steward. The situation was brought fully under control after a 'get-to-know-you sort of visit' by the district secretary. The convenor described the new situation, 'I see all overtime lists and vet them carefully. If any excess overtime is needed, management must convince me it is necessary and I countersign any letter they send to the District Office.'[25]

This was, then, a considerable crisis of control for stewards. Among a section of the membership, wage dissatisfaction increased to an extent which could not be 'managed'; basic trade-union principles were at stake, and stewards resigned when they were violated. However, this situation was shortlived and stewards were apparently able, within a short period, to mobilize sufficient support to be re-elected and to reassert control over the distribution and level of overtime working.

In informal follow-up interviews, it became apparent that respondents were very aware of the evasion of policy constraints by employers and workers in other small toolrooms in the area, and that this, as well as the perception of falling living standards, fuelled their discontent and encouraged fault-finding with stewards. Members also felt that they were a 'year behind' in that, almost as they settled for 5 per cent, other groups of workers were pressing well-publicized claims for 10 per cent and above. To some extent, this was a problem for management, who were unable to recruit sufficient skilled craftsmen.

The solution to all of these difficulties was found in the adaptation, as at A, of payments made in Group 2 to the particular needs of the plant. All AUEW members were paid 12.3 pence per hour in September 1977, for 'significant technical change'. There was also a lump-sum backpayment to cover the previous three months. Unlike Plant A, payments to skilled and unskilled workers were equal, not *pro rata*; this was necessary on comparative grounds, as the TGWU workers in the plant also settled for 12.3p. However, as at A, the change involved was in some cases purely notional. As the convenor remarked, 'of course, there will not be much change, if any. The management realize this, but even they admit that to get the best of craftsmen they must pay out some cash.'[26] No detailed measurement of change was undertaken. Items cited as instances of change included 'The developing use of the metric system . . .' and 'Flexibility: New manufacture and higher demands on the engineering resource requires greater flexibility of the membership between the various engineering sections than has been necessary in the past, and more versatile use of skills.'[27] Moreover, the agreement itself involved only 'flexibility', 'best working practices' and 'utmost cooperation'—exceedingly vague notions.

TABLE 7.11
*Movements in Earnings subsequent to Interview*

|  | *Factory A* | *Factory B* |
|---|---|---|
| November 1976 | Lump Sum payment | |
| April 1977 | Phase II settlement | |
| July 1977 | + 12.3p settlement | Phase II settlement |
| August 1977 | Lump sum payment | |
| September 1977 | | + 12.3p settlement |

At B, the solution to pay pressures was, from the stewards' point of view, unlooked for. They had sought various means of increasing the pay of their members—such as a reference under Schedule 11 of the Employment Protection Act—but the ultimate solution was found in a rise which maintained pay-rise parity internal to the company, rather than one which solved the particular problems of the union at Factory B.[28] This may be contrasted to some degree with the situation at A, where the convenor's pressure actively modified a rise elsewhere to fit in with the equity conceptions of AUEW workers: here also, the power of comparison within the company caused the generalization of rises.

In summary, then, the increase in earnings in the two case-study plants in this period subsequent to structured interview are described in Table 7.11.

CONCLUSION

The pattern of bargaining subsequent to the interviewing is as might have been expected given the analysis in the previous chapters. There are three main things to note.

First, on steward control. Subsequent to the interviews, membership pressure on stewards at both plants increased. At A, this
pressure arose out of an invidious comparison with pay rises ac-
corded to certain SOGAT workers; at B, it was a continuation of the
wage dissatisfaction noted at the time of interview, fuelled at least to
some extent by disadvantageous local comparisons. The crucial difference is that at A this pressure was resolved by stewards, whereas
at B there was apparently a 'palace revolution' which resulted in the
stewardship passing to those who were less concerned to control
overtime working.

Secondly, on the use of comparisons: at A, subsequent events
provided a good example of the 'manipulation' of comparisons by
stewards: an 'informal' comparison was made by members with
SOGAT workers, which was 'translated' into the appropriate bargaining comparison by the convenor, i.e. with engineers elsewhere
in the company. The success of this can be gauged by the construc-
tive response elicited from management. At B, there was no corresponding manipulative use of comparisons: 'informal' and
'bargaining' comparisons coincided, and there appeared no means
of acting upon them. At both plants, the importance of management collusion in pay matters was demonstrated in the co-operation
on flexibility arrangements for the '12.3p' deal: in the interests of
maintaining pay-rise parity within the company, management were
prepared to encourage 'new work' deals and to accept comparisons
made with similar workers elsewhere in the company. This readiness
clearly explains the success of stewards at both plants in using such
comparisons. The coercive power of company-internal comparisons
is demonstrated by the spread of the '12.3p' settlement at the risk of
Department of Employment disapproval.

Thirdly, on the impact of incomes policy. Subsequent activity
appears to confirm the decreasing popularity of incomes policy over
time. Much dissatisfaction prior to the interviews at B, and subsequent to it at A, arose out of uneven application of policy: the
simple equality of treatment on which the policy was based was seen
to be absent in both locations. This added to dissatisfaction with a
policy which was seen to erode living standards. Although there is
no data on this, it seems plausible to suggest that the company's collusion in the spreading of the 'new work' increase and the absence of
critical analysis of—much less hard bargaining over—the work
changes at both plants was prompted by a desire simply to avoid the
trouble resulting from the application of the policy. In any event,
the three 'extra-curricular' settlements I have discussed indicate how
important bargaining flexibility *within* a formal adherence to the

guidelines remained throughout the period: stewards still retained an important role in determining the pay of their members even where it might seem that the important decisions had been taken at national level.

These findings have important policy implications. Stewards try to pursue trade union principles, but their relationship with their constituents helps to define the extent to which they may do so. Any change in law or policy that affects the steward–member relationship is of great significance for the process of wage determination, and different types of incomes policy may effect this relationship in different ways. These policy implications are assessed in the next chapter.

## CHAPTER 8

# FAIRNESS AND INCOMES POLICY

## INTRODUCTION

In this study so far, I have tried to demonstrate the links between workers' views on fairness and unfairness and the activities of their representatives in bargaining. In Chapter 7, I tried to relate these views directly to the incomes policy measures which acted as a constraint on bargaining activity in the case-study plants, and in this chapter I want to take the discussion a little further by assessing the relevance of the findings for future stages of incomes policy. The central question is—what light can the case-study data shed on the reasons for the acceptance or rejection of incomes policy measures and what implications do they have for the design of such measures in future? I shall try to answer this question first of all by summarizing the relevant attitudinal data and assessing the behaviour of the two bargaining units under the Social Contract. These considerations indicate the importance of steward leadership for the success of incomes policy and consequently the inherent perishability of incomes policy measures. The latter part of the chapter looks at the sorts of changes necessary to prevent this decay, and assesses the possibilities for a more permanent national incomes policy.

## THE ACCEPTABILITY OF THE SOCIAL CONTRACT

One of the firmest conclusions to be drawn from the data was the importance of steward leadership for the success of incomes policy. The episodes described in the previous chapter indicate the consequences of successful and unsuccessful leadership attempts. Moreover the outcomes of these episodes show a clear relationship to the attitudinal data presented earlier. Although there were strong membership feelings about the need for cost-of-living indexation, about the importance of establishing a single rate for the job, and about the necessity of a co-operative basis for incomes policy—all of which I shall discuss in more detail below—many of the issues with which policy makers were concerned were strictly 'leadership' issues. Members formed no common idea about the size of FFPR, nor did they possess a single frame of reference for the assessment of differentials: they chose a range of informal comparisons, and differed in those they found most salient. The policies of the Social Contract did not enjoy their limited success because they mirrored in some way the perceptions and values of respondents: they succeeded because they were also supported by stewards.

In fact, one could argue that these measures succeeded *despite* the form they took. There was no attempt in the Social Contract to guarantee indexation or to move towards one rate for the job: Phases I and II were simply wage restraint. The 'normatively central' views of members were not accommodated. Moreover the exception clauses of Phase II (and indeed Phase III) were based on bargaining arguments—job change and increasing productivity—which did not appear as equitable to respondents. The upshot of this was that both bargaining units followed other groups through the loopholes in the policy, seeking collective bargaining opportunities where they could, irrespective of eligibility in policy terms. They were able to do so without giving much away, since pay increases in both instances helped solve management problems. The attachment of both groups to the policy and its exceptions was purely pragmatic. The reaction to the advancement of other salient groups via the loopholes was not an admission of the fairness of the special case, but can attempt to use the loophole in turn.[1] Incomes policy exception clauses encouraged the widening of orbits of comparison, not the resolution of anomalies or inequities.

The success of the policy measures thus relied on the commitment of steward leadership on the shopfloor, just as more widely it relied on the commitment or acquiescence of the formal unions and the TUC. It was thus also important that steward leadership be sustained, and it is significant that, despite the rigidity of the Social Contract pay norms, stewards could continue to bargain under incomes policy in the case-study plants.[2] The extent of this bargaining and the maintenance of steward leadership were related, as were the extent of leadership and the degree of wage satisfaction of the membership under incomes policy.

However, an incomes policy which relies mainly on steward leadership is fragile, because to the extent that it reduces living standards, violates wage expectations, or generates anomalies, it undermines such leadership. Policies of wage restraint are, to judge from the data, inherently perishable; in both plants, one of the most pronounced features of responses was the increasing unpopularity of consecutive policy measures. Since this tendency has been identified by others who have assessed the failure of incomes policies on a larger scale, it is perhaps worth discussing in some detail; in particular, to place the case-study findings in the wider context.

John Corina suggests that it is possible to distinguish phases in the necessary decline of incomes policies: from 'installation' through' consolidation' and 'maturation' to 'collapse'. These phases are distinguished in terms of the changing behaviour of the wages round. The principal causes of collapse—at least for his classic analysis of the 1948–51 policy—lay partly in the inability of the TUC to impose a policy on member unions and partly in the necessary response of negotiators to inequities generated by wage drift.[3] Thus; 'A time limit must be set to tight guidance because restraint inevitably decays and has to be relaxed under explosive socio-economic conditions . . . A policy must be judged by whether it succeeds or fails in decelerating the rate of breakdown'.[4] Similarly, Gennard identifies a 'life-cycle' of incomes policy in which initial suspensions of bargaining behaviour (the 'on hard' phase) are much more successful than subsequent ('sophisticated') phases which seek to modify bargaining behaviour.[5]

Such a 'decay' is evident in both case-study plants. The Social Contract was supported at first by the establishment of a high wage norm and by the level of steward leadership commitment to it. Subsequently, rising living costs and the perceived inequity of the exception clauses put this leadership under considerable membership pressure. During the period of observation, these pressures were resolved at Factory A, but in the longer term they seemed likely to build up again. At B, they caused severe problems even in the short term. While membership pressure may be accommodated by steward leadership, in the not-so-long term, such leadership will disappear, and with it the incomes policy which it supports.

This very sharp decline in the acceptability of incomes policy at the two plants[6] corresponds closely to changes in opinion within the AUEW (Engineering Section) more generally. The National Committee had fully supported the Labour government's counter-inflation policy in 1976, although it had also opposed 'any form of statutory wage restraint', and pledged itself 'to reassert the principle of free collective bargaining as soon as the economic circumstances permit'.[7] However, by mid-1977 the committee was calling for an immediate return to free collective bargaining at the end of Phase II and for further action if this policy were not accepted by the TUC.[8] Similarly, Congress in 1975 accepted that 'for the next 12 months only, pay increases should be limited to a single flat rate figure with protection for the lower paid', but in 1976 called for a 'planned' return to free collective bargaining and by 1977 for free collective bargaining with the '12-month' rule.[9]

Although the two case studies were small, and did not appear to have any great involvement with or dependence on the formal organization of the AUEW, it appears that the changing climate of opinion in the two plants could be a barometer for the pressures building up within the AUEW which were eventually to explode at Congress. The seeds for the ultimate rejection of the policy by the AUEW, the decline of any commitment on the shopfloor, seem to have been sown as early as 1977, after the expiry of the £6 phase. If events at the case-study plants are indicative of more widespread trends, attachment to the policy became increasingly pragmatic and commitment increasingly perfunctory from then on.[10]

The extent of declining acceptability and its role in the ultimate demise of incomes policies seems established. But the question then arises; must this always happen, or is it possible to devise some policy for wage and salary determination which will be effective in the long term, and promote a stable basis for the structure of earnings in the United Kingdom? I shall deal with some of the main considerations underlying this question in the next section.

AN ACCEPTABLE INCOMES POLICY

It might be supposed at the outset that *in principle* the problem of devising an acceptable incomes policy is simple; if the main reason for decay is rank-and-file dissatisfaction, and one has elicited a set of pay principles of which the membership *do* approve, then, practical difficulties aside, their incorporation in some policy measure would remove dissatisfaction and constitute a solution. But a number of problems arise. First, these views quite simply might not be more general; I shall discuss this later in this chapter. Secondly, these views cover only part of the necessary ground. I have stressed already the importance of steward leadership in generating commitment to incomes policies. A solution to the problem would need to work with rather than against the institutions of collective bargaining and be compatible with their continued development. Furthermore, if a policy can strengthen steward leadership and support collective bargaining institutions, members' normatively central views may become less important. The design of such a policy is thus something of a balancing act; it would need to incorporate widely-held views about fairness, be compatible with collective bargaining developments and still achieve the economic ends set for it by government. The conceptual problems are, therefore, quite complex.

*(a) Fairness*

Two pervasive features of the pattern of workers' responses were, first, the extent to which both craft and non-craft workers felt that the craft qualification was important and, secondly, the importance of cost-of-living compensation as a justification for pay rises. Both of these views have featured as elements in relatively systematic approaches to fair pay in the past, which encourages the suspicion that they may be the basis for incomes policies in the future.

For example, the 'scholastic' ideas about the just wage discussed by Fogarty specify principles of equity which refer to social categories rather than individual participants to the effort bargain. In terms of such ideas, 'The right principle is equal pay for equal working capacity, not simply equal pay for equal work. Pay is to be related to the social value of the labour employed, not to its value to the individual employer, and the employer who underuses his labour force must pay the full price all the same.'[11] The wage is not seen simply as a transactional element, but as the expression of the employee's status in the social order as a whole. Moreover, scholastic principles refer to the maintenance of real living standards; thus, 'The scholastic's second great test of fair pay . . . is that an employee should be able to maintain out of it a stable standard of living at a customary level.'[12] These ideas are important for two reasons. First, similar principles have been encapsulated in incomes policy measures both in the United Kingdom and abroad, with varying degrees of success, in the form of indexation and comparability arrangements.[13] Secondly, both the 'scholastic' originals and these later developments appear to have been *codifications* of more widely held views on fair pay.[14] These points then raise the question: could not an incomes policy generate acceptability by incorporating such widely held principles? Broadly, there are three sets of difficulties involved.

First, although elsewhere there might be a wider basis of acceptability, the United Kingdom data I have quoted is from craft respondents. One could suggest historical reasons—to do with the integrity of craft skills—why AUEW craftsmen might adhere to the 'rate for the job' principle.[15] Others may not; even other craftsmen—such as those in print—might argue that workers with the same craft qualifications ought, for various reasons, to be paid at different rates. While indexation would probably be acceptable if it acted as a floor rather than a ceiling for wage increases, equalization of wages within occupational or skill categories might not be.

Secondly, these two principles do not provide an adequate basis for any incomes policy on their own: they are necessary but insufficient. The scholastic theory operated with other principles as well,[16] while both the United Kingdom evidence and the Australian experience quoted by Brown indicate the need to cope with the pressures of the labour market and changes in labour productivity.[17] A rigid, index-linked hierarchy of skill differentials in a changing economy is a spectre with which to haunt any government.

Thirdly, it is a feature of both the British and Australian experience that the operation of these other principles could lead to problems. Productivity bargaining and job changes have disturbed patterns of relativities in both countries: such piecemeal changes run counter to the 'one rate' principle. In fact, the United Kingdom evidence is that even the operationalization of those principles about which there *is* some agreement has been problematic. Comparability has been important in the determination of pay in the public sector for some time, and is undoubtedly influential in pay bargaining in the private sector, but there does not seem to be agreement about the role of comparability as an element in public policy. Under successive incomes policies, the role of comparability was both restricted and confused, while, with a return to 'free' collective bargaining, the elaboration of 'acceptable bases of comparison' for public sector pay by the Clegg Commission has been truncated by the present government.[18] In general, those concerned to take an overview of the pattern of wage settlement have shied away from any reliance on comparability, presumably on the assumption that, at least in the short term, such reliance would involve an open-ended commitment to higher wage claims. Given the scatter of earnings within occupational categories in the private sector and the diffuseness of informal comparisons, this avoidance makes some sense.

Similarly, while certain industries have sustained indexation agreements in the past, the attempt to generalize indexation in the form of threshold arrangements under the last Conservative incomes policy is generally agreed to have been highly inflationary.[19] At present, the Government feels that 'indexation is not a satisfactory means of determining pay' in the public sector.[20]

Thus, certain obstacles stand in the way of the realization of principles of comparability and indexation. Many have argued that these obstacles reside in the structure of bargaining arrangements. So, comparability is seen to be unstable because there is no generally agreed basis on which comparisons can be made, and threshold arrangements have been unsatisfactory because they do not preclude bargaining at different levels. The structure and practice of collective bargaining has been inimical to the realization of such principles

and thus to the operation of an acceptable incomes policy. However, it now seems that those features of collective bargaining which
obstructed incomes policies in the past are disappearing, and the
prospects for policy success are consequently increasing.

### (b) Collective Bargaining

Put at its simplest, the argument claims that the co-ordination of
collective bargaining is a sufficient condition for the establishment
of a long-term incomes policy. Previous policies collapsed since they
failed to control earnings increases because of a mismatch between
their policing mechanisms and the structure of collective bargaining: as the structure of bargaining is rationalized, successful policies
become attainable.

The keystone of this argument is the identification of a 'Dono-
vanesque' reform of plant and company bargaining, rationalizing
pay structures within plants, using techniques of work-study and
job evaluation, and shifting bargaining over pay away from the
shopfloor to company level.[21] This has two important implications
for incomes policies. Firstly, the number of points of negotiation re-
quiring control decreases and the size of agreement increases, thus
increasing the cost and visibility of settlements beyond an incomes
policy norm.[22] Secondly, the institutional basis for wage drift is
removed.

Inequities generated by wage drift have frequently been important elements in arguments about the decline of policy measures.
For example, Corina attributes the breakdown of the 1948–51
experiment in wage restraint largely to differential wage drift, which
generated claims *within* drift-prone industries and from those industries where bargaining arrangements prevented drift; piecework
payment systems were clearly important.[23] More recently, Clegg
has offered the opinion that 'One of the greatest obstacles to a
reasonable and fair system of pay in the country as a whole is the
injustice and absurdity of many of our plant and company pay
structures.'[24] But with the shift to plant-wide bargaining and
authoritative company agreements, the problem of drift receded.[25]
Clegg has spelt out the implications of this for incomes policies in
the early 1970s; 'If the Social Contract has controlled pay more successfully than Heath's policy did, one of the reasons may be that he
handed over to the Labour government a system of pay bargaining
more amenable to control than the system they had bequeathed to
him in 1970.'[26] The success of incomes policy is thus seen as closely
related to the ease with which pay developments can be monitored.
Following this line of argument, one might see other trends such as

the growth of authoritative joint shop-stewards' committees and management 'sponsorship' of shop steward organizations in terms of a widespread move towards the sort of bargaining structure alleged to be the basis for incomes policy success.[27]

This argument has a great deal of appeal, since centralized, authoritative collective bargaining on pay has been associated with the development of long-term incomes policies abroad.[28] Moreover, the use of job evaluation techniques in company wide bargaining would go some way towards satisfying the 'rate for the job' principle favoured by respondents here (indexation being quite another matter). Thirdly, if the evidence here is anything to go by, large companies attempting to move towards centralized bargaining *do* try to stick to incomes policy norms. But I think that there are three sets of problems with the argument that changes in the collective bargaining structure in manufacturing industry will facilitate the acceptance of incomes policy. These have to do with the opposition of craft workers, the use of job evaluation and the nature of the consensus which would underly incomes policy.

Within the case-study company, the trends outlined above had not progressed very far; in two Groups, sectional bargaining survived, neither case-study plant had a JSSC or plant-wide bargaining, and job evaluation had been rejected by both case-study groups. Although the Company was making moves towards an integrated system, there were great obstacles in the form of worker opposition. This may make the case studies atypical of more general patterns of change, but it does point to one problem with the argument above. If the Company moves towards an integrated system, it will do so by overcoming the opposition of many craft groups committed to local, autonomous bargaining; the change is likely to be coercive rather than spontaneous, and to have deleterious effects on steward leadership and commitment to bargaining arrangements. There are likely to be continued pressures from the union side for decentralization of bargaining structures and, given the level of organization of craft workers within the Company, they may be considerable. If this pattern of change and commitment has been more general within those companies which have moved over to company-wide bargaining, it will provide a shaky basis for long-term incomes policy reliant on authoritative centralized agreements.

Problems with the use of job evaluation arise from similar grounds. The opposition of craft groups to job evaluation is by now well established; it is reflected in the level of coverage of craft groups by job evaluation schemes of various types.[29] One could argue on the basis of the case studies that this opposition stems rather from a distaste for the bargaining arrangements generally associated with the implementation of job evaluation on the part of shop stewards than with a feeling on the part of the membership that it would distort fair pay relativities. But there are two more general problems with the use of job evaluation as a tool for the reform of pay structures and a basis for incomes policy. The first has to do with the role played by job evaluation in reform, the second with the nature of workers' attachment to job evaluation schemes.

While few are nowadays seduced by the idea of a national job evaluation scheme covering all industries and occupations, there are those who suggest that separate job evaluation schemes can be matched by the comparison of 'key' jobs between different companies and industries.[30] This would provide a national 'rate for the job', but would virtually relegate collective bargaining to a concern with non-monetary issues. The 'bargaining reform' argument does not suggest this; it seeks 'rational' structures *within* companies which could act as the building blocks for a long-term policy. It does not, therefore, have such dire consequences for the role of trade unions; but because it is more piecemeal and there is no obvious role for the co-ordination of strategies between companies, the possibility of disordant comparisons persists. They might arise between firms whose pay levels differed because of product market differences; in fact, job evaluation might increase the visibility of relative pay levels, so increasing the likelihood of such comparisons. Or they might arise from informal references to workers *outside* the rationalized sphere of bargaining arrangements made by large corporations.[31] In this case the 'rate for the job' principle is not achieved. The job-evaluated basis for incomes policy would thus be likely to fall between two stools; either it would be seen as an attempt to 'freeze out' trade unions from the pay-determination arena, or it would generate very visible (and rigid) pay relativities.

Moreover, it cannot be assumed that the extension of job evaluation indicates the existence of a consensus on relative occupational worth of the sort which would support long-term incomes policy. I have presented data already which indicates the limits of this consensus and, as Walker has shown, the spread of job evaluation schemes is not necessarily associated with it.[32] Job evaluation is a managerial technique which is seen by trade unionists merely as a collective bargaining tool, not the basis for a fair pay hierarchy; it may be accepted as a compromise and therefore need not provide the basis for a lasting solution to the problem of fair pay.[33] Its use may make it more difficult for bargainers to breach incomes policy guidelines, but there is no reason why it should increase their commitment to them.

Consequently, although there is some basis for the construction of a longer-term incomes policy, a number of problems remain which have to do with the nature of workers' values and their relationship to collective bargaining. The important question concerns their importance; would they prevent any form of policy success, or are there means of overcoming them? I think that such means do exist; they involve the creation of consent in the development of a policy.

## (c) Incomes Policy

The problem of consensus is in fact central to the whole discussion of incomes policy. There is clearly a difference between an agreement made in a crisis to halt or control the rate of wage increases and a thoroughgoing commitment to a long-term mechanism for the regulation of wages and salaries. I have argued that the former is extremely perishable; it is the form of consensus which has preceded past attempts at incomes policy. It is extremely uncertain whether the latter exists; certainly, the evidence presented above would discourage the assertion that it exists in the form of any generally agreed hierarchy of relative occupational worth, or that this is in fact a useful way to think about the problem. This underlying consensus is so indeterminate that it contains sufficient disruptive potential to wreck any attempt at incomes policies. Hierarchies of worth are generally acknowledged, but there is disagreement about specifics of the ranking order. Informal comparisons are generally restricted, but they often generate feelings of inequity. Moreover, these agreed hierarchies and restricted comparisons are associated with severely restricted information about the pay, conditions and job content of other groups of workers.

However, important though these problems are, they do not necessarily imply that a long-term incomes policy is completely inviable. The salience of comparisons under job evaluation and the commitment of workers to company bargaining arrangements will depend on the activities and influence of their bargaining representatives; and the translation of an indeterminate consensus into conflict over pay or into commitment to a specific set of norms, exception clauses and restraints depends on the activities of trade-union representatives opposed or committed to restraint. The sort of consensus which must underly incomes policy in the long term is thus not spontaneous; it cannot simply be a latent property of the way social actors perceive and rationalize the world. It must be continually sustained by those in a position to influence workers' views. As Corina notes;

If consensus is taken to imply a high degree of agreement upon goals and means, then, if this is to be more than a temporary truce in the orthodox pattern and behaviour of collective bargaining, it is more likely to be a changing product of political activity (the outcome of explicit views, disagreement, conflict and compromise) than a stable condition.[34]

The form of policy implied by the need for this sort of consensus needs to make use of a chain of commitment; of rank-and-file workers to their trade-union organizations[35] and of those organizations to the goals of the policy (or to the avoidance of an unwelcome alternative). This commitment involves the tolerance of a great deal of uncertainty and the foregoing of bargaining opportunities on the part of workers and their representatives; they must, therefore, be sure that the basis of the policy is sound. For workers, it must not involve them with principles they do not share, for representatives, it must not implicate them in unwelcome bargaining arrangements.

It is essential, therefore, that incomes policy be framed so as to minimize this uncertainty, and the most efficient way of achieving this is to ensure that those affected by the policy have a hand in its development. The data above indicate that it is not possible to produce any programmatic statement incorporating the views on fairness of these two small craft groups. The task of codifying the contradictory views on fairness of British society generally may be safely seen as impossible. The important point is that there be constant 'disagreement, conflict and compromise' in the administration of the policy, and that all relevant bodies be involved in it. And if the administration of the policy is to involve the constant articulation of viewpoints and decisions about their relative merits, some consistency is essential. These two considerations imply the need for a body representing employers, unions and government, making authoritative decisions about differentials and relativities on a consistent basis. The advocacy of this sort of body is by no means new; previous advocates include Hugh Clegg and Sir Henry Phelps-Brown.[36]

In summary, then, a successful long-term incomes policy would be designed and implemented so as to incorporate trade-union organizations in its administration and would support trade-union leadership to the extent of satisfying members' requirements about fairness. To this end it would:

(i)   be presented by a government acting with the co-operation of the trade-union movement, and administered by a body on which trade union interests were represented, acting in accordance with a consistent set of principles;
(ii)  incorporate those general feelings about fairness on which there appears to be some consensus by:
(a)   incorporating cost of living compensation;
(b)   applying comprehensively and without exception to all wage and salary earners;
(c)   reducing intra-occupational differentials.

The major problems facing the administrative body would arise as the *planning* of change began. Even perishable policies have had some success in administering even-handed 'freezes' or flat-rate norms. But difficulties will arise in the development of exception clauses; both the case-study data on a small scale and international experience of incomes policies more generally have indicated how difficult it is for policy makers to respond to changes in job content or in productivity and to accomodate labour market pressures. Unfortunately, aside from indicating how pragmatic was workers' attachment to the exception clauses of Phase II, the data give little guidance in these areas.

One of the key problems is the development of guidelines for productivity bargaining. The experience under the National Board for Prices and Incomes is generally agreed to have been less than satisfactory, at least in part because of the general feeling that the productivity exception was applying unevenly[37] But the experience of productivity bargaining under Phase III of the Social Contract, subsequent to the interviewing, was by no means so bad.[38] Without the burdens which were apparently laid on the productivity exception during the Wilson incomes policy, it appears not to have operated as a general escape clause under the Social Contract, even though there was no general guidance issues by the Department of Employment and the trade-union movement as a whole was not at that time committed to pay policy.[39] Given this commitment, and an agreed set of consistent guidelines for productivity bargaining which relied on the tri-partite form of monitoring suggested above, it might be possible for this hitherto troublesome exception to perform acceptably as part of a flexible, agreed policy, particularly if the number of points of negotiation at which such deals may be struck continues to decrease.

However, it should be emphasized that even policy measures which strive to incorporate all of these 'best features' are likely ultimately to face crisis, and the reasons for this are sociological.

They have to do with the nature of the underlying consensus and the limits this sets to the possibilities for trade-union initiatives. In considering these reasons, and the scope for the creation of consent on incomes policies, I shall, as indicated in the first chapter, be comparing sociological and more policy-oriented industrial relations approaches.

In the opening chapter, I criticized industrial relations work on comparisons and fairness for a failure to concern itself with the views of rank-and-file workers. This failure has been seen by Goldthorpe as characteristic of an entire 'reformist' school of industrial relations analysis which has tended to ignore 'the importance of the orientations and motivations of the actors involved at grass-roots level'.[40] This ignorance has tended to encourage the identification of clearly-defined 'problems' for which institutional solutions may be developed. By looking more closely at the 'view from below', Goldthorpe concludes that the preferred solutions of institutional reform and the application of incomes policies might both crumble because they are in fact *ex parte* attempts to impose order on a relatively chaotic industrial scene which would not attract the general support of the workers involved.[41]

The argument I have described at some length in this chapter—which sees the basis for a long-term incomes policy in the reform of collective bargaining structure—is in fact a species of the 'reformist' analysis of which Goldthorpe was so critical. It does not deal at all with the nature of the reform—the extent to which management, union and workers related to new institutional forms and old; nor with the impact of reform on the relationship between unions and their members—specifically, the impact on steward leadership; nor with the attitudes of the rank and file to incomes policies and fairness which have been the subject of this book. It is concerned to identify the institutional problems of previous incomes policies and to suggest that their eradication is not merely a necessary but a sufficient condition for the success of a long-term policy.

But I also criticized sociological work on fairness in Chapter 1 for failing to take account of the processes involved in collective bargaining. The work I reviewed there ignored such processes completely. Goldthorpe could hardly be accused of this, but throughout sociological work on incomes policy there has been a tendency to underemphasize the influence of trade-union representatives in ensuring the success of an incomes policy to which they are committed. Arguments tend to run from the identification of feelings of inequity or, broader still, the suggestion that the structure of inequality is broadly unlegitimated, to the conclusion that incomes policy is not viable. The presumption is that incomes policies are not viable merely because the *potential* for disruptive behaviour exists. In ignoring collective bargaining processes, the analysis leaves uninvestigated the mechanisms by which this potential does or does not become realized. This analysis notes that incomes policies have failed, identifies the absence of a normative basis for inequality and assumes that the two are causally related. In Goldthorpe's critique of Fox and Flanders, the persistence of feelings of inequity where reference groups are limited, and the existence of a *'wider structure of inequality which has no rationale whatsoever'* are noted, as is the absence of consent on pay principles and the use of varied arguments in pay negotiations,[42] but the links between legitimacy, consensus and bargaining behaviour remain unclear.

The data here indicate that a potential for disruption exists. Consensus and restricted reference groups are associated with an absence of information about other groups. The provision and use of such information could render extremely fragile the basis on which incomes policy could rest. But the issue here is surely one of salience. There seems to be no obstacle to the aquisition by respondents of *some* information about white-collar groups; one must assume that they chose to ignore it because it was of little use or interest. They were disturbed by the wages of other manual groups doing similar work; this is a problem familiar to 're-formists'. Moreover, the data indicated the power of stewards in handling wage information about dissimilar groups which *was* discordant; they could manage the difficulties created without dire consequences.

The collection of both kinds of data—on attitudes and on institutions—and an analysis of the ways they interact, illustrates the value of borrowing from both approaches. Certainly, incomes policy measures have a limited life-span. But there is a role for purposive policy making, adapting the best features of incomes policy to ensure longevity. The issue of greatest importance is the *involvement* of worker representatives in policy development. Incomes policies based on this involvement could feed off their own success; a measure that succeeds for some time might, on its demise, provide foundations for the next venture.

## CONCLUSION

Much has been left unsaid, in that the conclusions have not specified the sufficient conditions for the success of long-term incomes policies; but I think that I have gone as far as is reasonable in generalizing from a small sample. The degree of acceptability of incomes policy is essentially a question of trade-union politics. Because there is considerable indeterminacy in views about fair pay, there are a range of policy options open within the constraints I have identified. The success of a chosen option depends largely on how it is handled by policy makers—their accomodation of trade-union views of their own organizational interests and those of their members. Unions must be highly committed to incomes policy, or fearful of the alternatives, if it is to succeed. But the data indicate that some basis for an acceptable incomes policy does exist. One can introduce greater rationality into the industrial pay structure given that one takes account of the origin, structure and influence of workers' views of fairness.

# APPENDIX I

Several different techniques were used in combination. In detail, they are as follows.

## (1) Structured Interviews

All members of the two case-study organizations were to be interviewed, on the basis of the schedule reproduced as Appendix 2. This schedule is comprehensive and involves some deliberate overlap. The average time taken to complete each interview was about one hour.

## (2) Unstructured Interviews

These were of two types.

(a) Information-eliciting interviews, concerned to ascertain the industrial relations background and practices. These were conducted with representatives of other trade unions in the two plants studied, full-time officers of the AUEW, managers within the case-study plants, and staff at the company head office.

(b) Follow-up interviews, concerned to maintain contact with respondents to monitor continuing developments. At their broadest, these were simply social encounters at which problems that arose in work were discussed, but an attempt was made to discuss the specific issues with which the analysis was concerned. An attempt was made to have some sort of social encounter with respondents prior to administering the structured interview schedule, but this was not always possible. This type of interview assumed particular importance as it became apparent that observation would be curtailed by the type of access offered. At both plants, the impetus for access came from officers of the domestic organizations, in particular from the two convenors, and from their associates on the Combined Committee. In both plants, the initiative of these officers was ultimately accepted by management to some degree. Nevertheless, having been to some extent 'sponsored' by the steward organizations, there was a danger that I would come under their influence or under the influence of particular personalities. Consequently, every attempt was made to make contact with respondents away from the influence of shopstewards.

## (3) Observation

Observation techniques were seen as having three main functions:
- (a) the understanding, from a non-engineering outlook, of the act of work and what this implied in the broadest sense, and of the terminology respondents used about work,
- (b) to establish a form of rapport with respondents, and

(c) actual data collection. This was to be far more systematic, involving recording of arguments and contacts at negotiating meetings, and meetings of official and unofficial trade-union organizations.

In the event, observation was severely curtailed. The more diffuse functions of observation were compensated for by an increase in the number of unstructured interviews outside work. However, the more specific aspect of observation in negotiating situations is more central with regard to access to 'bargaining comparisons' and the absence of information on this is a substantial loss, particularly since it was not always possible to elicit comments on negotiations from both sides when no solution was immediately reached.

### (4) Documentary Analysis

Records of meetings, relevant correspondence, agreements, job descriptions and statements of proposed job changes (where available), statements of company policy and media coverage of company affairs were all monitored and used where necessary. Publications by the Department of Employment on the implementation of incomes policy were also monitored. All available, relevant wage data were analysed, including that produced by management within the company and by official and unofficial trade-union organizations. In addition, the more generalized data published by the Department of Employment (the New Earnings Survey) was used.

### PROBLEMS

The centrepiece of the empirical analysis was the structured interview schedule (see Appendix 2) which was piloted in January, 1976, in a small engineering plant in the Merseyside area which was part of a large multi-plant enterprise producing car-components.[1] Attempts to base the main study within this company failed as management refused further co-operation once the pilot study had been completed.

Subsequent approaches to other companies similarly failed on the question of managerial co-operation; the principal objections were that too much managerial time would be involved, and that detailed studies of income differentials were potentially explosive, and might have unpleasant repercussions for collective bargaining.[2] The usual response, where a joint approach to management and shopfloor union was made, was for the union side to grant co-operation, but for management to refuse it. There was, therefore, some delay between piloting and the main study. In the event, the access granted for the case studies was partial, but sufficient for completion of the main elements in the research design. Briefly, access was as follows:—

*Plant A*: interviewing was permitted during lunch breaks and at the end of shifts, either in the canteen or social club area. Access to the work area itself was limited to the arranging of interviews: access to negotiating situations was refused completely; in certain circumstances, which I shall discuss below, access to earnings information was withheld.

*Plant B*: interviewing was permitted in the work area during and beyond working hours. Access to the work area itself, and to all documentation required, was complete. However, access to negotiating situations was, as at A, refused.

As a consequence of the less complete access at Plant A, the completion of interviewing was a protracted affair; interviewing took place from late June to mid-August, 1976. In Plant B, where access was better, all of the interviewing was completed in April 1977.

In both cases, the projected programmes of structured interviews were completed and access to documentation was all that could be asked, although this was often provided by stewards and convenors even when it originated with management. However, access to the relevant earnings information was restricted as follows:

(1) AUEW shop stewards' quarterly earnings returns were refused by both of the District Committees concerned;

(2) At Plant A, detailed information about merit payments to SOGAT and NGA members was refused;

(3) The company declined at that time to disclose information about the 'league table' of earnings between its plants: this was partially compensated for by the provision of less complete data by the officers of the Combined Committee.

This may seem to be an extensive list. However, as all of the necessary unstructured interviews were completed and a high response rate was achieved in both plants for the structured interviews and, moreover, all of the earnings information and documentation immediately relevant to the two groups was collected, the data required by the research strategy were obtained. The main casualty was the observational element. It could be argued that the failure to complete the observational element was a serious deficiency, particularly since the model developed in Chapter 2 is obviously influenced by the work of Batstone *et al.* which relied to a considerable extent on observation techniques. In fact, at the outset, the role of observation was seen to be far more limited than it was for Batstone *et al.* There are two main reasons for this. Firstly, the model deviates from the approach favoured by Batstone *et al.* in that steward leadership is seen to be issue-specific, rather than a feature of a generalized role-orientation. The isolation of issues at the outset on which attention was to focus meant that 'open-ended' observation was less important: structured and unstructured interviews combined with a limited amount of observation could cover the relevant issues where these were isolated and defined at the outset, so that one was analysing behaviour in specific situations rather than general orientations towards behaviour in a role. The second reason involves the practical question of resources: I felt that it was wiser to rely on intersubjectively testable, more 'accountable' structured techniques rather than observation where I was performing the analysis alone. Observation may have introduced too large an element of bias where there was no opportunity for discussion and corroboration of observations with another analyst, and would certainly have involved more time than was available.

In fact, the major problem arising out of the limitation on observation was that negotiating situations themselves were inaccessible, rather than that I was unable to analyse steward behaviour or membership attitudes. It is therefore important to stress the methodological implications of the focus of the thesis. I have been concerned to look at, in particular, the implication of members' values for steward behaviour in bargaining. Had I been concerned with either manual workers' values or steward bargaining behaviour in isolation, then the mixture of techniques I have advocated may not have been necessary. Either of these separate focuses may have encouraged more reliance on observation techniques—on the one hand, in negotiations, on the other, within the framework perhaps of some form of network analysis documenting in detail the pattern of contacts from which comparisons might have arisen. However, my focus was broader than either of these. It is thus of the greatest importance that response rates to both structured and unstructured interviews were good, and that most of the documentary evidence required by the research design was made available.

# APPENDIX 2

## THE INTERVIEW SCHEDULE

In the schedule which is reproduced below, I have attempted to give some idea of the ways in which questions were asked and the 'prompts' which were given, by including some notes on completion: I have also indicated which responses were not used in the analysis and tried to show why.

In some instances, the wording of questions presented in tables in the body of the text differs from that of the questionnaire itself. Because, when presented in isolation, the wording would not make sense as it does when the questions are asked sequentially in the schedule, the changed, fuller wording in the text is adopted for ease of comprehension.

INTERVIEW SCHEDULE
LOCATION:
DATE:
TIME:
DURATION:

Q1. What department do you work in, and what is your job title?
(The question was asked in this form at Factory A, but it was not necessary to ask about department at Factory B because of the pronounced toolroom—maintenance split and because respondents were frequently interviewed within their own departments.)

Q2. Have you ever held a job other than your present one within this factory?
YES/NO
If YES, get details
(Responses were only coded YES if the job was outside the present department.)

Q3. How long have you been with this firm?

Q4. Why did you take this job in the first place?

Q5. Could you please tell me about the jobs you held before you came to work in this factory?
Date    Location    Company    Job title    Description
(I probed back as far as respondents' memories would allow: quite often the location and job were remembered, but the company and date were not.)

Q6. At what age did you leave school?
Grammar/Secondary/Elementary/Other

Q7. What was your first job after leaving school?

Q8. Have you ever served an apprenticeship?
YES/NO
If YES, get details; Location/Company/Type of apprenticeship

(Situations where respondents had started but not completed apprenticeships were also noted.)

Q9. Have you ever attended college on a day-release basis from work?
YES/NO
If YES, establish period.
(Block release was also noted.)

Q10. Have you ever held a white-collar job?
YES/NO
If YES, get details.

Q11. Have you ever been a shop steward?
YES/NO
If YES, get details.
If NO, ask why not?
(Respondents were asked whether they would be interested in doing the job in future. Stewards at A and stewards and shop committee members at B were asked to describe their experience; an attempt was made to elicit their satisfaction with their role and their plans for the future.)

Q12. How old are you?

Q13. Are you married?
YES/NO
If YES, ask how many children do you have?
Is your wife employed?

Q14. How would you describe your job; can you give me examples of the tasks you are expected to complete?
(Responses to this question were of little use at Factory A and it was omitted at Factory B.)

Q15. What abilities does a man need, in your opinion, to do your job well?

Q16. Do you think that these abilities are fairly rewarded in your job by the pay you get?
Why/Why not?

Q17. What amount of money would you say would be fair top-line pay for the work currently involved in your job?
(It was made clear that this was to be *gross* pay for a forty hour week.)

Q18. What amount of money or what percentage of earnings do you think would represent a fair pay increase for the work you are doing, over the next year? (It was made clear that *gross* weekly or hourly amounts were required.)

Q19. How would you judge if a pay award were fair or not?
Prompt—would you look at what it would buy, what you got last time, what others were getting, or something else?

Q20. What are your prospects of promotion out of your present job?

Q21. Which jobs in the factory should, in your opinion, receive about the same amount of pay as your own?

Q22. Do you know how much these jobs actually *are* paid?

Q23. Which jobs in the factory do *actually* receive about the same amount of pay as your own?

Q24. Is it fair that this/these job(s) should be paid about the same as yours?

Q25. Would you be prepared to tell me what your top-line pay was last week to the nearest £?
For how many hours?

Q26. What has your average top-line pay been over the last 4 weeks, to the nearest £?
And for how many hours per week is that?

Q27. Some people might say that the differences in pay between everyone employed here—on the shopfloor, in the offices and in management—are fair, others that they are not. What do you think?

Q28. Are differentials among manual workers in this factory fair?
Why/Why Not?

Q29. I'd like you to look at the following list of occupations in your factory, which are listed in no particular order. First, on the left of the list, I'd like you to write in the amount you think an average worker in that group *actually gets*, to the nearest £, as top-line pay in this factory for a normal working week. Secondly, will you please write in on the right of the list the amount you think would be *fair* top-line pay for a normal week, for the work involved in each job.
Factory A
        time-served 4-colour printer
        maintenance electrician
        HGV driver (class 1)
        brakehand
        unskilled labourer
        personnel manager
        production foreman
        machine setter/operator
        records clerk
        factory manager
Factory B
        time-served turner
        maintenance electrician
        HGV driver (class 1)
        die-setter
        unskilled labourer
        personnel manager
        production foreman
        semi-skilled production worker
        records clerk
        factory manager

Q30. Are there any jobs in the factory which are, in your opinion, under-paid relative to the others?

Q31. Why do they deserve more pay?

Q32. Are there any jobs in the factory which are, in your opinion, paid too much relative to the others?

Q33. Why do they deserve less pay (or the others deserve more)?

Q34. (a) Sometimes pay claims are justified by claiming that some workers' pay has fallen 'seriously out of line' with the pay of another group. In your own case, whose pay you look at to see whether your own was out of line?

(b) Why this/these groups/people in particular?

(c) Do you think that your steward would support you in making this comparison?
Why/Why Not?
(Where respondents were stewards, changes were made to part (c) of the question; at Factory A, stewards were asked whether 'the other stewards' would support them, at Factory B all respondents were asked whether 'the shop committee' would support them.)

Q35. Have you ever used the rates of another group of workers as an argument in a pay claim?
YES/NO
If YES, when was this and who were the other group?

Q36. Are there any other factories in the area which employ people in jobs similar to your own?
Names          Location          Jobs

Q37. How does your pay in this factory relate to the pay for similar work in other factories in the area?

Q38. (a) Why do you think that differences exist between factories for the same or very similar jobs?

(b) Is it fair that these differences in pay should exist?
(This question only asked where differences were identified in response to Q37.)

Q39. If you knew of a vacancy in any of these factories for work similar to your own, would you move from here to there, and what for?

Q40. What are the things which most attract you to any job?

Q41. (This was asked in a different form at the two locations.)
Factory A: Should there be just one rate for skilled workers, another for semi-skilled and a third for unskilled, or should there be more or fewer differentials than this?
Factory B: There are 3/4 rates for skilled men here; do you think that this is about right, or would you like to see more or less?

Q42. Do you think that your payment system is a fair one? Would you like to see it changed in any way?

Q43. Do you think that any other system would be fairer?
(Response to this question were too patchy to use in the main analysis.)

Q44. In the last year or so, have there been any changes in the general rate of payment in the factory?
YES/NO
If YES, what was the change?
How did it affect you?
Do you think that it made pay more or less fair?

Q45. Here is a list of things on which your pay could be based. Could you

show me how important you think each one of them is by assigning
each one a number?

| | | | | | |
|---|---|---|---|---|---|
| Payment according to skill | 1 | 2 | 3 | 4 | 5 |
| Payment according to movements in the cost of living | 1 | 2 | 3 | 4 | 5 |
| Payment according to the profitability of the firm | 1 | 2 | 3 | 4 | 5 |
| Payment according to effort | 1 | 2 | 3 | 4 | 5 |
| Payment according to productivity | 1 | 2 | 3 | 4 | 5 |
| Payment according to family size | 1 | 2 | 3 | 4 | 5 |
| Payment according to seniority within the firm | 1 | 2 | 3 | 4 | 5 |

(It was necessary to clarify that item 5 referred to *individual* productivity.)

Q46. I would like you now to turn your attention to work outside of
engineering. Which jobs in other industries should, in your opinion,
receive about the same amount of pay as your own?

Q47. Do you know how much these jobs actually *are* paid?

Q48. Which jobs in industries other than your own do *actually* receive
about the same amount of pay as your own?

Q49. Do you think that this is fair? Should they be paid more or less?

Q50. Are there any jobs in the country generally which are, in your opinion,
underpaid?

Q51. Why do they deserve more money?

Q52. Do you think that there should be a nationally-set minimum wage,
and if so, how much should it be?
(It was again made clear that gross weekly or hourly amounts were
required.)

Q53. Are there any jobs in the country generally which are, in your opinion,
too highly paid?

Q54. Why do they deserve less pay (or others deserve more)?

Q55. Do you think that, in the period before pay policy came into opera-
tion, any group in the country generally was setting the pace for pay
increases?
YES/NO
If YES, which group?
If NO, what did set the pace for pay increases?

Q57. Do you think that a skilled craftsman should always be paid more than
a labourer?
If YES, what do you think should be the size of the differential?
If NO, why not?

Q58. Are skilled workers always paid more than semi-skilled and unskilled
workers in this factory?
(I established whether respondents were referring to basic rates or to
earnings, and whether they included bonus and overtime payments in
their considerations.)

Q59. I want to give you another list, and I'd like you to do the same with this as with the last one; estimate the top-line earnings of each, then tell me what would, in your opinion, be fair pay for each. These are occupations with which you may not be familiar, so if you feel that you don't know enough about any of them, just leave a blank.

> headmaster of a secondary school
> British Rail ticket collector
> time-served welder
> unskilled car assembly worker
> insurance collector (door-to-door)
> semi-skilled machinist in an engineering factory
> underground miner (face worker)
> production manager
> gas fitter
> foreman fitter

(In answering this question and Q29, respondents were generally unable to supply amounts for actual income of the named occupations. It was not possible to use this information in the main analysis.)

Q60. (a) In assessing how good or bad your own pay is, do you ever make comparisons with workers in other industries and, if so, which workers?

(b) Why these groups of workers?

(c) Do you think that your steward would support you in making this comparison?

(Notes to Q34 apply here also.)

Q61. Do you ever use the rates of workers outside of the industry as an argument in pay claims?

YES/NO

If YES, when was this, and who were the other workers involved?

Q62. I'd like now to shift the focus back to this factory;

Do you attend union meetings?

Site: how often?

Branch: how often?

Q63. Are you in favour of the present policy of the steward organization within this factory?

Q64. Is your steward effective in getting what you want personally?

Q65. Does the steward himself decide what action should be taken over an issue, or do the members decide at a meeting?

Q66. Has your steward ever refused to raise an issue with management?

YES/NO

If YES, what sort of an issue was this?

Q67. Do the stewards have a policy on differentials and, if so, what is it?

(At Factory B, this question referred to the 'stewards' committee'.)

Q68. Do you think that this is a fair policy?

Why/Why not?

Q69. What do you think is management policy on differentials?

Q70. Would you say that this factory experiences good industrial relations?

YES/NO

Why is this so?

Q71. Has the outcome of recent pay negotiations in the factory appeared to favour any group of workers in particular?

YES/NO

If YES, which workers?

Q72. What would you consider to be a fair reason for a pay rise at the present time?

Q73. What arguments for a pay rise do you think are most likely to sway management?

Q74. At the present time, are there any reasons other than the pay policy why management could fairly refuse you a pay rise?

YES/NO

If YES, what are they?

Q75. I'd like to close by asking you a few questions about government policy;

What do you see as the general reason for government pay policies?

Do you think that such policies work?

Q76. Do you think that union leaders should continue in the next phase to co-operate with government to formulate an incomes policy, or would you prefer that they do not get involved?

Q77. Some people say that the main cause of the country's economic problems is high wage settlements; would you agree?

YES/NO

If NO, what do you think is the major cause?

Q78. Why do some people say that it is wage claims?

Q79. What do you think of the '£6' policy?

Was it necessary and fair?

Did it lead to an erosion of differentials?

Q80. What do you think of the Phase II settlement of a percentage increase with a monetary limit?

Q81. What do you think the third phase should look like?

(This was only asked at Factory B.)

Q82. Would you like to see a return to free collective bargaining?

Q83. Could you please indicate your agreement or disagreement with the statements on this card?

'Management and workers are really on opposite sides.'

strongly agree/agree/don't know/disagree/strongly disagree

'Industry should pay its profits to workers, not to shareholders.'

strongly agree/agree/don't know/disagree/strongly disagree

'Most management have the welfare of their workers at heart.'

strongly agree/agree/don't know/disagree/strongly disagree

'Worker participation in management could only do the firm harm.'

strongly agree/agree/don't know/disagree/strongly disagree

(Both the numer of items and the number of response categories are reduced from Blackburn and Mann's original set of measures. The measures here are thus less flexible, but respondents appeared to find no great difficulty with the fixed-choice questions. However, the 'either-or' nature of the worker-shareholder opposition in item 2 was unwelcome; 13 per cent at A and 22 per cent at B felt only that *more* profits should go to workers and *less* to shareholders. Provision was made for the inclusion of this response; it was coded as midway between 'agree' and 'don't know and scored accordingly.)

# APPENDIX 3

## THE COMBINED COMMITTEE

The Combine in question covered AUEW and EETPU workers throughout the product groups and the capital equipment group. At the time of interview, more than forty plants were affiliated. The Committee began in the early 1960s and grew steadily in the fifteen years following. Its coverage was thinnest in Group 2 where group-level bargaining occurred, and best in the capital equipment group where the largest AUEW bargaining units were.

The Committee met regularly, had a formal constitution and elected officials: meetings were minuted and regular information bulletins containing earnings information, information about the company and about incomes policy, were distributed. The organization was developing during the course of the interviewing: it was decided to hold an AGM and to elect an Assistant Secretary to cope with increasing administrative loads, and a number of sub-committees covering particular groups and regions were set up.

Formally, the committee was unrecognized by the Company and by the formal union. Most of the combine activists were AUEW members: given the structure of that union, and the importance of District Committees, Combines must remain strictly speaking, unrecognized, since they can have no formal contact with the Executive Council. But Combine officers seemed to work within the union rather than against it. Officers were on good terms with the National Officer dealing with the Company, who on occasion visited their meetings.

Similarly, the Combine was not recognized by management, but it exerted considerable influence on national negotiations. The turning point was perhaps the signing of the Engineering Agreement with the company in 1972, which established minimum rates and common conditions for AUEW and EETPU workers at national level. The trade-union side of negotiations was composed mainly of lay representatives elected by a National Delegate Conference: most of these are convenors active in the Combined Committee. One major consequence of this is that the Combine is not simply an earnings information bureau: it develops policies on conditions of employment settled nationally which strongly influence the claims forwarded by the AUEW in national negotiations.

# APPENDIX 4

The occupational composition of the two subsamples varied slightly. These differences are summarized in Table A 4.1. They stem less from differences in production technology than from differences in the contours of union organization and the scope of the maintenance function.

## TABLE A4.1
### Occupational Composition of the Sample

| Job Title | Factory A (per cent) | Factory B (per cent) |
|---|---|---|
| Chargehand | 5(12.5) | 3(6.0) |
| Toolmaker/Machine Worker | 2(5.0) | 35(70.0) |
| Maintenance Fitter/Welder | 18(35.0) | 11(22.0) |
| Fitter's Mate | 4(10.0) | — |
| Storesman | 4(10.0) | 1(2.0) |
| Boilerhouse Labourer | 7(17.5) | — |
| Total | 40(100) | 50(100) |
| Total % engaged on skilled work | (62.5) | (98) |
| Total % of time served | (60.0) | (94) |

*Source:* Question 1 of Structured Interview Schedule.

*Note:* This classification itself involves some compression. 'Fitters' at Factory A include those maintaining the production machinery as well as pipefitters and garage fitters: at Factory B the term refers to work on the production machinery and to 'development' work on new machinery. Included in the toolmakers at B are several 'line engineers' who are directly involved in maintenance/supervision of the production lines: the category appears to be peculiar to the industry, and was regarded by both management and union as a species of toolroom work.

In plant A, AUEW membership extended to workers in the boilerhouse and encompassed fitters' mates and storesmen. At B, fitters mates were no longer employed, as a consequence of past agreements on manning levels. Other unskilled maintenance workers were organized by the TGWU, which accounts for the very few unskilled respondents at B. The different occupational composition of the two units also reflected, to some extent, their different functions. While the AUEW unit at A performed an 'orthodox' maintenance function, at B this was supplemented by the production of fine-limit machine parts both for other company plants and on a commercial basis: consequently the toolroom was bigger than it would otherwise have been. This led to rather different distributions of workers at the two plants: at B, all the AUEW workers were concentrated in two adjacent rooms—the toolroom and maintenance sections—with the exception of the line engineers (14 per cent of the sample) who worked on their particular can lines. At A, workers were positioned near the machinery they were to service: there were a number of departments, spread across the factory.

As one might expect, the craft dominance of both bargaining units set considerable limits on the patterns of occupational mobility within the plants. At A 27.5 per cent of the sample and at B 14 per cent had changed jobs within the factory, excluding promotions to chargehand within the same department (Question 2). All the movements at B and all the movements of skilled men at A can be accounted for in terms simply of interdepartmental shifts of staff. Of the unskilled mobile at A, a number of older workers had been moved from fitter's mate to the physically less exacting job of storesman, and a number of other workers had used their previous engineering experience as the basis for a move across from production work when redundancy threatened. At both plants, a significant number of skilled men had served their apprenticeship with the company and consequently never worked elsewhere: at A 28 per cent and B 34 per cent of skilled men had done so. At A nearly 50 per cent of the unskilled (17.5 per cent of the whole sample) had started some form of apprenticeship, not necessarily in engineering, but had never finished it (Question 58). In demographic terms, the subsamples are very similar indeed. Table A4.2 shows a remarkable similarity of age and length of service distributions, while further chi-square tests revealed no significant difference in marital status and family size (Question 13).[1] Educational levels were similar across

TABLE A4.2
*Demographic Characteristics of the Sample*

|  | *Factory A* | *Factory B* | *Over-all* |
|---|---|---|---|
| Average Age (yrs.) | 42.3 | 42.3 | 42.3 |
| Average Length of Service (yrs.) | 12.3 | 17.04 | 14.63 |
| No Respondents | 40 | 50 | 90 |

*Source:* Questions 3 and 12 of the Structured Interview Schedule.

*Notes:* (1) Chi-square tests revealed no significant differences between the age distributions of sub-samples A and B (chi-square = 7.896, $\alpha$ = .05, d.f. = 5) or the length of service distributions (chi-square = 9.129, $\alpha$ = .05, d.f. = 5).

(2) The lower average length of service at A does not appear to be attributable solely to the presence in the sub-samples of a proportion (37.5 per cent) of unskilled workers ($\bar{X}$ skilled length of service 13.3 years, unskilled 10.7 years. In addition, very few respondents had much experience of work outside of engineering in the post-war period: at A 27 per cent of respondents and at B only 6 per cent had worked for more than 6 months consecutively at any one job outside of engineering work. This difference is wholly attributable to the occupational differences between samples, since none of the skilled workers at A had worked outside of engineering.

the whole sample: most respondents had left school at the statutory minimum age, so that observed differences were related to movement in this minimum over time (Question 56). Similar age distributions imply similar educational attainment distributions. In addition, 37.5 per cent of respondents at A and 40 per cent of those at B had attended college on a day-release basis during their apprenticeship: this represents a larger proportion of *skilled* respondents at A than B (Question 59). Very few respondents in either sub-sample had any experience of white-collar work: at A 7.5 per cent of the sample had done so, and at B, 12 per cent. This exludes any clerical work performed during national service and short spells in the drawing office during apprenticeship (Question 10).

Both sets of respondents tended to be pessimistic about their chances of promotion. The National Economic Development Office found that the absence of any widespread perception of a valuable 'career' in engineering work was one of the causes of labour shortages in the industry: in certain respects the data here bear out their contentions, although few of the sample manifested any disposition to leave their jobs (Question 39).[2] At A, 82.5 per cent and at B, 66 per cent of respondents felt that their chances of promotion were 'nil' or 'poor' (Question 20), the lower percentage at B is explicable in terms of the 'merit' system which operated there, since a number of respondents interpreted 'promotion' as movement through the merit grades.

# APPENDIX 5

## EARNINGS INFORMATION; FACTORIES A AND B

TABLE A5.1

*The AUEW Rate Structure Factory A: July 1976 (exclusive of the Effects of Overtime)*

| Grade | Basic Hourly Rate* (p) | Gross Hourly Earnings†** | | Gross Weekly Earnings‡ | | Percentage differentials§ | |
|---|---|---|---|---|---|---|---|
| | | 2 shift (p) | 3 shift (p) | 2 shift (£) | 3 shift (£) | 2 shift | 3 shift |
| Chargehand | 152.32 | 199.7 | 214.92 | 79.88 | 85.97 | 112 | 111.98 |
| Craftsmen | 134.8 | 178.3 | 191.92 | 71.33 | 76.77 | 100 | 100 |
| Storesman | 112.75 | 151.2 | — | 60.46 | — | 84.8 | — |
| Fitter's Mate/Boilerman | 110.00 | 148.4 | 159.37 | 59.35 | 63.75 | 83.23 | 83.35 |

*Source:* Company Records: Convenor's Records.

*Notes:*

\* The basic hourly rate is the negotiated rate. It does not refer to an amalgamation of items including a national minimum, but stands as a house rate. It is used merely as a base, since pension entitlement, holiday earnings and overtime all refer in their different ways more directly to shift-enhanced gross hourly earnings.

† Gross hourly earnings at the time of interview are calculated by applying the shift premium to the basic hourly rate and subsequently adding an amount to represent the Phase I supplement. The calculations are as follows:

Gross Hourly 2-shift earnings: (Basic Hourly × 1.2125) + 15p.
Gross Hourly 3-shift earnings: (Basic Hourly × 1.3125) + 15p.

‡ Gross weekly earnings are flat week earnings derived from this: i.e. they are gained by multiplying the gross hourly figures by 40. There is no consideration of overtime in this table.

§ The percentage differentials are calculated on the basis of gross hourly earnings. If calculated on the basis of basic hourly rates, the percentages widen very slightly: this is a consequence solely of the exclusion of the £6 per week flat-rate supplement from this calculation.

\*\* The gross figures presented here are thus effectively hourly 'APNOR' as described in Table 4.8.

## TABLE A5.2
### The AUEW Rate Structure at Factory B: April 1977
### (exclusive of the Effects of Overtime)

| Grade | Basic Hourly* Rate (p) | Gross Hourly† Earnings (p) | Gross Weekly‡ Earnings (£) | % differentials§ |
|---|---|---|---|---|
| Chargehand | 149 | 164 | 65.6 | 106.49% |
| Top Rate | 139 | 154 | 61.6 | 100% |
| Middle Rate | 135 | 150 | 60.0 | 97.4% |
| Bottom Rate | 131 | 146 | 58.4 | 94.8% |
| Starting Rate | 128.5 | 143.5 | 57.4 | 93.18% |
| Unskilled | 113 | 128 | 51.2 | 83.12% |

*Source:* Company Records: Convenor's Records.

*Notes:* * The basic hourly rate is again the negotiated rate. Its status in this respect is similar to that at A. However its importance as a basis for overtime pay, holiday earnings, etc., is greater here, as shifts are not worked.

    † Gross Hourly Earnings are derived by a simple addition of 15p per hour, representing the Phase I supplement.

    ‡ Gross Weekly Earnings are flat week earnings derived from this. Again, they exclude overtime.

    § The percentage differentials are calculated on the basis of gross hourly earnings. Again, if calculated on the basis of basic hourly rates, the percentages widen slightly: the movement is a little more pronounced than at A because of the greater proportional impact of a £6 supplement in this case.

## TABLE A5.3
### Manual rate structure, Factory A, 1975–1977:
### Gross Hourly Earnings (excluding overtime)

| | April 1975 (per cent) (£) | April 1976 (per cent) (£) | April 1977 (per cent) (£) |
|---|---|---|---|
| (1) 3-shift workers | | | |
| AUEW Skilled | 1.769 (100) | 1.919 (100) | 2.075 (100) |
| EETPU Skilled | 1.769 (100) | 1.919 (100) | 2.075 (100) |
| SOGAT Class I—Slitter | 1.436 (81.1) | 1.586 (82.6) | 1.665 (82.6) |
| SOGAT Class I—Fork Lift Driver | 1.525 (86.2) | 1.675 (87.3) | 1.759 (87.3) |
| AUEW—Unskilled | 1.444 (81.6) | 1.594 (83.1) | 1.674 (83) |
| EETPU—Unskilled | 1.404 (79.4) | 1.555 (81) | 1.633 (81) |
| SOGAT Class III Gravure Ass. | 1.290 (72.9) | 1.440 (75) | 1.512 (75) |
| (2) 2-shift workers | | | |
| AUEW Skilled | 1.635 (100) | 1.785 (100) | 1.874 (100) |
| SOGAT Class I—cutter | 1.493 (91.3) | 1.643 (92) | 1.725 (92) |
| SOGAT Class I—Diemaker | 1.511 (92.5) | 1.661 (93.1) | 1.744 (93.1) |

| | April 1975 (per cent) (£) | April 1976 (per cent) (£) | April 1977 (per cent) (£) |
|---|---|---|---|
| SOGAT Class I—Fork Lift Driver | 1.416 (86.6) | 1.566 (87.8) | 1.644 (87.8) |
| AUEW Unskilled | 1.344 (81.6) | 1.484 (83.2) | 1.558 (83.2) |
| SOGAT Class II | 1.298 (79.4) | 1.448 (81.1) | 1.520 (81.1) |
| SOGAT Class III—Gravure Ass. | 1.174 (71.8) | 1.324 (74.2) | 1.390 (74.2) |
| SOGAT Class III floor man | 1.190 (72.8) | 1.340 (75.1) | 1.407 (75.1) |

*Source:* Company Records: SOGAT Records.

*Notes:* (1) Gross hourly earnings include all shift premia, merit money and machine extras but exclude overtime earnings.

(2) The uniformity of the table is assured to some extent by incomes policy. The 'vintage ranking' pattern which is implied here is not accurate however, since the jobs included as examples of SOGAT rates were not those which renegotiated 'machine extras' over the period ('Merit' deals were prevented by the policy). The relationship between AUEW earnings and those of SOGAT jobs thus fluctuate in the short term.

(3) The SOGAT figures quoted thus illustrate a more complex structure. NGA rates are not quoted as they were withheld. All indications are that they were much higher than those in the table. Other maintenance work carried the same rate as the AUEW. HGV drivers were on a grade of the general workers agreement (see Table A5.4).

## TABLE A5.4
### Manual Rate Structure, Factory B, 1975–1977: Gross Hourly Earnings (Excluding Overtime)

| | July 1975 (per cent) (£) | July 1976 (per cent) (£) | July 1977 (per cent) (£) |
|---|---|---|---|
| AUEW top rate | 1.39(100) | 1.54(100) | 1.616(100) |
| middle rate | 1.35(97.1) | 1.50(97.4) | 1.575(97.4) |
| bottom rate | 1.31(94.2) | 1.46(94.8) | 1.533(94.8) |
| starting rate | 1.285(92.5) | 1.435(93.2) | 1.506(93.2) |
| unskilled | 1.13(81.3) | 1.28(83.2) | 1.344(83.2) |
| TGWU grade 5 | 0.986(70.94) | 1.136(73.77) | 1.198(74.17) |
| 4 | 0.093(64.96) | 1.053(68.38) | 1.116(69.1) |
| 3 | 0.872(62.72) | 1.022(66.35) | 1.084(67.12) |
| 2 | 0.851(61.22) | 1.001(65) | 1.064(65.88) |
| 1 | 0.83(59.71) | 0.98(63.64) | 1.043(64.58) |

*Source:* Company Records.

*Notes:* (1) There are no shift or merit additions to basic rates.

(2) All other maintenance workers were on AUEW rates: part-time female workers are excluded.

(3) The uniformity of the table is somewhat artificial. July was the AUEW settlement date, but the rates for each July for the TGWU are effective in all cases from the previous October.

# NOTES

## CHAPTER 1

1. B. Wooton, *The Social Foundations of Wage Policy* (1962), p. 100, and D. Lockwood, 'Arbitration and Industrial Conflict' (1955).
2. R. Hyman and I. Brough, *Social Values and Industrial Relations* (1975), p. 1.
3. W. W. Daniel, 'Wage Determination in Industry' (1976), p. 1.
4. H. Clegg, 'The Scope of Fair Wage Comparisons' (1961), p. 211.
5. J. H. Goldthorpe, 'Social Inequality and Social Integration in Modern Britain' (1969).
6. J. H. Goldthorpe, 'The Current Inflation, Towards a Sociological Account', (1978).
7. Hyman and Brough, *Social Values,* p. 108; H. Phelps-Brown, 'A Non-Monetarist's View of the Pay Explosion' (1975).
8. Goldthorpe, 'The Current Inflation'.
9. J. Corina, 'Can an Incomes Policy Be Administered?' 290–1 (1968).
10. W. G. Runciman, 'Justice, Congruence and Professor Homans' (1967).
11. B. Williams, 'The Idea of Equality' (1962).
12. See both Runciman, 'Justice, Congruence and Professor Homans', and W. G. Runciman, *Relative Deprivation and Social Justice* (1972).
13. The close relationship between the two terms stems from the fact that they both refer to grievance generated by inequality (or conceivably by the absence of it). Runciman defines relative deprivation as follows: 'we can roughly say that $A$ is relatively deprived of $X$ when (1) he does not have $X$ (2) he sees some other person or persons, which may include himself at some previous or expected time, as having $X$ (whether or not this is or will in fact be the case), (3) he wants $X$ and (4) he sees it as feasible that he should have $X$'. (*Relative Deprivation*, p. 11). His terminology is not adopted here because of the modifications which will be suggested to the concept of a 'reference group' and because, whereas the term 'relative deprivation' refers only to grievance generated by inequality, the use of the 'fairness—unfairness' dichotomy can also succinctly indicate satisfaction with it. In other ways, the meanings of the two terms are convergent.
14. Ibid., p. 298.
15. Ibid., pp. 307–23.
16. G. A. Withers, 'Social Justice and the Unions', (1977).
17. J. W. Chapman, 'Justice and Fairness' (1963).
18. Runciman, *Relative Deprivation*, pp. 299–302.
19. Ibid., p. 304.
20. H. Behrend *et al.*, *Incomes Policy and the Individual* (1967); H. Behrend *et al.*, *Views on Incomes Differentials and the Economic Situation* (1970).
21. D. T. B. North *et al.*, *Report on a Study of Some Aspects of National Job Evaluation* (1973).
22. Given that there may be considerable variance of earnings within any group, it is difficult to see what criteria the analysis could have used to decide whether fair pay as stated by respondents corresponded to actual pay. Measures of central tendency would obviously not accommodate to the fact that respondents may have stated amounts based on personal knowledge of individuals in the 'tails' of any occupational distribution.
23. Runciman *Relative Deprivation*, pp. 232 and 263.

24. W. W. Daniel, *'The Next Stage of Incomes Policy'* (1976), p. 33.
25. Chronologically, H. Behrend, 'Price and Income Images and Inflation' (1964); H. Behrend, 'Price Images, Inflation and National Incomes Policy' (1966); Behrend *et al.*, *Incomes Policy and the Individual* (1967); H. Behrend, A. Knowles and J. Davies *'Views on Pay Increases, Fringe Benefits and Low Pay'* (1970); H. Behrend, 'The Impact of Inflation on Pay Increase Expectations and Ideas of Fair Pay' (1974); H. Behrend, *Attitudes to Price Increases and Pay Claims* (1974).
26. See her 'Public Acceptability and a Workable Incomes Policy' (1972), and *Incomes Policy, Equity and Pay Increase Differentials* (1973).
27. P. Fosh and D. Jackson, 'Pay Policy: What Britain Thinks' (1974).
28. W. W. Daniel, 'The P.E.P. Survey on Inflation' (1975), pp. 3, 8.
29. H. Clegg, *The Changing System of Industrial Relations in Great Britain* (1979), p. 355.
30. See John Corina, 'The British Experiment in Wage Restraint 1948–51' (1961).
31. S. M. Lipset and M. Trow, 'Reference Group Theory and Trade Union Wage Policy' (1957), p. 391.
32. W. Brown and K. Sisson, 'The use of Comparisons in Workplace Wage Determination' (1975) pp. 23–51.
33. A. M. Ross, *Trade Union Wage Policy* (1948).
34. W. A. Brown, 'Incomes Policy and Pay Differentials' (1976), and 'Engineering Wages and the Social Contract 1975–1977', (1979).
35. Ross, *Trade Union Wage Policy*; R. Lester, 'A Range Theory of Wage Differentials' (1952); M. Reder, 'The Theory of Union Wage Policy' (1952); H. Levinson, *Determining Forces in Collective Wage Bargaining* (1966); Brown and Sisson, 'The Use of Comparisons'.

## CHAPTER 2

1. Hyman and Brough, *Social Values and Industrial Relations*, p. 203.
2. I. Bernstein, *Arbitration of Wages* (1954). Ross, *Trade Union Wage Policy*.
3. Wooton, *The Social Foundations of Wage Policy* (1962), Ch. 4.
5. C. W. Mills, 'Situated Actions and Vocabularies of Motive' (1963), p. 439.
6. H. Gerth and C. W. Mills, *Character and Social Structure* (1954), p. 112.
7. Ibid., p. 118.
8. Allan Flanders, 'Collective Bargaining: A Theoretical Analysis' (1970), p. 230.
9. W. Baldamus, *Efficiency and Effort* (1961).
10. Ibid., p. 99.
11. Ibid., p. 26.
12. Ross, *Trade Union Wage Policy*.
13. W. A. Brown, 'A Consideration of "Custom and Practice"' (1972); W. A. Brown, *Piecework Bargaining* (1973); M. Rimmer, *Race and Industrial Conflict* (1972).
14. Rimmer, *Race and Industrial Conflict*, pp. 3–4.
15. Brown, 'A Consideration of "Custom and Practice"', p. 46.
16. M. Terry, 'The Inevitable Growth of Informality' (1977).
17. Brown, *Piecework Bargaining*, p. 136.
18. M. J. Pedler, 'Shop Stewards As Leaders' (1973).
19. E. Batstone, I. Boraston, S. Frenkel, *Shop Stewards in Action* (1977).
20. Ibid., p. 35.

21. P. Willman, 'Leadership and Trade Union Principles: Some Problems of Management Sponsorship and Independence' (1980).
22. Pedler, 'Shop Stewards as Leaders', p. 56.
23. The term 'domestic organization' is defined, after Batstone *et al.*, as referring 'not merely to a particular shop-steward organization within a plant, but also to the members the shop stewards represent' (p. 10).
24. E. Batstone, I. Boraston, S. Frenkel, *The Social Organisation of Strikes* (1978), p. 220.
25. Ross, *Trade Union Wage Policy*, p. 18.
26. Ibid., p. 39.
27. Ibid., p. 33.
28. So, for Ross, a good bargain is not the one which yields the largest pay rise, nor necessarily that which keeps the employment level highest. Principally, it is 'a successful resolution of the political pressures which are focused on the leadership in the bargaining process' (ibid., p. 95).
29. Ibid., p. 38.
30. Batstone *et al.* note, 'Leader stewards gain their relative independence from the membership because they have a higher rate of success at bargaining' (*Shop Stewards in Action*, p. 100).
31. Pedler, 'Shop Stewards as Leaders', p. 47.
32. B. Partridge, 'The Activities of Shop Stewards' (1977), p. 32.
33. Hyman and Brough, *Social Values and Industrial Relations*, p. 90.
34. As Brown notes, 'The management opponent is unlikely to pay attention to the comparison unless the worker can persuade him that the group concerned is a legitimate comparative reference group for the worker' (*Piecework Bargaining*, p. 72).
35. As in the 'Bermudan dreams' of Batstone *et al*'s interviewees (*Shop Stewards in Action*, p. 126) or the 'Great Train Robber' comparisons identified by Nichols and Armstrong's interviewees (T. Nichols and P. Armstrong, *Workers Divided* (1976), p. 74).
36. Ross, *Trade Union Wage Policy*, p. 38.
37. Brown, *Piecework Bargaining*, p. 77.
38. Brown, *Piecework Bargaining*, p. 77; Behrend, 'Price and Income Images'.
39. Lipset and Trow, 'Reference Group Theory', p. 403.
40. Brown and Sisson, 'The Use of Comparisons'; Ross, *Trade Union Wage Policy*, p. 52.
41. Brown, *Piecework Bargaining*, pp. 78–9, 143.
42. H. Clegg, *The System of Industrial Relations in Great Britain* (1972), p. 31.
43. J. Goodman and T. W. Whittingham, *Shop Stewards* (1973), p. 174. Brown treats work group formation as issue specific, so that it becomes axiomatic that a bargaining unit will contain several (*Piecework Bargaining*, p. 132).
44. J. T. Dunlop, 'The Task of Contemporary Wage Theory' (1957), p. 129.
45. H. Beynon, *Working for Ford* (1973).
46. Batstone *et al*, *Shop Stewards in Action*, p. 151.
47. I. Boraston, H. Clegg and M. Rimmer, *Workplace and Union* (1975).
48. Clegg, *The System of Industrial Relations in Great Britain*, p. 20.
49. W. Brown, R. Ebsworth and M. Terry, 'Factors Shaping Shop-steward Organization in Britain' (1978).
50. For some general figures on this see Clegg, *The System of Industrial Relations in Great Britain*, p. 14.
51. Brown, Ebsworth and Terry, op. cit., p. 142.
52. Brown, *Piecework Bargaining*, p. 104.

53. Batstone *et al.*, *Shop Stewards in Action*, p. 169.
54. M. Terry, 'The Emergence of a Lay Elite?' (1978); Willman, 'Leadership and Trade Union Principles'.
55. L. Clements, 'Wage Payment Systems and Work Group Frames of Reference' (1976); D. I. MacKay *et al.*, *'Labour Markets under Different Employment Conditions'* (1971), p. 113.
56. Brown, *Piecework Bargaining*, p. 156.
57. However, note the remarks of D. Robinson and W. Conboy, *Local Labour Markets and Wage Structures* (1970), p. 215–60; 'It is clear from the great disparity in wage levels and structures that the internal bargaining strength of specific occupations is not merely a reflection of their external economic position as determined by supply and demand considerations.' (p. 259.)
58. J. W. Kuhn, *Bargaining in Grievance Settlement* (1961).
59. Incomes Data Services, *The Timing of Pay Increases*, 1977.
60. Clements, 'Wage Payments Systems'; on the opacity of piecework, Brown, *Piecework Bargaining*, p. 73.
61. L. C. Hunter and D. Robertson, *The Economics of Wages and Labour* (1969), p. 106.
62. Goodman and Whittingham, *Shop Stewards*, p. 138.
63. JSSC's are noted by Beynon, *Working for Ford*; and Batstone *et al.*, *Shop Stewards in Action*; it is possible however that such developments, and other features such as 'parallel unionism' are more likely to be found in the car industries.
64. W. Brown and M. Terry, 'The Future of Collective Bargaining' (1978).
65. Brown, *Piecework Bargaining*, p. 144.
66. Boraston *et al.*, *Workplace and Union*, p. 24.
67. Batstone *et al.*, *Shop Stewards in Action*, p. 208, Boraston *et al.*, *Workplace and Union*, p. 15.
68. Boraston *et al.*, *Workplace and Union*, p. 188.
69. Batstone *et al.*, *Shop Stewards in Action*, p. 156.
70. Boraston *et al.*, Workplace and Union, p. 22.
71. Dunlop, 'The Task of Contemporary Wage Theory', p. 131.
72. H. A. Turner, 'Inflation and Wage Differentials in Great Britain' (1957).
73. See D. Robinson, 'External and Internal Labour Markets', pp. 28–68 in Robinson (ed), *Local Labour Markets and Wage Structures* (1970), on the absence of uniformity of wage increases in a local labour market. Also R. F. Elliot, 'The National Wage Round in the U.K.: a sceptical view' (1976).
74. D. Robinson, 'Differentials and Incomes Policy' (1973); this line of reasoning may also be extended to include what are characterized as 'linked' differentials.
75. Ross, *Trade Union Wage Policy*, p. 18–20, notes that, within an area, equalization of wages is most likely to be sought where, (a) trade unions centralize their wage policies; (b) separate plants are brought under common ownership; (c) government intervenes in wage determination; (d) rival unions compete for members; or (e) unions or employers ally to form their respective associations.
76. D. Robinson, 'Differentials and Incomes Policy' (1973); Pay Board Advisory Report No. 2 *'Relativities'* (1974).

## CHAPTER 3

1. Batstone *et al.*, *Shop Stewards in Action*, p. 3.
2. D. Mackay, 'Internal Wage Structures' in Robinson (ed), *Local Labour Markets and Wage Structures*, pp. 127–68.
3. Brown, 'Incomes Policy and Pay Differentials', and 'Engineering Wages and The Social Contract'.
4. P. Willman, 'The Growth of Combined Committees: A Reconsideration' (1981).
5. D. Gowler, 'Socio-Cultural Influences on the Operation of a Wage Payment System' in Robinson (ed), *Local Labour Markets and Wage Structures*, pp. 100–27.
6. There are exceptions to this: in certain plants the AUEW does not have negotiating rights for the EETPU members, but their terms and conditions of employment are those of the Engineering Agreement.
7. There are NGA members in Group 1 on BPIF terms and conditions employed where printing on cans take place.
8. P. E. Lloyd, 'The Impact of Development on Merseyside' (1970); J. Salt, 'The Impact of the Ford and Vauxhall Plants on the Employment Situation of Merseyside, 1962–5', (1967).
9. At one the AUEW were involved in production work analogous to that performed by the NGA at A; they were, moreover, on staff conditions.
10. D. Rake, 'Spatial Changes in Industrial Activity in the East Midlands since 1945: I. Changes through growth and changes through acquisition,' (1974) and 'IV. The Engineering Industry,' (1976).
11. At the time of interview, TGWU representatives reported 90 per cent membership but stressed that this had only been obtained recently.
12. Similarly, 87.5 per cent of respondents at plant A and 90 per cent at plant B felt that their respective plants experienced 'good' or 'reasonable' industrial relations (Question 70).
13. There was a skill-based difference in response rate at A. The skilled response rate was 74 per cent and the unskilled 63 per cent. But unskilled workers were more likely to work a three-shift system and high levels of overtime.
14. These were either non-union or members of TASS at both plants.
15. e.g. North *et al.*, *Some Aspects of National Job Evaluation*; Daniel, 'The Next Stage of Incomes Policy'.
16. W. H. Walker, 'The Cultural Distribution of Income in Industrial Organizations' (1965); H. Phelps-Brown, 'Inter Industry Job Evaluation and Collective Bargaining', in Foundation for Business Responsibilities, *Approaches to National Job Evaluation* (1971); B. Livy, *Job Evaluation: A Critical Review* (1975).
17. C. Craig, 'Towards National Job Evaluation?: Trends and Attitudes in Britain and the Netherlands' (1977); A. Bowey and J. Eccles, 'Relativities, National Job Evaluation and Collective Bargaining' (1975); A. Bowey and T. Lupton, *Job and Pay Comparisons* (1973).
18. This approach is adopted from Behrend, *Views on Income Differentials and the Economic Situation* 1970.
19. i.e. a reversal of pairing of occupations between any two respondents would only produce $d^2 = 1$.
20. Although this also had to do with a rejection of group-level pay bargaining by the stewards.
21. Daniel, 'The P.E.P. Survey on Inflation', and 'The Next Stage of Incomes Policy'.
22. J. S. Adams, 'Inequity in Social Exchange' (1965); M. Patchen, *The Choice of Wage Comparisons* (1961).
23. The questions were also asked in reverse order; respondents were asked to name

jobs of equal pay and asked about their worth. Combining internal and external comparisons, 66 per cent at Factory A and 50 per cent at Factory B minimized dissonance. Among those who did not, there was again a tendency to quote disadvantageous comparisons (Questions 23-4, 48-9).

## CHAPTER 4

1. One shop committee member was absent for the entire interviewing period.
2. He had over twenty years service as a steward on various sites. His three stewards averaged only 2.7 years each—all of it in Factory A.
3. This effectively bypassed a succession of personnel managers.
4. An unskilled man was elected steward soon after the interviewing was completed.
5. At A, those members who had been stewards averaged more experience than present incumbents of the office (3.5 years to 2.7). At B, the average for past stewards was 3.7 years compared with 3.9 for present incumbents.
6. The 'Hackney rate' had been a leading rate—one higher than the other graded rates—for the TGWU/GMWU general workers' agreement in the past. The stewards kept an eye on this, the best-paid general worker group in the company.
7. Members also tended to feel that profitability of the firm was not of the greatest importance; see Table 4.6.
8. He acknowledged pressure on earnings, but felt that this was the case for all groups; craft workers felt increasing dissatisfaction at collapsing differentials, while unskilled workers felt the pressures of rising living costs more keenly.
9. At A, the factory manager acknowledged the past use of local rates—'about four years ago'—and at B the personnel manager acknowledged use of other company plants as comparisons 'before we became the best paid'.
10. Members of both plants were quite realistic about the sorts of arguments used. They felt that management would grant pay rises on a cost of living basis, in return for a productivity increase, or to keep up with earnings elsewhere in the Company. The pattern of response was very similar at both plants (Questions 69, 70).
11. For comparable developments elsewhere, see W. A. Brown, 'Incomes Policy and Pay Differentials' (1976).
12. This argument was that fitters' mates were semi-skilled, in terms of wider union policy, so that differentials ought to be narrower; 100-87.5 per cent rather than 100-80 per cent. The local District Secretary felt that things were a little more complex than this; the mates' rate varied in the area between 82.5 per cent and 90.0 per cent of the fitters' rate; he noted, 'it's a matter of negotiation . . . you've got to be very careful you don't get too close to the skilled rate.' The convenor's revealed preference was also for a convergence of rates. He noted: 'We don't want to argue amongst ourselves, we want to raise everybody's pay using the rates of the strongest group.'
13. There were fifteen different merit rates in Plant B in 1968. This was down to eight by 1972, and the four-rate system had operated since 1974.
14. Those who felt differentials were unfair at A were mainly concerned with print earnings (see Chapter 5).
15. Dunlop 'The Task of Contemporary Wage Theory', p. 129.
16. Adams, 'Inequity in Social Exchange'; R. D. Pritchard, 'Equity Theory: A Review and Critique' (1969).
17. E. Jaques, *Equitable Payment* (1967). Notable critiques include A. Fox, *The Time-Span of Discretion Theory: An Appraisal* (1966). The literature is reviewed in S. Cameron, *Felt-Fair Pay* (1976).

18. Cameron, *Felt-Fair Pay*; R. Richardson, *Fair Pay and Work* (1971). For the APWR–FFP relationship, Cameron obtains a coefficient of 0.83 ($p = .0001$): for his AP–FFP relationship Richardson obtains a correlation of 0.862 (significance level not given). Their measures differ slightly from those used here. Cameron's APWR is actual pay from wages records—gross pay for a standard week including any regular bonus, but excluding overtime: it is thus identical to APNOR. Richardson is vaguer about his AP measure, describing it simply as 'The base salary being paid each subordinate at the time of his interview' (p. 36).

19. Jaques's ideas could not be tested, since no independent time-span measure could be taken. Despite methodological problems, in Jacques's own work, high TSD-FFP correlations have been obtained by others using sounder methods and one could not rule such a relationship out here. But given the occupational homogeneity of the sample, the necessary range of TSD is unlikely to exist.

## CHAPTER 5

1. For a description of the operation of an AUEW district, see Boraston, Clegg and Rimmer, *Workplace and Union*, Ch. 2.
2. Interview with District Secretary, 19 November 1976.
3. The District Committee was apparently concerned rather more with the *level* of pay than with the pattern of differentials proposed by an agreement. According to the Merseyside ADO. 'The AUEW has no commitment to any particular wage structure. They do have a commitment to improve members' pay as best they can.'
4. A number of issues settled nationally (i.e. at company level) did not go through the District Committee, however, see Chapter 7 below.
5. This is to be contrasted with the print societies in Factory A. The NGA Officers noted that 'there's very few sources of information outside the branch'. In both SOGAT and NGA, the branch controls the local labour market. Aside from the branch, print officers were involved, on the one hand, in a local lithographical trades committee, and, on the other hand, in a local SOGAT FOC fellowship. They were both isolated from any company-internal organization. While the officers of print societies were thus involved with the branch, there is, however, some reason to believe that members of the print societies were as unlikely to attend branch meetings as their AUEW counterparts.
6. The convenor attended many broad left, Communist Party and Trades Council meetings. He would have affiliated to a local area shop-stewards' committee, but the membership objected to its political affiliations.
7. Interview, District Secretary, 16 September 1977.
8. In particular, 'call-out' payments and 'double-time' arrangements at weekends.
9. The major print machines in the plant in the South-West were operated by TGWU members, not SOGAT.
10. There was considerable personal antipathy between the NGA officials and the SOGAT FOC.
11. They wanted this despite the fact that they were, in their own eyes, the best-paid printers in the company and area. Apparently, such unofficial organizations are seen to have a long-term utility.
12. There was an all-embracing safety committee, but stewards and FOCs did not serve on it, because it would increase their already heavy negotiating workload.
13. There were also shift premia, which differed slightly from those of the AUEW (two-shift, + 20%; three-shift, + 33%).
14. In the spring of 1976, SOGAT negotiated the redundancy of about twenty mem-

bers, on the basis of these productivity arrangements. The AUEW refused to negotiate redundancy and took industrial action.

15. The FOC of SOGAT remarked in interview that he could not stop 'litho' doing whatever that department wanted. He stressed that he wanted to move away from departmental bargaining, but apparently management wanted to retain it on the grounds that its 'productivity' basis assured some 'return' on pay rises.

16. Particularly since practically all manual workers at the plant were on time rates. The only bonus payments were paid to two small groups of SOGAT workers (1) in the 'knocking out' section, payment by results operated, but output limitation had controlled this at £8 per week for several years, (2) the cheque unit operated a thirteen-week output bonus.

17. All Group 1 and 2 plants had delegates who voted in 1971 for or against the job evaluation scheme: the majority decision was for acceptance.

18. All of those at B who expected shop-steward rejection of their comparison choice mentioned comparisons other than those with toolroom workers elsewhere in the area. Of those who anticipated such rejection at A, 18 per cent out of 21 per cent made comparisons with print societies.

19. In detail, the major responses categories were as follows: at A, 25 per cent pointed to maintenance workers as underpaid, and 27.5 per cent to cleaners and canteen staff. A further 10 per cent felt that no jobs were underpaid within the factory, and 27.5 per cent could not respond. At B, 24 per cent felt that toolroom staff were underpaid, and a further 14 per cent felt that AUEW members were: 18 per cent felt that unskilled workers in the factory were underpaid, and 24 per cent pointed to 'most jobs'.

20. In detail, the major response categories were as follows: at A, apart from the 42.5 per cent pointing to print workers, 12.5 per cent pointed to white-collar jobs, 20 per cent replied that one could not be overpaid, and 22.5 per cent could not respond. At B, 26 per cent pointed to management jobs; 36 per cent replied that one could not be overpaid and 32 per cent could not respond. The 4 per cent pointing to another manual group pointed to maintenance workers.

21. As does for example Daniel, 'The Next Stage of Incomes Policy'.

22. Respondents were distributed between the two branches in the area on a roughly equal basis.

23. In the East Midlands, the unemployment figures were as follows at the time of interview: 1977, March 4.9 per cent; April, 4.9 per cent; May, 4.7 per cent (Department of Employment Gazette).

24. This development had been monitored by the AUEW District Committee and Secretary. Such firms were able to avoid the constraints of incomes policy both because they were 'new' firms and consequently offered 'new' jobs, and because of the purely practical difficulties involved in controlling them.

25. Interview with previous convenor, 12 April 1977.

26. Respondents at both plants interpreted 'the industry' as referring to engineering rather than print or can-making.

27. Patchen, *The Choice of Wage Comparisons*; P. Goodman, 'An Examination of the Referents Used in the Evaluation of Pay' (1974).

## CHAPTER 6

1. See in particular K. Sisson, *Industrial Relations on Fleet Street* (1975).

2. The critical feature in this respect in the table is the number of times an organization 'scores' 2 as opposed to 1; i.e. where the difference is in the achievement of

a policy rather than the disposition so to do. Thus organization A scores 2 on control over redundancy because the convenor would not negotiate it and had successfully resisted managerial attempts to do so in the past. Some years previously, however, the convenor at B had negotiated redundancy. It was explicitly the policy of both organizations not to do so. This demonstrates the fundamental relationship between job control and pay principles. In the past, the lower demand for labour in the company had 'lost' jobs, now higher demand encouraged higher levels of overtime working; the convenors attempted to resist the effects of both in the interests of reducing the uncertainty inherent in their constituents' relationships with management.

3. SOGAT permitted redundancy provided the wage bill did not diminish, and maximized job opportunities for displaced members by strict entry control through the branch.

4. Management stated in interview that they would have increased pay rates to engineers if they could have done so 'legally'.

5. There is no 'hard' data on this. However, it was the opinion of the convenor, the factory manager and the District Secretary—as well as of a number of members at A—that since 1972 the AUEW had improved its position relative to other workers on site. The convenor and factory manager further concurred that the position had improved relative to other AUEW members in the company.

6. R. Blackburn and M. Mann, 'Ideology in the Non-skilled Working Class' (1975). Their items were 'political in the sense that they were designed to tap alternative images of society, ranging from the proletarian radical left to the deferential conservative right. However, the statements were clearly set in an industrial context, in preference to political questions of an abstract or party-political nature. The intention was to make questions relevant to the workers' experience and to reduce standard responses to familiar political ones' (p. 133). The findings depicted in table 6:4 replicate those of Blackburn and Mann in that they appear to show that 'coherent consistent ideologies in the conventional sense do not exist' (p. 156). In this respect, they appear to be 'ambivalent' as characterized in the model in the fundamental sense that they demonstrate allegiance to both 'left' and 'right' ideas. Stewards are simply *less* ambivalent. The data on steward tenure presented in Chapter 4 may explain the differences between stewards at different plants.

7. Daniel, 'Wage Determination in Industry', p. 19.

8. There had been four personnel managers in the previous two years.

## CHAPTER 7

1. Brown, 'Incomes Policy and Pay Differentials', p. 44.

2. Brown 'Engineering Wages and The Social Contract'.

3. This effect was visible, though less pronounced, at Factory A.

4. Daniel's conclusions from a sample-survey study are not supported by the findings quoted here. He found that: 'Union representatives at plant level who have such a major influence on pay determination in industry tended to be hostile to the idea of incomes policy in principle. It may well be that they now represent the only section of British Society where a substantial proportion of people are opposed to incomes policy in principle' (Daniel, 'The Next Stage of Incomes Policy', p. 12). While the first statement may well be accurate, the second appears to be an overgeneralization.

5. The basis of this division is as follows; in Table 7.5 response categories 1 and 4 are favourable, the remainder unfavourable. In Table 7.6 categories 1 and 2 are favourable, the remainder unfavourable.

6. Corina 'Can an Incomes Policy be Administered?'.
7. Nevertheless, only 42 per cent of respondents at B were opposed totally to the idea of another year of pay restraint. The remaining 58 per cent put forward proposals for a third phase; 18 per cent wanted to see some flexible form of policy which would re-establish differentials; 14 per cent were happy with another percentage policy and 8 per cent wanted cost of living indexation of wages; 12 per cent wanted a further flat rate policy—the amounts mentioned generally were large. This question was not asked at A where the idea of a third phase had at the time little salience (Question 81).
8. Daniel, 'The Next Stage of Incomes Policy', p. 14.
9. This period was, because of constraints on resources, of unequal duration at the two plants. It extended until September 1977; consequently it was of thirteen months duration at A, but only six months at B.
10. *The Attack on Inflation*, Cmnd. 6151 (1975).
11. *The Attack on Inflation: The Second Year*, Cmnd. 6507 (1976).
12. Cmnd. 6151, paragraph 8.
13. See *Employment News*, July 1975. For a different interpretation which treated 1 September 1975 as the principal 'stoppage' date in both cases, see Confederation of British Industry, *The New Anti-Inflation Policy: Guidance for Employers* (1975). Further discussion of the transitional arrangements can be found in the *Reports* published by Incomes Data Services Ltd. August 1975 to February 1976, where the inconsistency of the Department of Employment in the interpretation of individual cases is remarked upon.
14. See the Department of Employment statement quoted in IDS, *Report*, No. 219, October 1975, p. 27, and subsequent criticism of the Department's failure to observe this restriction to specified figures or formulae in IDS, *Report* No. 221, November 1975, p. 3.
15. This is an extract from the written submission made by the convenor at the final stage of the disputes procedure.
16. These extra payments were considerable: Class 1 operatives, £6; Class 2, £4; and Class 3, £2 per week.
17. Both sides asserted the existence of a definite 'forward commitment', but that this was merely verbal. The Department of Employment responded that there was no requirement for such an agreement to be in writing, but that it was 'unusual' for it not to be so. Management presented evidence of forward commitment in the form of minutes of negotiating meetings. As the convenor put it: 'These were news to me'.
18. The dispute went into procedure on 11 March 1977. According to the convenor, this was the first time that he had put a dispute into procedure, and the first time that the local full-time officer (FTO) had been involved in a wage problem at Factory A during his own tenure of office. Under the terms of the company procedure, the local FTO had to be called in to talk with local management within five days of the above date. The second stage involved the local FTO and a national officer in discussion with management at group level, and the third and final stage involved the same union personnel with top management at company headquarters. This dispute ran the whole course, but reached final stage only in August 1977, which was considerably later than the fifty-nine day maximum stipulated in procedure. Because of the change of personnel at each stage of procedure, and the high turnover of local personnel officers at Factory A, the AUEW convenor was the only individual to reach the final stage who had been involved in the dispute from the beginning.
19. The stewards' case rests on the claim that 6p per hour should have been paid from

1 April 1975, and that they qualified for this, since the previous settlement date was September 1974. Management's 'prior commitment' case sets the payment date in October 1975. However, the basis of the second award is management's claim to have *included* the 6p per hour in the settlement of 28 April 1978. The convenor disagreed: he felt that the April 1975 award was intended to consolidate threshold payments, achieve parity with the electricians and 'reward' the change of settlement date. In any case, it is clear that the two settlements are inconsistent: either the 6p was included in the April award, in which case no 'prior commitment' need have been made, and the four-week second award is sufficient, or a prior commitment *was* made, in which case this second award is baseless. The two payments are mutually exclusive.

20. See Cmnd. 6507, and *Labour Research*, April 1976, p. 84–5.
21. Quoted from a 'Combined Committee Information Bulletin' n.d., but circulated during September 1977.
22. Ibid.
23. The Combined Committee Policy, or at least anticipation of Combined Committee activity by management, may have something to do with this. The Secretary notes: 'it appears that management have taken the decision to pay engineers and electricians who can prove they have had significant changes of job content'. Instances of change are adaptation to new safety procedures and 'Flexibility—which already exists.' The advice is to 'only negotiate on existing practices *not* on any introduction of new practices which could be regarded as sig. job change. If you do negotiate for more than the 12.3p per hour claim'. (Bulletin, n.d., circulated September 1977.)
24. 'Joint Report between the AUEW and * * * * Management on Significant Change for Engineers', n.d., but produced in May 1977. All references below to the substance of the changes which justified the 12.3p increase are based on this.
25. Letters from the Convenor, dated between 13 August 1977 and 20 May 1978.
26. Letter dated 20 October 1977.
27. Extracts from 'Significant Change for Engineers', document dated July 1977. The document describing the basis of the deal for electricians—'Technical Change Report—Electrical Department' is purely descriptive of a set of working practices and makes no mention of any changes.
28. The TGWU at B received a rise of 12.3p on 1 September 1978. They were in some respects 'closer' to the origins of the deal that AUEW members, in that they were covered by the same 'independent agreement' as Group 2 general workers. The pattern of diffusion of the deal appears to have been: production workers in Group 2 to all workers therein, via these to all those covered by the Independent Agreement to the Engineering Agreement, and so to all workers in the company.

## CHAPTER 8

1. Exactly as Clegg suggests: H. Clegg, *How to Run an Incomes Policy: and Why We Made Such a Mess of the Last One*' (1971).
2. This capacity may have been widespread. See Brown, 'Engineering Wages and the Social Contract', p. 52. Daniel, 'Wage Determination in Industry', p. 40.
3. Corina, 'The British Experiment in Wage Restraint'. The 'wage drift' argument is probably less important now (see pp. 148–51).
4. J. Corina, 'Discussion', in F. Blackaby, 1972 op cit p 84.
5. J. Gennard, 'Incomes Policy; Problems and a Proposal' (1976).

6. The entire period of study, both interviews and observation, lasted only fifteen months from the start of interviews at A to the end of observation at B.

7. National Committee, *Reports*, 1976.

8. National Committee, *Reports*, 1977. In both years, National Committee policy became National Conference policy for the whole AUEW, except that part of the 1977 resolution which called for recall of the National Committee after TUC.

9. TUC, *Report*, 1975, p 570–1, Composite 8; 1976, p. 637, Composite 7; 1977, p. 589, Composite 7 (proposed by Hugh Scanlon).

10. In Brown's sample under Phase II 'a smaller proportion of firms undershot and a higher proportion exceeded the limit for most occupations than in the previous phase' ('Engineering Wages and the Social Contract' p. 55).

11. M. Fogarty, *The Just Wage* (1961).

12. Ibid, p. 263.

13. W. A. Brown, 'Antipodean Contrasts in Incomes Policy' (1979).

14. Brown, 'Antipodean Contrasts', p. 103; Fogarty, *The Just Wage*, Ch. 1.

15. J. B. Jefferys, *The Story of the Engineers, 1800–1945* (1945).

16. Fogarty, *The Just Wage*, Appendix 1.

17. Clegg, *How to Run an Income Policy*: Brown, 'Antipodean Contrasts', pp. 113–5.

18. Standing Commission on Pay Comparability (Clegg Commission) *Report No. 9* (1980).

19. See F. Blackaby, 'Incomes Policy' p. 360–401 in F. Blackaby (ed), *British Economic Policy 1960–1974* (1978).

20. Clegg Commission, *Report No. 9*, p. 49.

21. Clegg, *How to Run an Incomes Policy* Ch. 1; Brown and Terry, 'The Future of Collective Bargaining'; W. A. Brown, 'The Structure of Pay Bargaining in Britain' (1980).

22. W. A. Brown and K. Sisson, *A Positive Incomes Policy* (1976).

23. Corina, 'The British Experiment in Wage Restraint'. He distinguishes 'market conditioned' drift (due to excess demand) and 'payment-system conditioned' drift (due to piecework).

24. Clegg, *How to Run an Incomes Policy*.

25. Brown, 'Engineering Wages and the Social Contract'.

26. Clegg, *The Changing System of Industrial Relations*, p. 372.

27. Brown, Ebsworth and Terry, 'Factors Shaping Shop Steward organization'; M. Terry, 'The Emergence of a Lay Elite' (1978).

28. Craig 'Towards National Job Evalution'; Organization for Economic Cooperation and Development, *Socially Responsible Wage Policies and Inflation* (1975).

29. National Board for Prices and Incomes, Report No. 83, *Job evaluation* (1968).

30. G. Webb, 'National Job Evaluation' in Foundation for Business Responsibilities, *Approaches to National Job Evaluation*; Bowey and Lupton, 1973 op, cit.

31. i.e. as at Factory B. This may cause widespread problems under incomes policy since the union/non-union differential tends to fall in policy'on' periods and rise in 'off' periods; D. Metcalf, 'Unions, Incomes Policy and Relative Wages in Britain' (1977).

32. Walker, 'The Cultural Basis of Income Distribution'.

33. For examples of the pragmatic trade-union response, D. Whitaker, 'Job evaluation' (1967); Trades Union Congress, *Job evaluation and merit rating* (1975 edition).

34. in F. Blackaby (ed), *An Incomes Policy for Britain*, pp. 70–1.

35. Goldthorpe, 'The Current Inflation', pp. 207.

36. Clegg, *How to Run an Incomes Policy*, p. 69; Phelps-Brown, p. 37–41 in Blackaby, *An Incomes Policy For Britain*.

37. Clegg, *How to Run an Incomes Policy*, p. 39.
38. The operation of the productivity exception may in fact have delayed pay deals under Phase III. Very few productivity deals were signed in the first half of the policy year although there was a sharp rise in the second; by July 1978 the Department of Employment had been notified of 1,500 deals (Income Data Services, *Reports*, 269, 274, 278, 288, November 1977—September 1978).
39. For Phase III the Department of Employment issued guidelines only as advice to those companies requesting it (Income Data Services, *Report*, 267, October 1977). For the subsequently unsuccessful Phase IV the intention was to work from a general published set of rules (Income Data Services, *Report*, 287, August 1978).
40. J. H. Goldthorpe, 'Industrial Relations; A Critique of Reformism' (1974).
41. Ibid., p. 425.
42. Goldthorpe, 'Social Inequality and Social Integration', p. 224–7; his emphasis.

## APPENDIX I

1. There were eight respondents in the pilot study, 8.9 per cent of the final sample, selected non-randomly on a departmental basis to include skilled, semi-skilled and unskilled respondents. A number of changes to the questionnaire were made on the basis of this piloting.

2. In addition to approaches to a number of individual firms, the North-West region of the Engineering Employers Federation were approached, and the District Committee of the AUEW. Both were prepared to co-operate, but not to assist the negotiation of access.

## APPENDIX II

1. Chi-square = 10.313, $\alpha$ = .05, d.f. = 5.

2. At A 76.5 per cent and at B 72 per cent replied that they would not change. Of those who would do so, the most commonly mentioned reasons were money (A 27.5 per cent, B 10 per cent) and better employment conditions (A 5 per cent, B 6 per cent). See National Economic Development Office, (1977). *Engineering Craftsmen: Shortages and Related Problems*

# BIBLIOGRAPHY

J. S. Adams, 'Inequity in Social Exchange' in L. Berkowitz (ed), *Advances in Experimental Social Psychology*, Vol. 2 (New York, Academic Press, 1965), pp. 267–99.

*The Attack on Inflation*, Cmnd. 6151, HMSO, July 1975.

*The Attack on Inflation: The Second Year*, Cmnd. 6507, HMSO, July 1976.

Amalgamated Union of Engineering Workers (Engineering Section), *National Committee Reports*, 1975–1977.

W. Baldamus, *Efficiency and Effort* (London, Tavistock, 1961).

E. Batstone, I. Boraston, S. Frenkel, *Shop Stewards in Action* (Oxford, Blackwell, 1977).

E. Batstone, I. Boraston, S. Frenkel, *The Social Organisation of Strikes* (Oxford, Blackwell, 1978).

H. Behrend, 'Price and Income Images and Inflation', *Scottish Journal of Political Economy*, II (1964), 85–103.

_____, 'Price Images, Inflation and National Incomes Policy', *Scottish Journal of Political Economy*, 13 (1966), 273–96.

_____, H. Lynch, H. Thomas, J. Davies, *Incomes Policy and the Individual* (Edinburgh, Oliver and Boyd, 1967).

_____, A. Knowles, J. Davies, *Views on Incomes Differentials and the Economic Situation* (Dublin, Economic and Social Research Institute, 1970).

_____, A. Knowles, J. Davies, *Views on Pay Increases, Fringe Benefits and Low Pay* (Dublin, Economic and Social Research Institute, 1970).

_____, 'Public Acceptability and a Workable Incomes Policy' in F. Blackaby (ed), *An Incomes Policy for Britain*, (London, Heinemann, 1972), pp. 187–217.

_____, *Incomes Policy, Equity and Pay Increase Differentials* (Edinburgh, Scottish Academic Press, 1973).

_____, 'The Impact of Inflation on Pay Increase Expectations and Ideas of Fair Pay', *Industrial Relations Journal*, 5 (1974), 1–17.

_____, *Attitudes to Price Increases and Pay Claims* (London, NEDO Monograph 4, HMSO, 1974).

I. Bernstein, *Arbitration of Wages* (Berkeley, University of California Press, 1954).

H. Beynon, *Working for Ford* (Harmondsworth, Penguin, 1973).

F. Blackaby (ed), *An Incomes Policy for Britain* (London, Heinemann, 1972).

_____, (ed), *British Economic Policy 1960–74*, (National Institute of Economic and Social Research, Cambridge University Press, 1978).

R. Blackburn and M. Mann, 'Ideology in the Non-Skilled Working Class', in M. Bulmer (ed), *Working Class Images of Society* (London, RKP/SSRC, 1975), pp. 131–63.

I. Boraston, H. Clegg and M. Rimmer, *Workplace and Union* (London, Heinemann, 1975).

A. Bowey and J. Eccles, 'Relativities, National Job Evaluation and Collective Bargaining', *Journal of Management Studies*, 12 (1975), 83–94.

A. Bowey and T. Lupton, *Job and Pay Comparisons* (London, Gower Press, 1973).

W. A. Brown, 'A Consideration of Custom and Practice', *British Journal of Industrial Relations*, 10 (1972), 42–61.

_____ *Piecework Bargaining* (London, Heinemann, 1973).

_____ 'Incomes Policy and Pay Differentials', *Oxford Bulletin of Economics and Statistics*, 38 (1976), 27–51.

_____ 'Engineering Wages and the Social Contract', *Oxford Bulletin of Economics and Statistics*, 41 (1979), 51–61.

_____ 'Antipodean Contrasts in Incomes Policy' in J. K. Bowers (ed), *Inflation, Development and Integration; Essays in Honour of A. J. Brown* (Leeds, Leeds University Press, 1979), pp. 101–17.

_____ 'The Structure of Pay Bargaining in Britain', in F. Blackaby (ed). *The Future of Pay Bargaining* (London, Heinemann, 1980).

_____, R. Ebsworth and M. Terry, 'Factors Shaping Shop Steward Organisation in Britain', *British Journal of Industrial Relations*, 16 (1978), 139–60.

_____ and K. Sisson, 'The Use of Comparisons in Workplace Wage Determination', *British Journal of Industrial Relations*, 13 (1975), 23–54.

_____ and K. Sisson, *A Positive Incomes Policy*, Fabian Tract 442, May 1976.

_____ and M. Terry, 'The Changing Nature of National Wage Agreements', *Scottish Journal of Political Economy*, 25 (1978), 119–33.

_____ and M. Terry, 'The Future of Collective Bargaining, *New Society*, 23 March 1978.

S. Cameron, *Felt-Fair Pay*, Department of Employment Research Paper No. 1 (London, HMSO, 1976).

J. W. Chapman, 'Justice and Fairness', *Nomos VI* (1963).

H. A. Clegg, 'The Scope of Fair Wage Comparisons', *Journal of Industrial Economics*, 9 (1961), 199–214.

_____ *How to Run an Incomes Policy and Why We Made Such a Mess of the Last One* (London, Heinemann, 1971).

_____ *The System of Industrial Relations in Great Britain* (Oxford, Blackwell, 1972).

_____ *The Changing System of Industrial Relations in Great Britain*, Oxford, Blackwell, 1979).

L. Clements, 'Wage Payment Systems and Work Group Frames of Reference', *Industrial Relations Journal*, 7 (1976), 40–9.

Confederation of British Industry, *The New Anti-Inflation Policy: Guidance for Employers* (London, CBI Publications, August 1975).

J. Corina, 'The British Experiment in Wage Restraint, 1948–51' (D. Phil. Thesis Oxford University, 1961).

_____ 'Can an Incomes Policy be Administered?' in B. C. Roberts (ed), *Industrial Relations: Contemporary Issues* (London, Macmillan, 1968), pp. 257–91.

C. Craig, 'Towards National Job Evaluation? Trends and Attitudes in Britain and the Netherlands', *Industrial Relations Journal*, 8 (1977), 23–36.

W. W. Daniel, 'The P.E.P Survey on Inflation', Broadsheet No. 553, Vol. XLI (London, PEP, July 1975).

_____ 'Wage Determination in Industry', Broadsheet No. 563, Vol. XLII (London, PEP, June 1976).

_____ 'The Next Stage of Incomes Policy', Broadsheet No. 568, Vol. XLII (London, PEP, December 1976).

J. T. Dunlop, 'The Task of Contemporary Wage Theory', in G. W. Taylor and F. W. Pierson (eds), *New Concepts in Wage Determination* (New York, McGraw-Hill, 1957), pp. 117–39.

R. F. Elliot, 'The National Wage Round in the United Kingdom: a Sceptical View', *Oxford Bulletin of Economics and Statistics*, 38 (1976), 179–203.

*Employment News*, June–August 1975.

A. Flanders, *A Policy for Wages* (London, Fabian Society, 1950).

_____ *Management and Unions* (London, Faber, 1970).

M. P. Fogarty, *The Just Wage* (London, Chapman and Hall, 1961).

P. Fosh and D. Jackson, 'Pay Policy: What Britain Thinks', *New Society*, February 1974.

Foundation for Business Responsibilities, *Approaches to National Job Evaluation*, London, 1971.

A. Fox, *The Time-Span of Discretion Theory: An Appraisal* (London, Institute of Personnel Management, 1966).

J. Gennard, 'Incomes Policy: Problems and a Proposal', *Three Banks Review*, 110 (1976).

H. Gerth and C. W. Mills, *Character and Social Structure* (London, Routledge and Kegan Paul, 1954), Ch. 5, pp. 112–29.

J. H. Goldthorpe, 'Social Inequality and Social Integration in Modern Britain', *Advancement of Science*, 26 (1969), 190–202.

_____ 'Industrial Relations: A Critique of Reformism', *Politics and Society*, 4 (1974) 419–52.

_____ 'The Current Inflation: Towards a Sociological Account' in F. Hirsch and J. H. Goldthorpe (eds), *The Political Economy of Inflation*, (London, Martin Robertson, 1978), pp. 186–214.

J. T. B. Goodman and T. W. Whittingham, *Shop Stewards* (London, Pan, 1973).

P. Goodman, 'An Examination of the Referents Used in the Evaluation of Pay', *Organisational Behaviour and Human Performance*, 12 (1974), 170–95.

D. Gowler, 'Socio-Cultural Influences on the Operation of a Wage Payment System', in Robinson (ed), *Local Labour Markets and Wage Structures* (London, Gower Press, 1970), pp. 100–27.

L. C. Hunter and D. Robertson, *The Economics of Wages* (London, Macmillan, 1969).

R. Hyman and I. Brough, *Social Values and Industrial Relations* (Oxford, Blackwell, 1975).

Incomes Data Services Ltd., *Reports*, August 1975–September 1978 (Nos. 214–88).

Incomes Data Services, Study No. 158, *The Timing of Pay Increases*, November 1977.

E. Jaques, *Equitable Payment* (Harmondsworth, Penguin, 1967).

J. Jeffreys, *The Story of the Engineers, 1800–1945* (London, Lawrence and Wishart, 1945).

J. W. Kuhn, *Bargaining in Grievance Settlement* (New York, Columbia University Press, 1961).

R. Lester, 'A Range Theory of Differentials', *Industrial and Labor Relations Review*, 5 (1952), 483–500.

H. Levinson, *Determining Forces in Collective Wage Bargaining* (New York, Wiley, 1966).

S. M. Lipset and M. Trow, 'Reference Group Theory and Trade Union Wage Policy', in M. Komarovsky (ed), *Common Frontiers in the Social Sciences* (Glencoe, Free Press, 1957), pp. 391–439.

B. Livy, *Job Evaluation: A Critical Review* (London, Allen and Unwin, 1975).

P. E. Lloyd, 'The Impact of Development on Merseyside', in R. Lawton and P. Cunningham (eds), *'Merseyside: Social and Economic Studies'* (London, Longman, 1970), pp. 374–410.

D. Lockwood, 'Arbitration and Industrial Conflict', *British Journal of Sociology*, 6 (1955) 335–47.

D. McKay, D. Boddy, J. Brack, J. A. Diack and N. Jones, *Labour Markets under Different Employment Conditions* (London, Allen and Unwin, 1971).

D. Metcalf, 'Unions, Incomes Policy and Relative Wages in Britain: *(British Journal of Industrial Relations*, 15 (1975), 157–75.

C. W. Mills, 'Situated Actions and Vocabularies of Motive', in D. Horowitz (ed), *Power, Politics and People* (Oxford, Oxford University Press, 1963), pp. 439–52.

National Board for Prices and Incomes, Report No. 83, *'Job Evaluation'*, Cmnd. 3772 (London, HMSO, 1968).

National Economic Development Office, *Engineering Craftsmen; Shortages and Related Problems* (London, NEDO, 1977).

T. Nichols and P. Armstrong, *Workers Divided* (London, Fontana, 1976).

D. T. B. North, C. J. Woods, R. W. Brewer and W. D. Webb, *Report on the Study of Some Aspects of National Job Evaluation* (London, Working Together Campaign, 1973).

Organization for Economic Cooperation and Development, *Socially Responsible Wage Policies and Inflation* (Paris, 1975).

S. R. Parker, *Workplace Industrial Relations 1973* (London, Office of Population, Censuses and Surveys, HMSO, 1975).

B. Partridge, 'The Activities of Shop Stewards', *Industrial Relations Journal*, 8 (1977/78), 28–43.

M. Patchen, *The Choice of Wage Comparisons* (Englewood-Cliffs, Prentice Hall, 1961).

Pay Board Advisory Report No. 2, *Relativities*, Cmnd. 5535 (London, HMSO, 1974).

M. J. Pedler, 'Shop Stewards as Leaders', *Industrial Relations Journal*, 4, (Winter 1973/4), 43–61.

H. Phelps-Brown, 'A Non-Monetarist's View of the Pay Explosion', *Three Banks Review*, 105 (March 1975), 3–25.

R. D. Pritchard, 'Equity Theory: A Review and Critique', *Organisational Behaviour and Human Performance*, 14 (1969) 176–211.

D. Rake, 'Spatial Changes in Industrial Activity in the East Midlands since 1945: I. Changes through Growth and Changes through Acquisition', *East Midlands Geographer*, (1974) 1–16 and 'IV. The Engineering Industry', *East Midlands Geographer* (1976) 265–75.

M. Reder, 'The Theory of Union Wage Policy', *Review of Economics and Statistics* 34 (1952), 34–46.

I. Reid, *Social Class Differences in Britain: A Sourcebook* (London, Open Books 1977), Ch. 2.

R. Richardson, *Fair Pay and Work* (London, Heinemann, 1971).

M. Rimmer, *Race and Industrial Conflict* (London, Heinemann, 1972).

D. Robinson (ed), *Local Labour Markets and Wage Structures* (London, Gower Press, 1970).

———, 'Differentials and Incomes Policy', *Industrial Relations Journal*, 4 (1973), 4–21.

A. M. Ross, *Trade Union Wage Policy* (Berkeley, University of California Press, 1948, 2nd ed. 1953).

W. G. Runciman, *Relative Deprivation and Social Justice* (Harmondsworth, Penguin, 1972).

———, 'Justice, Congruence and Professor Homans', *European Journal of Sociology*, 8 (1967), 115–28.

J. Salt, 'The Impact of the Ford and Vauxhall Plants on the Employment Situation of Merseyside, 1962–5', *Tidjschrift voor Economische en Sociale Geographie*, 58 (1967), 255–64.

K. Sisson, *Industrial Relations in Fleet Street* (Oxford, Blackwell, 1975).

Standing Commission on Pay Comparability (Clegg Commission), Report No. 9, Cmnd, 7995, London, HMSO, 1980.

M. Terry, 'The Inevitable Growth of Informality', *British Journal of Industrial Relations*, 15 (1977), 76–90.

———, 'The Emergence of a Lay Elite', Warwick University *IRRU Discussion Paper*, November 1978.

Trades Union Congress, *Job Evaluation and Merit Rating* (London, Congress House, 1975 edition).

H. A. Turner, 'Inflation and Wage Differentials in Great Britain' in J. T. Dunlop (ed), *The Theory of Wage Determination* (London, Macmillan, 1957), pp. 123–35.

W. H. Walker, 'The Cultural Basis of Income Distribution in Industrial Organizations' (Birmingham University Ph. D. Thesis, 1965 (unpublished)).

D. Whitaker, 'Job Evaluation', *AEU Journal*, May 1967.

B. Williams, 'The Idea of Equality', in P. Laslett and W. G. Runciman (eds), *Politics, Philosophy and Society*, Second Series (Oxford, Blackwell, 1962).

P. Willman, 'Leadership and Trade Union Principles: Some Problems of Management Sponsorship and Independence', *Industrial Relations Journal*, 11 (1980), 39–50.

———, 'The Growth of Combined Committees: A Reconsideration' *British Journal of Industrial Relations*, 19 (1981), 1–13.

G. A. Withers, 'Social Justice and the Unions: A Normative Approach to Co-operation and Conflict under Interdependence', *British Journal of Industrial Relations*, 15 (1977), 322–38.

B. Wooton, *The Social Foundations of Wage Policy* (London, Allen and Unwin, 1962).